Remaking Cities

Remaking Cities

An introduction to urban metrofitting

TONY FRY

Bloomsbury Academic
An imprint of Bloomsbury Publishing Plc

B L O O M S B U R Y
LONDON · OXFORD · NEW YORK · NEW DELHI · SYDNEY

Bloomsbury Academic

An imprint of Bloomsbury Publishing Plc

50 Bedford Square	1385 Broadway
London	New York
WC1B 3DP	NY 10018
UK	USA

www.bloomsbury.com

BLOOMSBURY and the Diana logo are trademarks of Bloomsbury Publishing Plc

First published 2017

© Tony Fry, 2017

Tony Fry has asserted his right under the Copyright, Designs and Patents Act, 1988, to be identified as Author of this work.

British Library Cataloguing-in-Publication Data

A catalogue record for this book is available from the British Library.

ISBN:	HB:	978-1-4742-2416-1
	PB:	978-1-4742-2415-4
	ePDF:	978-1-4742-2418-5
	ePub:	978-1-4742-2417-8

Library of Congress Cataloging-in-Publication Data

Names: Fry, Tony.
Title: Remaking cities : an introduction to urban metrofitting / Tony Fry.
Description: New York : Bloomsbury Academic, 2017. | Includes bibliographical references and index.
Identifiers: LCCN 2016053855 (print) | LCCN 2016054923 (ebook) |
ISBN 9781474224154 (paperback) | ISBN 9781474224161 (hardback) |
ISBN 9781474224178 (Epub) | ISBN 9781474224185 (Epdf)
Subjects: LCSH: Urban ecology (Sociology) | Sustainable urban development. |
City planning–Social aspects. | BISAC: ARCHITECTURE / General. | ARCHITECTURE /
Urban & Land Use Planning. | ARCHITECTURE / Sustainability & Green Design. |
DESIGN / History & Criticism.
Classification: LCC HT241 .F797 2017 (print) | LCC HT241 (ebook) | DDC 307.1/216–dc23
LC record available at https://lccn.loc.gov/2016053855.

Cover design by Eleanor Rose
Cover images © Tony Fry

Typeset by RefineCatch Limited, Bungay, Suffolk

Contents

Preface

The future of humanity – the conditions under which our collective fate is decided – cannot be divided from the planetary determinates within which the majority of the world's population now lives: life in cities. The mineral and biological resources of the planet are sucked into cities. The transformation, use and abuse of these resources to sustain human beings has created a situation of deep ambiguity wherein this process is taking futures away as fast as it creates them. One can name this indivisible relation between creation and destruction 'the dialectic of Sustainment'. When the human population was small and its destructive capability delimited by simple technologies, planetary systems were able to absorb the impacts of this action. This is no longer the case. Our species now exists in such numbers and with such amplified technological means for resource utilization that this process is putting our very future in the balance. If one views this situation from the perspective of the dialectic of Sustainment, it becomes clear that the city is positioned as a fulcrum. Currently, its movement is weighted towards destruction. The weight of destruction has to be reduced to restore some kind of balance, and for this to happen the negative impact of cities and city life has to be dramatically reduced. The 'remaking of cities' is the name of this process, with 'metrofitting' as it means.

From the start, let's be absolutely clear: this is not merely an instrumental technical exercise. For cities to be remade, the very nature of what a city is and does requires to be rethought – new thinking is the key to such transformative action – and the ambition of this work is directed towards this end. By implication, what is to be presented cannot be but a starting point of a vast task – one that completely depends on establishing a new praxis.

Current redemptive approaches to cities: sustainable cities, liveable cities, smart cities, resilient cities and the like, by degree, have practical merit. But, as will be shown, they do not have the corrective force to deal with the critical situations cities are increasingly facing. Such approaches are really not confronting the scale and the complexity of the intellectual challenge of remaking cities to become 'futural' (understood here as constructed environments enabling the advancement of viable futures). In the face of the need to take practical action, this intellectual exercise is not an indulgence, digression or avoidance but an essential and integral means to direct informed practice: hence the claim to praxis.

Today, cities are tremendously varied in scale, form and operation. They are in good and bad condition, more or less threatened, at various levels of function or dysfunction, and situated in enormously different environmental, economic, social, cultural and security contexts. It follows that there can be no single theory, strategy or practice of remaking cities. Moreover, whatever thinking is done has to be brought to a situated context wherein it becomes directive of, and corrected by, research *in situ*.

Against these caveats, metrofitting is presented as a way to frame the thinking and means of remaking the city. It has no universal template, fixed method, specific practice or proposed closed concept. Rather, it centres on: (i) a situated recognition that the remaking of cities is increasingly an imperative that arrives from the convergence of numerous 'defuturing' impacts (like climate change, population pressures, geopolitical instability, resource stress, and social and individual technologically linked cultural transformations); and (ii) redirective, reparative and reconstructive action to transform what relationally exists (materially, operationally and socio-culturally). As defuturing affirms, it does this in the knowledge that as finite beings, the negative impacts of our collective actions on the environments of our dependence are reducing the duration of our earthly existence. So understood, the agenda of metrofitting spans an engagement with every aspect of the form, life and function of a city in order for it to deal with existing and coming impacts of the unsustainable.

The unsustainable is now dominantly characterized as those damaged environmental systems and natural resources impacted by human conduct. Thereafter, much that travels under the auspices of sustainability takes such a characterization as self-evident. Perceptions, policies and practices are then instrumentally mobilized to deal with this situation, with mixed results. Overwhelmingly, the sensibility at work here is based on the proposition that it is possible to retain and extend the 'benefits of modernity' while reducing its negative impacts. Such thinking and associated instrumental action exposes a failure to grasp the depth, trajectory and ontologically inscriptive power of the unsustainable.

In contrast, the intellectual project of remaking cities embraced by metrofitting does not accept the unsustainable as being sufficiently understood. The reverse is in fact the case, and the disclosure of its complexity has to be a fundamental part of its project.

There are a number of people whose help and support during the course of the project has been appreciated. I am indebted to Philippe d'Anjou, Atlantic University, Florida for his constructive comments on a draft of the book. On events associated with the case studies, thanks to Mary Beth McGrew,

University Architect, University of Cincinnati, and Larry W. Falkin, Director of the Office of Environmental Quality, City of Cincinnati. The material for the Cairo case study would not have happened without the help of Anne-Marie Willis, German University Cairo and Waleed Ghamry, Halwan University. Finally, I would like to thank D Wood for her editorial help and James Thompson at Bloomsbury for his insights and support.

List of figures

Introduction

For most of us cities seem so familiar an environment, yet they are also mysterious. So much escapes our attention; so much remains hidden – appearances deceive. The city we thinkers think we know is obviously not a perception shared by all its inhabitants. Notwithstanding exceptions, most people do not look up from their sightline of concern. The architecture and planning of the city is invisible in its visible presence and its problems are found easy to ignore by the unaffected. For the most part the synthetic metabolism of the city is taken for granted and as such remains unconsidered and so out of sight and hearing. Meanwhile people just go about their business knowing what they functionally need to know. Geo-culturally and existentially the city is not one thing. The proper name misleads, thus cities like Berlin, New York, Mumbai, Lagos, Cairo, London, Sydney and above all Tokyo projected as singularity of place, are misnomers. The place is always more than what the name can signify. It is evident that at the extreme nobody can actually know a city of tens of million of people. Urbanization has in actuality overtaken the city and now subsumes it. Yet the 'city', while an empty signifier, retains an economic and sign value.

What is taken to be the normality of the city does not define a condition of stability. The reverse is true: continual change is required to maintain the status quo. Interconnected economic growth, building development, technological progress, retail expansion and consumerism, all converge to create conditions of turmoil which *enframes* the contradictory aspiration of 'the masses' from the richest to the poorest. In so doing these aspirations become 'set in place' and thereafter produce the conditions of the broken in all its manifest forms, from the squalid and unsightly to the excessive so often concealed in the beautiful.

Architecture, urban design and planning, all now show themselves to be unable to adequately deal with the 'normal' city and the critical complexity of the urban. Certainly the age of the European city as the design paradigm of modernity is dead. The largest cities in the world will belong to Asia and Africa, as will the epicentre of the unfolding disaster of the city (nineteen of the most at-risk cities in the world exposed to sea level rises are in Asia).

. . .

The city is a ruin – some are seen as ruins, some are full of elegant buildings, then again many are not. Dealing with what already exists requires remaking this ruin. But in the context of remaking the city, guided by its intellectual project of new thinking, there is a seeking out of the broken of normality. In this setting, metrofitting will be revealed as predicated upon an ethos grounded in an order and spirit of conviviality in difference. It can but start modestly, learning from a liberation of ideas and knowledge enabling an unlearning and relearning in a situated context.

What the intellectual exercise of remaking cities means in this context is, in large part, just learning what there is to learn (especially in relation to the ontologically directive forces of the nature and conditions of exchange of matter and the psycho-social cultures of the city).

The health of cities, environments and people is indivisible. This relation seems an obvious foundation for design, enfolding as it does the directive actions of the life of the body, the city and all elements of the total environment. This relation in many ways is captured by the notion of 'vital nourishment' (meaning 'to feed one's life'), a common term within ancient Chinese thought.[1] But reason directing the form and operation of cities, while striving to secure them as functional, seems unable to recognize the obvious. Rather, reason is employed to serve non-reasonable ends. Again the intellectual (epistemological) project of remaking cities needs to come to the fore.[2]

The imperative of the remaking of cities is, of course, indivisible from securing the future of human habitation on this, our planet. The challenge and urgency of doing this is absolutely huge but not widely recognized in any substantial way. But what are the implications of these remarks? What is actually to be remade, and how can it be done? Engaging these questions will overarch all that follows, but with the qualification that the answers presented will not be purely instrumental.

Contextually, the concern with remaking cities cannot be divided from understanding the agency of a cluster of convergent future-shaping climatic, environmental, geopolitical, demographic and economic forces as they relationally interconnect and impact on multiple levels. In acknowledging these forces one immediately finds oneself unavoidably immersed in a

---

[1] Theorized by Zhuangzi (370–286 BCE) – see François Jullien (2007), *Vital Nourishment: Departing from Happiness* (trans. Arthur Goldhammer), New York: Zone Books, p. 9.
[2] The language of the city is riven with organic metaphors in significant part due to urban sociology constructing a view of the city as an organism. This thinking embodied a contradiction – the reduction (to a discipline) of an expanded field of complexity where the biological metaphor, while exposing complexity and equally obstructed its recognition.

situation of escalating complexity. Metrofitting is put forward here as a way to start to bring this complexity together with a response to the imperative of remaking cities conceptually and practically. As such, it strives to register a way forward to advance dealing with a challenge as great as, or greater than, any our species has ever faced. Even trying to find where to begin is a very substantial ambition. It cannot but start with an effort to think the assumed and the unthought. Thereafter small steps can be taken and modest change enacted to vitally nourish larger ambitions. What is already beginning to be recognized is that such critical action will come out of responding to the conditions of crisis and abandonment.[3]

Remaking: the project of metrofitting

The question of remaking of cities needs to begin by reconsidering the very idea of the city as used to name plural and mutating modalities of environmental, economic and political life and forms of socio-cultural mass habitation. Cities have been, and clearly are, both conditions and forces of transformation. Not only does the category of a place as a city enfold a great deal of difference of form, scale and function but emergent global circumstances mean that the idea of *what a city is*, or could be, needs to be open to reconsideration. Is a city with a population the size of a medium-sized nation really a city? Is it appropriate to name a refugee camp of a half a million people as a city? What does a vast informal sector of a megacity have in common with a refugee camp? These are a few questions drawn from the urban status quo.

As is well understood, the built form of cities has always been responsive to the geographic climatic variables of heat, cold, wind and weather patterns. Modern cities, of course, have employed engineering to modify such determinants. But the scales of the emergent and expected changes of the global climate will often now go beyond the economic and practical capability of an applied 'techno-fix'. As we shall see, enormous numbers of coastal cities, towns and villages will be lost in the coming decades and centuries to sea level rises. Likewise, many urban environments will find themselves climatically misplaced because their built form will no longer be able to cope with the extreme climate in which they find themselves. Added to this situation are problems of rapid urbanization, population pressures and myriad types of infrastructural and social dysfunction. Effectively what

---

[3] An example of this thinking is provided by Nabeel Hamdi (2004), *Small Change*, London: Routledge.

is starting to be identified is that by degree, and in varied ways, more and more cities will become 'broken'. Brokenness, as a precondition of disaster, is not necessarily an obvious condition reducible to built fabric or infrastructure in visible need of repair. It can be equally evident in a failing operational metabolism, social ecology, system of governance and inability to manage a crisis of structural unsustainability. All of these 'areas of failure' will be (re)thought and explored at length later, but for the moment they arrive to register that 'metrofitting', in the face of coming circumstances, has to gain the ability to embrace the repair of all the relationally interdependent elements of the city.

Repair and metrofitting

The most basic characterization of metrofitting is taking the concept of retrofitting (as applied to an existing structure, manufactured object or system) beyond its instrumental remit and up to an urban scale. Its fundamental premise is that there is an overwhelming priority to deal with cities, this as they currently exist in every respect. This priority does not exclude 'the new' – it simply puts it in its appropriate structural place.

Metrofitting aspires to engage everything within the life of the city, and whatever can be exposed to be 'at risk', broken or in 'in danger'. The aim is to begin to think about a process of repair that does not just mend and reinstate what things originally were but futurally redirects them to be able to deal or adapt to emergent conditions. As such, it begs to be viewed as becoming part of the everyday life of the state, non-governmental organizations, industry, the commercial sector and 'the people', and therefore integral to culture and economy. Thus metrofitting is not put forward as a project simply brought to a city but rather as an ongoing process of its directional change, be it that of the old cities of Europe and the rest of the world or the new and fast expanding new cities of Africa, Asia and Latin America (many of which are increasingly split between the formal and informal).

It should already be clear that the approach to writing about the city will not fall within normal genres that treat it as if it were a discrete object knowable through familiar theories of knowledge coming from architecture, urban design, urban geography, urban sociology, anthropology, environmental studies and so on. This is not to say that insights from these disciplines are rejected but rather that another more relational perceptual frame is needed – one that does not take the city as a given, and as framed by extant and dominant discourses, including those of utopianism and dystopia.

To this end, a concern with metrofitting will be woven into a crosscutting collection of narratives viewing it from multiple viewpoints. This approach will be made clear in Chapter 1, thereafter as a designing event (Chapter 2), in relation to what a city is (Chapter 3), as a city in time (Chapter 4), dealing with urban imperative in the face of change (Chapter 5), an object of imagination (Chapter 6), as a figure of the unfamiliar futures (Chapter 7), as a projection of projected post-sustainability knowledge (Chapter 8). At this juncture a number of key concerns with metrofitting will be consolidated by Chapter 9 and used to inform the remaining chapters. The focus of Chapter 10 will be on '*habitus*', visibility, learning and unlearning. The concept of metrofitting will then be further advanced (Chapter 11), as will ontological design (Chapter 12); city fictions will then be discussed (Chapter 13), followed by the nature of dwelling (Chapter 14). Questions on urban habitation and metrofitting will be readdressed in Chapter 15. The two final chapters are contrasting case studies – the first being of Cincinnati (USA), the second of New Cairo (Egypt).

Environmental impacts

No matter our race, gender or nationality, or if we live inside or outside the city, we are all increasingly exposed to environmental impacts, including those created by the combined forms of human intervention in the 'natural environments'.

We humans in our anthropocentric miasma are an animal now out of control. There is no check to our material excess, our acquisitiveness is unbounded, and we are in deep crisis. But this is not how 'we' see ourselves. So much deemed as environmentally critical is in fact attributable to the understated flaws in our being. From the very beginning of our making a world-within-the-world for our selves (the constructed world of the human epoch – the anthropocene[4]), a corresponding process of world unmaking commenced. It is only now in this age of the evident and coming disasters that this propensity is slowly becoming recognized. Without question what has amplified out impacts has been our sheer numbers. It is sobering to consider that it took some 160,000 years for our species to reach a population of one billion, only for it to double in a century. Thirty-five years later the number of three billion was reached, to get to four billion only took seventeen years, and four leaped to seven billion in just twelve years. By 2050 the projected global population will be eight billion (these figures are in line with the 'UN Secretary General's Report on Population and Food in 2012'). There is still a debate about whether the global population will stabilize at ten or eleven

---

[4] As the human is a plurality, the anthropocene is constituted by, and itself constitutes, difference in the world-within-the-world.

billion by 2100 or not. Of course a major war, global famine, mass pandemic or another kind of disaster could 'correct' this figure.

Raw population numbers are, however, only one element of the equation. The other is the multiplier coming from continually expanding global 'consumption' (people of the 'rich world' now consume over twenty times more per capita than they did a century ago). Moreover, the expectation is that by the end of this century eighty per cent of the world's population will exist within 'modern consumer culture'. Put mildly, the current situation is not sustainable; the prospect is pure catastrophe. For instance, the demand for food is expected to double by 2050, but global warming is going to dramatically reduce agricultural output, this especially because the availability of fresh water will fall. At the same time the cost of food is expected to rise significantly.[5] Such problems are not discrete. As is now clear from recent history in Asia, the Middle East and Africa, a lack of food and water acts to trigger conflict. Likewise, sea level rises also negatively impact on food production. Many of the world's richest and most productive soils are in delta regions, but they are equally placed most at risk from coastal flooding.[6] The projection now is three to four metres globally occurring over the next 200 years plus.[7] The actual number of towns and villages that will be lost will obviously be huge and the cost of such impacts is beyond current calculation.[8]

---

[5] Asia is the driest continent on the planet but has the fastest growing demand for water – for food, industrial production and domestic use. Brahma Chellaney (2012), *From Arms Racing to Dam Racing*, Washington, DC: Transatlantic Academy, Section 1. Additionally, 70 per cent of all irrigated land in the world is in Asia, p. 3.

[6] Recent NASA data has shown that the meltdown of the glacial system of the West Antarctic is now unstoppable and this means a much worse global prospect of sea level rises than the one metre rise projected by the end of this century. Suzanne Goldenberg (2014), 'Western Antarctic Ice Sheet Collapse has Already Begun, Scientists Warn', *The Guardian*, 12 May [https://www.theguardian.com/environment/2014/may/12/western-antarctic-ice-sheet-collapse-has-already-begun-scientists-warn]. This is the fastest rate of sea ice melting (67 gigatonnes per year) ever recorded. Sea level rises are also now being linked to increased deep-sea ocean temperatures. Recent research is also showing these events are also changing the planet's gravity.

[7] This process is already underway and eventually the coastline of every nation on the planet will be redefined with a subsequent loss of huge numbers of coastal cities, towns and villages. Moreover, residents of Pacific Islands, including Fiji, Kirabati, Tuvalu, Vanuatu, and the Marshall, Cook, Solomon and Maldives Islands are already being relocated. In 2007, the OECD ranked the top twenty most exposed cities to coastal flooding in the world. Fifteen of them were in Asia, headed by Kolkata (Calcutta) – with a population in 2014 of 4.5 million – three in Africa and two in the USA. OECD Report (2007), *Ranking of World's Cities Most Exposed to Coastal Flooding Today and in the Future*, Newark, CA: RMS.

[8] To take just one example: Miami was listed number nine in global cities at risk. As a city in the wealthiest of nations, it has the highest exposure to the loss of assets – which is currently $416.29 billion and projected to rise to $3,513.04 billion. The situation between now and when the report was issued in 2007 is clearly worse.

All these problems fold into each other and layer onto the geopolitics of international security (security analysts regard climate change as a major potential source of global or regional conflict). Added to this view, some of the proposed solutions to climate change such as geo-engineering look as dangerous as the problem they are proposed to solve.[9]

The kind of information that science presents on climate change, which mostly appears in academic journals, is obviously important; however, it is not given sufficient media or public attention. But even if this situation was corrected it would not give an adequate picture of the problem. For to properly understand the consequences of a changing climate equally requires a cultural perspective, and this gets almost no attention.

Consider this: from the very beginning, the development of our species was massively influenced by climate. In fact, we only survived as a species by our ability to adapt to a changing climate. As nomads we moved as the climate changed, especially in periods of dramatic heating or cooling, and in the search for food. Thus climate was a major determinant of our migration patterns. Our bodies adapted to different climatic conditions, as is evident in our various skin colours. Climate influenced our forms of shelter, the clothes we wore, the food we ate, our systems of belief and the character of rituals. What was true in the past may well be true in the future, so unless we change sufficiently to respond to changing circumstances many of us will die. By implication cities have to change. Not only are they now part of the problem but, as Paul Virilio has pointed out, the modern city is a 'catastrophe'.[10] As such it is viewed as a machine of 'progress' driving the ever-faster destruction of natural resources, the resilience of communities and the negation of time.

Contexts: time, space, image

The city is never seen as itself. It always arrives mediated by the image and the imaginary that goes ahead of it and frames it contextually. No matter its past or its fate, we only ever see it now, and whatever we do see is but a fragment and emplaced by idea – perceptually, the city exists via the idea.

As Paul Virilio recognized in his *Speed and Politics,* first published in France in 1977, history is defeated as time and space are compressed. All forms of recording 'now' are not really *now,* for redundancy travels towards us from the future at an ever-greater speed (via accelerating technological propulsion). But 'at the same time', change constantly overtakes the image, so what is

---

[9] Tony Fry (2012), *Becoming Human by Design,* London: Berg.
[10] Paul Virilio (2005), *City of Panic,* Oxford: Berg, p. 90.

seen now is always of the past seen in the present. So contextualized, we all live in what Walter Benjamin called the 'now-time' of the decentred seeing. What is seen is an image of the convergence of past, present and future.[11] 'Now' is thus that moment that captures all that travels in time.

Life lived in the 'now-time' constructs a mode of perception that traps us in an image that mediates the power of time in space.[12] In this way space and image were, as Benjamin realized, a force, an action, and energy. In other words, 'we' just see 'space-image' as if we were de-positioned from what we appear to see. Consequently our seeing is (in)formed by a 'reality' that screens the real in which we act. If this is correct, we simply do not 'see' the city but rather view it through the animatory energy of formed images that prefigure what we think we see and name 'city' – hence what is seen is through the screen of images. The image actually exists between us, and everything we see, but as a reflection not a projection, for the image is lodged in our mind – and as Plato first made clear, we see with our mind not with our eyes (as purely optical instruments, our eyes relay unprocessed information to our brain/mind).

The energy of the image cannot be divided from the power of technology. In continually increasing its instrumental presence in the world, it has constantly commanded the means and content by which 'the world' is viewed. Technology, as it gathers constructed space, time, distance, mind, memory, image and culture, takes something that seems to be so natural – seeing – and totally denaturalizes it.

If issues of climate change impacts, environmental transformations and related losses of biodiversity are brought to the city, the problem of image should become evident, but we simply do not see the problem, and more specifically what is broken and in need of repair. In part this is because the cultural production of that imagery enabling us to see climatic and other transformative forces of the city does not exist. Yes there are images of climate events, but they exist to constitute an image of discernible change from the historically familiar.

Cairo, Lagos, Caracas and Delhi are representative of many cities at the end of the space-time we learnt to see. The images of them available to us do not capture the extent of this state of dissolution. The fixed, the fluid and the immaterial are now in flux: a breaking down of their urban matrix is underway. So while striated (divided and controlled) space remains, spaces of informality become smooth, thus walls move and fall, structures dissolve, borders become mutable, borderlands form and thus zones of hybrid knowledge and 'epistemological disobedience' start to proliferate. The city appears, and is

---

[11] Kia Lindroos (1998), *Now-Time/Image-Space*, University of Jyväskylä: SoPhi, p. 248.
[12] Ibid., pp. 247–256.

visited, 'out-of-place'. One wonders where one can go, where one has been and what is fated. Certainly, the ontological designing of the experience of such cities becomes, like the cities themselves, increasingly disjointed. The notion carried by modernity that the modern city brings a modern subject into being has now long gone. The subjects of the 'cities of now' are of a time-space spanning an abandoned past to a beleaguered future. Nothing holds 'things' in place and the very notion of ruin changes appearances.

The systems of exchange that the city accommodates (as a nodal point of the global economy) become ever more plural. This context once taken to be coherent now confuses. The *telos* of 'stages of capital' has no longer any credibility and has been replaced by a far more relational picture of variable levels of formal and informal exchange in which all stages co-exist and arrive together digitally disrupted, as the informal into the formal fuse. However, overarching all the ways the entire history of economy arrives in the now, there are two insurmountable facts of contemporary urban economic life.

Fact one is that perpetual economic growth in a finite system of planetary resources is no more feasible than is perpetual motion. Fact two is that the discredited notion of imposing limits to growth is now not only credible but actually essential.[13] Notwithstanding being denigrated at the time of publication, and then more recently by reactionary environmentalist Bjorn Lomborg, current UN data show that contemporary figures almost match those created by the Limits to Growth study on the future of the planet conducted on behalf of the Club of Rome by Donnella Meadows, Dennis Meadows and Jorgen Randers in 1972. Whereas they suggested 2010 would be the tipping point into disaster, recent data project it to be between 2015 and 2030. These findings echo those reported by Earthinsight published by NASA's Goddard Space Center study in March 2014. The common message linking the Meadows' to the present data is very clear: there is a prospect of industrial civilization collapsing in the coming decades due to unsustainable resource exploitation.[14]

As technological development continually happens at a faster rate (as part of the hegemony of speed), critical perspectives continually get left behind,

---

[13] Here one can cite research by Graham Turner and Cathy Alexander presented in *The Guardian* in 2014 ('*Limits to Growth* was Right. New Research Shows We're Nearing Collapse', *The Guardian*, 2 September [http://www.theguardian.com/commentisfree/2014/sep/02/limits-to-growth-was-right-new-research-shows-were-nearing-collapse]) showing that the argument of Meadows *et al.*, put forward in their 1972 book *The Limits to Growth* (Donella Meadows, Dennis Meadows, Jorgen Randers and William W. Behrens, III (1972), *The Limits to Growth*, New York: Universe Books), was actually correct.

[14] Nafeez Ahmed, (2014), 'Nasa-funded Study: Industrial Civilisation Headed for "Irreversible Collapse"?', *The Guardian*, 14 March [https://www.theguardian.com/environment/earth-insight/2014/mar/14/nasa-civilisation-irreversible-collapse-study-scientists].

stranded and forgotten. Time to reflect is simply erased. The philosophy of technology is a good example: it just cannot keep up with the pace of change. More generally, the more 'the masses' become immersed in the technosphere, the less they think about it. It has become an absolute 'second nature'. Yet its ontological designing is having massive cognitive, memory and perceptual consequences deeply affecting mind, imagination and consciousness: a situation we have hardly begun to comprehend. These changes are acted out in the home, school, university, during leisure time and at the workplace – they are thus intrinsic to the city and its future.

De facto, technological dependence has become the default position of contemporary 'advanced' society. What this effectively means is a growing condition of vulnerability to the very dangers outlined. It matters not if we are discussing the ontological designing of hegemonic technology for the individual, community or city, as designing every level it is 'a holding in place' that fosters compliance and negates adaptability. What is not recognized is the 'we' are not (just) users of technology but are components within the operational field of the technosphere and its designing. As such, 'we' are constantly, unknowingly and increasingly located, mapped, monitored, measured, imaged, profiled, categorized and deployed as we all go about our daily life. This being done under the guise that technology will make our life better, safer, more pleasurable, more social and so on. But slowly an unsettling realization is arriving. Our life, our claim to an independent self-consciousness is being etched away. To be outside the reach of technology so characterized is to be abandoned. Such inclusion or abandonment is not incidental to the fate of the city but a structural feature of its future as a designing event.

There is no conspiracy, just system and compliance in the saddle. Certainly we are not waiting for some kind of Philip K. Dick, Arthur C. Clarke, William Gibson or now Ray Kurzweil science fiction or fact nightmare to overwhelm us. Whatever the danger is, it is already here, but is just not seen as such. Without any supporting evidence, faith is widely posited in a techno-fix solution to the problems of the planet.[15] Effectively what is being exposed is an act of technological nemesis. The adoption of a complete faith in technology not only is a failure to grasp that it is deeply implicated in extending the problems but also that problems have been created and are arriving for which there are no solutions.

Experientially, cities are domains of complexity, control, disorder, structure and breakdown, according to who and where you are. To be in the city is to be in this context of difference. The question to ask is thus: do we know this, do we see it, and so do we have a perspective?

---

[15] Fry, *Becoming Human by Design*, pp. 75–106.

Perspectives

Increasingly, the future of humanity is indivisible from the form and future of the city. So contextualized, an adopted point of view will always be a product of a perspectival ideological difference. What this means is that knowledge of the city, or lack of it, is becoming, or has become, a political issue for educators and communicators at all levels and in numerous media. By implication, while there are naive views of the city none are neutral, for what is actually observed is always refracted through the image and a theory of knowledge.

A positivistic view of the city objectifies it as structure (built fabric) and system (from its infrastructure to intersecting flows of people, materials, goods, capital, data, etc.). A constructivist perspective presumes the city is determined by competing and co-existing temporalities wherein matter and meaning are not necessarily connected to each other. This perspective accommodates a contestation of values within cities (not least between utopian and dystopic dispositions). Phenomenologically, how the city is seen and understood cannot be divided from how it is framed and experienced by a placement of difference (as, for example, posited by a geopolitical or geo-climatic destiny or the afterlife of the colonial matrix).

Existentially, the city can be claimed as a locus of belonging ('this is my city: I am a part of what it is, and it is part of what I am'). But conversely, it can be no more than a transitory and nomadic experience and treated as expediency dictates. Between these poles is a variability of investment in place.

Now once architecture is brought to presence, the city as such disappears – here is the essence of post-urbanism where the signature building is all and everything else can look after itself. Much architectural discourse repudiates this, but nobody is listening: it's just architecture talking to itself. Architecture always draws a line between creation and destruction, but mostly unknowingly. It celebrates creation – its own – and ignores what it destroys. The indulgent ego believes its creation justifies what it destroys, but it almost never does. Consider these words by two crusaders for the revitalization of architectural creativity:

> Architecture's presence proves creative productivity and the refashioning of an indeterminate nature towards purpose.[16]

These words do not come from a moment in the high point of the modern movement but have the smell of fresh printer's ink and an investment in

---

[16] Stephen Cairns and Jane M, Jacobs (2014), *Buildings Must Die: A Perverse View of Architecture*, Cambridge, MA: MIT Press, p. 52. The ecology of architecture they explore in this book veers between interesting insights and an overwhelming culturalist impulse to reinstate the architect as a creative hero within an uncritical and inappropriate Eurocentric paradigm.

conspicuous erudition. The ambiguity of architecture allows us to say in reply to their claim: 'Architecture's presence proves an unjustified destruction of ecologically determinate natural resources that continues unabated in the name of a misplaced creative practice'. The point to re-emphasize is that creation and destruction (which making makes unavoidable) are indivisible. Once this is fully understood, an ethical practice becomes recognized as 'destruction justified by its created end'.

Destruction, like creation, takes many forms, including the destruction of cities in the process of their recreation. As Justin McGuirk's book *Radical Cities* shows, Latin America is replete with such examples. They all exist within the 'dialectic of Sustainment' as it defines the inseparable relation that exists between creation and destruction.[17] This relation is identifiable contextually at every scale as contradiction. At the micro level, it is evident in the clearing of 'slums' to build modern structures that themselves become a new kind of slum. The massive Tlatelolco (hyper-Le Corbusier like) development opened in Mexico City in 1964 is a tragic example. In 1968 it was the site at which the Mexican military machine-gunned hundreds of student protestors gathered in the square a few days before the Olympic Games opened in the city. People massed from positions between the apartment blocks. The second tragedy of the development arrived as an earthquake in 1985. One block fell, others were demolished due to the scale of damage they suffered. By the 1990s the still vast area had become a 'no go zone'.

At the largest scale the double movement of the dialectic of Sustainment defines the character of so many Latin American cities.[18] Obviously it is not just confined to one geographic location. It can also, for example, be seen in China where a percentage of the population is getting wealthier and gaining international recognition while a whole other segment is in decline, becoming marginalized, living in the most basic of housing and forgotten. Meanwhile vast areas of cities, and some cities themselves, stand empty. Of course these people, and where they live, do not appear in the media because '. . . the mainstream media and cultural production are [sic] controlled by the state'.[19]

Idealism constantly turns to nothing. For instance, on one side we read the idealist aspirations of *A City for All: The Future of Human Settlement in Latin America and the Caribbean*, produced by the Latin American and Caribbean Commission on Human Settlement Report (Habitat II, 1996), which claimed

---

[17] Justin McGuirk (2014), *Radical Cities*, London: Verso.

[18] Ibid, pp. 1–8.

[19] Li Zhang (2010), 'Postsocialist Urban Dystopia?', in Gyan Prakash (ed.), *Noir Urbanisms: Dystopic Images of the Modern City*, Princeton, NJ: Princeton University Press, pp. 127–149.

that people had a 'right to the city' and this could be delivered by 'structural planning', creative financial management, and the bridging of the formal and informal sections of cities. But in reality what has actually happened a decade and a half later is otherwise, as is clear from research papers like 'The Fragmented City: Changing Patterns in Latin American Cities' by Axel Borsdorf and Rodrigo Hidalgo.

What Borsdorf and Hidalgo report is that a rapid modernization process has taken place driven by foreign investment.[20] This resulting in the creation of urban services owned by international companies providing high-quality standards of housing to middle- and upper-class customers. Additionally, this investment has supported imported lifestyles, leisure activities, privately owned motorways, industrial parks, shopping malls, entertainment centres, hotel chains and gated community developments. Meanwhile the state failed to intervene and completely neglected the public sphere, including public transport. This prompted the growth in car culture for those who could afford it and even more spatial fragmentation. In many instances rural migration went into reverse, the poor were forced out of the city by development or into informal settlements, which dramatically grew on the margins of cities. So in contrast to 'a city for all', what arrived was more corruption and increased inequity.

Ever loath to shy away from contradiction, the UN Human Settlement Program (UN Habitat) asserted urbanization to be a positive process notwithstanding the trauma, violence and environmental degradation it created. One wonders who benefited, besides those who profited from development projects.

It is projected that by 2050, ninety per cent of Latin America will be urbanized. What this means for cities of the region is that they will double or triple in size. This is a frightening prospect when it is recognized that Latin American cities are some of the most unequal and violent places in the world (forty of the top fifty most violent cities in the world are in Latin America). Does not this situation make UN talk of high-rise building as the path to the management of urban areas, and to sustainable development in Latin American cities seem farcical?[21]

While Latin America is becoming one of the most urbanized continents on Earth it, together with Sub-Saharan Africa, has the largest and fastest growing

---

[20] Axel Borsdorf and Rodrigo Hidalgo (2009), 'The Fragmented City: Changing Patterns in Latin American Cities', *The Urban Reinventors Online Journal*, Issue 3/09, pp. 1–18 [http://urbanreinventors. net/3/borsdorfhidalgo/borsdorfhidalgo-urbanreinventors.pdf].

[21] Paulo A. Paranagua (2012), 'Latin America Struggle to Cope with Record Urban Growth', *Guardian Weekly*, 11 September [https://www.theguardian.com/world/2012/sep/11/latin-america-urbanisation-city-growth], pp. 4–5.

informal sector in the world. In some cities some sixty per cent and more of all housing can be informal (and thus outside the structure of urban management), as is the urban economy. For example, in Bogota over half the workforce is informal.[22]

As is becoming increasingly apparent, and as philosophy has told us in so many ways, language prefigures perspective: we see with language because it acts as the concrete medium of thought. 'New urbanism' and its attempted radical remaking as 'entropic planning' is a cogent example.

In cities of wealth and social stability, 'new urbanism' is a planning idealism grounded in an antiseptic nostalgia and values that reduces the notion of community to a series of tropes of domestic architecture and planned neighbourhoods with walkable grids. It treats the city as an assemblage of isolates. In cities of inequity and instability new urbanism gives way to gated communities. In both these cases, and beyond a claim of style, new urbanism is neither new nor urban (in actuality these communities are nostalgia in form, disarticulated from the urban).

Entropic planning (besides doing violence to the concept of entropy[23]) is another kind of nostalgia and idealism that takes the 'chaos' of the medieval city, the Greek village and the Brazil favela as a design template. What it fails to recognize is that the order of the seeming visual disorder of such places is actually a product of a kinship structure layered onto a particular topography. Such places are reproduced by a 'look-alike' imposed architecture. The idealistic determinism of 'new urbanism' is misplaced. Perhaps the urban in-fill version is a little more defensible, but then how can any claim to difference from other innovatory in-fill actions be realistically made?

Almost every contemporary approach to planning now claims to contribute towards making cities more sustainable. The way they do this is by bringing an 'add-on' series of instrumental practices and technologies to the planning and architecture agenda: urban consolidation,[24] infrastructure localization, renewable energy and energy efficiency technologies, all to assist in the reduction of greenhouse gas emissions, the use of recycled and low environmental impact materials in building construction; water recycling, urban food production – these are some of the more familiar and favoured examples. Now all these

---

[22] Robert Albro (2014), 'The "Informal City" and Latin America's Urban Future', 17 April [https://aulablog.net/2014/04/17/the-informal-city-and-latin-americas-urban-future/].

[23] While based on the second law of thermodynamics, entropy has been developed and applied to many areas of scientific enquiry. At the same time it has become more widely applied to an understanding of the behaviour of systems in general, as they move organizationally from order to disorder wherein their energy becomes confined within the system and thus unusable. It is in this context that entropy becomes a metaphor of chaos.

[24] Urban consolidation while bringing some benefits also increases the risk of extreme weather events and pandemics.

actions are worth doing and are claimed to be fundamental to '. . . achieving progress towards sustainability' as an 'economy that concentrates on well-being'.[25] The claim is also widely made that changing behaviour and lifestyle is key to 'achieving a sustainable environment'. The limitation of the perceptual reach of such thinking is substantial.

First of all, creating the conditions that will sustain human being depends upon overcoming our anthropocentric centre of gravity and demands 'we find ways to become other than we are'. Next, sustainable development presumes sustainability can arrive by sustaining the status quo via moderate reform. Not only does this thinking fold back into upholding 'business as usual' but exposes a fundamental failure to understand that the unsustainable is itself grounded in the anthropocentric essence of human being. As this it requires to be brought to presence and redirected towards a structure of responsibility. The illogic of the hegemonic economy has no comprehension of functioning within conditions that are finitudinally delimited. Moreover, the dynamic of global population growth, and consumerist expansion, all totally outstrip advocated actions of 'gestural sustainability'.

To create the Sustainment of all that needs to be sustained requires the commencement of processes of relational cooperation that transgress those divisions of knowledge (like architecture and planning) that decouple action from the complexity that is foundational to working to advance the Sustainment, this as it is intellectually underpinned, culturally understood, well-communicated, enacted in practical projects, and directed at the negation of pure destruction (like ecocide, global conflict and poverty, ethnocide, and 'hyper-consumerism').

In sum: a created rigour of the thinking and practice of the project of the Sustainment needs to arrive, is slowly arriving, so as to displace the debased and hollowed-out language of 'sustainability'.

Just as current perspectives on destruction are massively circumscribed and as such not grasped at all adequately by almost all proponents of sustainability, so equally is creativity mostly unthought. This assertion is very evident in design and architectural education and practice. Creativity is dominantly assigned as something that a subject is endowed with, is evident and exercised in their practice, yet, as said, such action mostly is oblivious to its resultant destructive consequences.

Nothing now exposes a limited and vacuous understanding of 'creative' more than its conflation with class. The 'creative class' names something that is almost nothing. It has been employed in such broad and uncritical ways as

---

[25] Mike Jenks and Nicola Dempsey (2005), *Future Forms and Designs for Sustainable Cities*, Oxford: Architecture Press, p. 25.

to now sweep up almost all 'white collar' workers while overlooking the creative activities of most 'blue collar' workers. More than this, such a thinking of creativity fails to comprehend the creative spirit of liberated imagination, including those of indigenous cultures. It equally ignores the destructive force of modernity, and its latter-day regimes of management as they erase that human potentially which so much creativity rests upon. Neither does late modernity recognize how the cultures of compliance of modern education are so destructive of those modes of deviance which creative insight so often depends upon.

'Creativity' has now been become inducted into the language and mind-set of Eurocentric neo-conservatives and their spurious metrics. While the doyens of the 'creative class' promote themselves as innovators and transformers of cities, what they actually do is feed the destructive economy that contributes to the advancement of structural unsustainability.[26]

Change and a return to metrofitting

If, as is the case, humanity has to adaptively change in order to survive, then there have to be ontologically designing environments that prompt and support this process (for such change cannot come from an appeal to transformations of the consciousness of 'the masses'). Contrary to their current unsustainable propensity, there is no question that cities are the most influential of these potential designing environments.

But given what of the urban already exists, what exactly can change? Is it actually possible to change cities, and more generally the nature of human settlement? Can we, in all our differences, change if cities change? Is there a real understanding of what cities are and what they could become? Is there a future in prospect wherein there will be almost no form of human settlement but cities? How can we think these questions? The traversing of them, as they take various forms and arrive in various contexts, defines the direction of our journey through the outlined issues of concern and towards thinking and acting otherwise.

The agenda of metrofitting now starts to acquire a little more shape. As such, it has to explore the indeterminacy of the city, its fragmentation, its porous edges, its creative and destructive metabolism, the risks to which it is exposed, what has to be learnt, what thinking has to be abandoned, what is broken, what can be repaired, and by whom, the politics of change, and the

---

[26] See, for example, Richard Florida (2002), *The Rise of the Creative Class*, New York: Basic Books, and Charles Landry (2000), *The Creative City*, London: Comedia/Earthscan.

imperative of acting in time (the medium and in a recognition of the urgency of the plight of the human condition of unsustainability). Problems proliferate: even if solutions are identified is intervention possible, and if so where and how (this in recognition that the record of architects, planners, designers, developers and politicians to date is mostly appalling)? Can other ways of enabling affirmative change be found? But then what solutions already exist, and can they be replicated and communicated?

As should now be absolutely clear, this journey is one of enquiry and thus it refuses the promise of a 'how-to book of answers'. There are now bookshop shelves full of books telling would-be change agents how to create sustainable buildings, communities, villages, cities, products, businesses, agriculture and so on, yet en masse they have hardly made a dent in the problem. This book starts in another place. Rather than avoiding the complexity of the transformation of 'the human' (of human settlement) and then of settlement, it embraces such complexity. Unless 'we' change nothing will change, but as indicated unless the socio-cultural and politico-material environments in which we are formed change, 'we' will not change. Here, then, is a classic and unavoidable double-bind problem that this book will live with. In sum: the knowledge of what we are is not on the outside of the broken and often destructive world of human creation. Whatever we will or may become can only but come out of this world. This observation is not incidental to metrofitting but rather its essence. As suggested, the remaking of cities, as action and outcome, is a means of our own remaking.

PART ONE

Contexts of Change
The Limits of How We
See Cities Today

Informed by an understanding of the city as an increasingly plural object of incoherence – which all regimes and discourses of the city attempt to order by, for instance, the law, mapping, auditing, documenting and imaging – our starting point will strive to expose the value of a kaleidoscopic way of viewing the city. The mirrors of the kaleidoscope reproduce disorder as pattern to create an illusion of order. The city so managed likewise brings a lot of fragments into view, but any sense they form and hold an ordered whole is illusory. Patterns are projected onto disorder to construct symmetrical and non-symmetrical forms as a totality. The idea does its work and the assembly arrives with difference flattened.

What follows provides a variety of contexts and perspectives directed at assisting the grasping of the complexity of cities. Immediately one has to acknowledge that the true complexity exceeds all representational ambitions. In fact one does not know, and cannot quantify, the sum of fragments that constitute the difference that is the city.

The familiar reduction of the city to a pattern language by planning theory is a misplaced ordering. Such order does not hold. The forces driving urbanization, the nature of deepening unsustainability, and geopolitical flux continuously shatter the mirrors supporting the illusion. The only constant is continuous change. To walk the city so understood is to constantly digress.

1

Cities now

No matter how established the city seems as built fabric, infrastructure, population, culture and economy, as the world changes so too does it. The human-formed structure and life of the city always exist in this continual worldly flux. Likewise, a full picture of the city never appears. It can only arrive as fragments and impressions that can never be prised away from a seeing subject who looks and constructs his or her own images. By implication, different subjects of varied cultures, backgrounds, occupations, classes, genders do not see the city, their city, uniformly.

Seeing the city

Michel Foucault made clear in the Preface to his *The Order of Things*, with reference to a fictitious taxonomy of animals presented by Jorge Luis Borges, just how influential the seemingly logical, but actually illogical, constructed systems of classification are. Here are Borges's words as cited by Foucault:[1]

> . . .'certain Chinese encyclopedia' in which it is written that 'animals are divided into: (a) belonging to the Emperor, (b) embalmed, (c) tame, (d) sucking pigs, (e) sirens, (f) fabulous, (g) stray dogs, (h) included in the present classification, (i) frenzied, (j) innumerable, (k) drawn with a very fine camelhair brush, (l) et cetera, (m) having just broken the water pitcher, (n) that from a long way off look like flies'.

Borges mocks just how arbitrary acts of classification are. What now can guide the listing of the ways of seeing the city that can categorize its elements with any claim to an adequacy of representation? Certainly there will be no reference to things coloured, parks, trees and streetscapes, monuments, public art, urban bird life, lamp posts, waste bins, fountains and ponds, crime,

---

[1] Michel Foucault (1994 [1966]), *The Order of Things*, New York, Vintage Books, p. xv.

public transport, paving materials, etc., etc. But what will be presented are ways of seeing the city that assist the explication of a narrative of metrofitting in terms of what it should, could or might engage as a transformative practice, politics and urban heuristics. As will now be realized, such listing cannot be claimed as definitive. It has no particular place to start or finish and so is only indicative: so to begin.

The romanticization of the city of European modernity, with its supposed vitality and promise of a brave future, captivated the avant-garde. But illusion did not survive the death of idealism rendered by the First World War. The visualization of the city as an object of desire has never had much in common with its overall reality. Yet the city as attractor, which again is never more than just an imagined fragment of the whole, lingers on. People continue to migrate to the city with a sense of excitement, but not with the spirit that emanated from the first age of mass urbanization. As the 1951 Roy Hawkins song (made famous by B.B. King) says, 'The Thrill is Gone'. The city as idea is not what it once was: the dynamic of the modern has been displaced by the magnetic force of money. Nonetheless a residual hope of the city delivering a better life remains.

Those who professionally image the city – urban designers, urban geographers, planners, cartographers, transport engineers, urban sociologists and so on – can never provide an adequate picture. The delimitations of disciplinary perspectives obstruct the construction of a comprehensive image. While delivering a complete picture is impossible, creating a sense of scale and complexity of the city depends upon exposing an awareness of absence. The viewer in knowing the picture is incomplete knows there is more to see. So with all this in mind, 'here is the city'.

One is usually presented with the city as formally constituted structures, both material and institutional, that have been sanctioned by the rule of law. But increasingly alongside this city, especially in those poorer countries that are rapidly urbanizing, is the growth of the informal city. In a significant number of cities, the informal is overtaking the formal in scale and population. The formal, in exploiting the informal as a source of cheap labour and services, feeds its growth. Thus the informal becomes hybrid borderland wherein the illegal and legal fuse to constitute something neither command. At the same time, the informal instils fear, for it is outside the reach and rule of urban management (and in many cases the rule of law).

Obviously urban hybridization takes on many forms, and has done so for eons. In the city of privilege this takes on familiar material forms: retrofitted, the sheds of a railway works become a school of music or home to a cluster of new technology business incubators; a once commercial docklands becomes a marina and mooring for twenty-first-century houseboats; a section of a struggling industrial estate becomes the city's sex worker centre and then, within a few years, nightclubs, cafes and bars move in as welding shops, steel fabricators, auto-parts suppliers and plastic extruding factories move out. In a not so privileged city, an empty office block, factory or cluster of abandoned railway carriages on the edge of the informal area gets taken over by homeless people. So many designations of space that seem so fixed, rational and ordered transpire to be fluid. The industrial, domestic, commercial, the impoverished, blighted, abandoned, the luxurious, desirable and chic: none are assured to hold their use and ground in time.

The city has always been a draw for people seeking work, wealth, pleasure, the exotic, the erotic, anonymity, friendship, hope, shelter, drugs, fame. In this respect, accident and opportunity conflate. Even if created for a specific purpose, a city never holds to its initially posited destiny – its projected future becomes corrupted in the flow of endless change. The deployment of the organic metaphor to describe the life of the city is equally misplaced. There is too much of it that is toxic, mutant and unnatural. It does not function or cohere as an organism. Its life and death are not within a regenerative process but rather are a consequence of good or bad fortune, an economic opportunity or travesty, creative endeavour or violence. Capital decides what is nascent or terminal, to be fed or starved. Technology walks the line between life and death. Dominantly, it is not the good that die young but the poor and the malnourished.

As an environment, the city partly makes its own climate. As such it forms a climatic zone to which its waste heat, radiated heat from thermal mass, exhausted pollutants, wastewater, sewage, constructed windscapes and planted vegetation all contribute.

As already indicated, the city is an un-viewable object: what you see from the street is the street; seeing it from the air or space reduces it to an abstraction. A map and plans are other kinds of abstraction. Paintings, film and photography deliver fragments and impressions. Memory gets left behind. The only thing that stands in for the complete image of the city is it as idea.

The space of the city is existentially encountered as place (of the body, the senses and the intellect), as Henri Lefebvre made clear. It is a conflation of: the product of spatial practices, including those that actively construct it socially and occupy it culturally; the agency of the representation of space which orders it as plan, sign, code and imaged objectified relations; and representational spaces in which coded and non-coded elements of the symbolic order of the city are made to appear.[2] All such spaces as they constitute the city, again as Lefebvre recognized, are inscriptions in time (as it is understood as plural).[3]

---

[2] Henri Lefebvre (1991 [1974]), *The Production of Space* (trans. Donald Nicholson-Smith), London: Blackwell, pp. 33–39.
[3] Henri Lefebvre (1996), *Writing on Cities* (trans. and ed. Eleonore Kofman and Elizabeth Lebas), London: Blackwell, pp. 16–17.

As a habitat the city is obviously a complex ecology in which we co-exist in the company of many life forms from the large and visible to the microscopically unseen. The city as habitat goes mostly unseen, it is ignored, and 'the environment' is talked of as if somewhere else. Likewise, the city as metabolic process is equally overlooked. As is the city as a sewer, as rot and decay, as a harbinger of disease, and as a machine of destruction – this is all kept out of mind and placed beyond the gaze. Dominantly the reach of the metabolically visible only goes as far as viewing goods in the shops, food on the shelves of supermarkets, the content of the waste bin, the garbage truck and the excrement in the toilet bowl. The speed at which everything passes through the metabolic machine of destruction that is intrinsic to the city, as fed and managed by an industry, mostly takes place in the domain of the invisible. Concerns reside elsewhere expressed, depending on class, in table talk are of reality TV, the price of bread, the quality of the wine, the time it took for the pizza delivery to arrive or of the latest and most fashionable restaurant to visit. Meanwhile fast foodies speed things along with a constant stream of food waste, discarded plastic eating utensils, empty cans and packaging.

The city is of course image, sign and semiosphere. We (all of us who live in cities) are all part of it as image: we are the imaged, image-makers, readers and writers of the city as text. Each of us knows a little of the city as a story (every such story is a travel story[4]), but few of us know 'the real story' of the city. What is seen populates memory, wherein map and experience merge and in so doing create a sense and relation to place. In the positive and negative ways in which it is experienced, and thereafter coded, the city is created as narrative and memory. It follows that as experience changes, so does place. We may live in the same city but we don't know it as the same place.

The city is equally seen in time: it is an assemblage of visually discernible matter of different moments. Know it or not, what is seen is constantly being read in time – the cityscape is thus also always a timescape.

Yet the city is also more than time and place: it is also (a compound) event, as such it is theatre. It is watched, although most of what is staged is banal, but drama is always awaited, expected, hoped for and, from time to time, happens. The theatre, of course, is not silent: all the stages of the cityscape are also soundscapes. The city is heard, occasionally attentively but mostly not. There is recoil from the way it assaults by sound, but then again its sound is also enjoyed.

The city is also a socio-political landscape where ethnicity and class are territorial determinates, and together with gender and religion, are generative of its cultures and the variability and viability of its communities. The socio-

[4] Michel de Certeau (1988), *The Practice of Everyday Life* (trans. Steven Rendall), Berkeley, CA: University of California Press.

political relations of the city are indivisible from how issues of inequity and poverty, social justice, crime and 'race', housing and homelessness, the state of the local environment and public health, as well as the economy and employment are all seen, and by whom. What all of these relations express is that while the population of the city may live in the same urban conurbation, existentially they do not live in the same socio-political place. The reality of this difference is equally territorially inscribed. Depending, be they the rich or the poor, the powerful or the marginalized, there are various parts of the city that these people never visit. By implication, most people do not stray far from their socio-economic and cultural enclaves. The sacred and the profane, capital and lack of it, fear and panic all lay a semiotic veil over the city that while not completely visible is continually read.

Much of what has been touched on in this partial and impressionist characterization of the complexity of the city will be picked up and over in far more detail as our narrative moves on. But at this stage there are two important ways to see the city that beg registration. The first is seeing the city as technology. Here in such a city (of relative affluence) is found a trench map where power, water, gas, waste and fibre optic cable travel a wandering journey. Then there are the even more invisible multiple-frequency telecommunication signals travelling through its skies. Of course, between that which is below ground and in the sky there is the vast road, rail and air transport infrastructure along with street lighting, the technology of traffic management, the infrastructure of emergency services and now the omnipotent technologies of the police, and national security surveillance. Every one of these technologies constitutes its own picture of the city within which 'we' continually appear as nodal points as users, travellers, suspects, victims, bystanders, customers. Yet in the city where poverty dominates, where infrastructure dysfunction constitutes a massive structure of limitation, transcending such negative conditions of life is a daily struggle for survival.

The fate of cities: seeing dangers

Urban life is only a mark of a recent episode in the history of human earthly habitation. Put in the perspective of the history of our species: we, *Homo sapiens*, came into being some 160,000 years ago and for most of this time were nomadic, whereas human settlement commenced approximately 10,000 years ago and the first city, Uruk, was created a mere 7,000 years ago.[5] During the entirety of this period, the fate of cities has never been assured.

---

[5] Çatalhöyük – a very large Neolithic and Chalcolithic proto-city settlement in southern Anatolia (Turkey) – is around the same age as Uruk but not of the same urban status.

Although cities of the past have been exposed to, and sometimes been destroyed by, the ravages of war and nature, they have never confronted the level of uncertainty about their future that now exists as a result of the combination of massive population pressures, environmental impacts (not least from climate change), insecure food security, and geopolitical reconfiguration in an age of ever-accelerating technological change, including its unprecedented destructive power. We humans have never been so many and destroyed so much. So framed, and in recognition of the placement and construction of many cities in inappropriate geological or climatic locations, there is now a slow realization that many cities around the world are at ever-increasing risk.

Three stark consequences arrive out of these observations: some cities will be abandoned in whole or in part, some will be transformed (hence metrofitting), and new modes of earthly habitation and city forms will have to arrive.

Danger and uncertain futures

There are immediate discernible dangers that can be instantly identified and acted upon when they are encountered: ice on the road, fallen power lines, an aeroplane with engine problems, a home invader and so on. But then there are dangers that are known but prompt no action because they seem abstract and seem not to pose any immediate threat. Even when they are viewed and felt as threatening they do not galvanize action, as they are deemed by most people to be beyond the reach of the individual. Dividing these two situations is just the difference between knowledge grounded in direct experience versus knowledge mediated by 'experts', often scientific. The latter is also not given due attention because it so often looks to be in the distant future and thus not pressing. As Friedrich Nietzsche recognized, human beings are 'chronophobic' – we fear time, only have a very limited ability to think in time (unless we learn to do so), and live with an illusion of permanence.[6] So framed, the city is seen as rock-like, as something solid. But in time rocks weather away, crack from tectonic movement and turn to sand. A seeming appearance of normality can also negate a willingness to think and act futurally.

Yet future threatening dangers are now increasingly unsettling ever more people. But which of these dangers loom the largest? Some would say, for example, climate change, global conflict, a nuclear disaster or a pandemic. But such answers immediately beg qualification. First, these dangers, and most others, do not exist independently from each other. They are in fact relationally

---

[6] On chronophobia and permanence, see Bernd Magnus (1978), *Nietzsche's Existential Imperative,* Bloomington, IN: Indiana University Press, pp. 190–195.

connected. Climate change, for instance, can mean large numbers of people crossing borders illegally looking for food and water (because their sources of both have failed) and being met with violence. Likewise, such displaced people living in poor sanitary conditions may become exposed to vector-borne diseases carried by insects, rats and bats whose numbers increase dramatically due to an increased food supply coming from warmer conditions.

For many millions of people, the kinds of dangers just considered are not lodged in the future: they are already here and having a dramatic impact on their lives. For instance, this situation is true for those people living in the delta region of Bangladesh who are dealing with the impact of sea level rise. They have few options: the nation's border with India is fenced and patrolled by Indian troops; if they migrate to the hills they are met with hostility; and having nowhere to go, some flee as boat people. In such contexts, researchers are questioning the contribution played by climate change in the rise, spread and fatal consequences of Ebola in West Africa, and the relation of increased temperatures to rising levels of conflict in East Africa. Then there are the millions of people made refugees by conflict in Syria, Afghanistan and Iraq where violence, the destruction of cities and natural resources, massive environmental damage, together with a lack of food and water, all combine to force people to leave their homeland.

The phenomenal manifestation of such dangers and disasters is hard to comprehend, as are the efficacious forms of practical response. Harder to grasp though is how to deal intellectually and psychologically with the prospective dangers. The most threatening to humanity, if long term, is at the start of the planet's sixth major extinction event[7] – this prompted by the impact of human unsustainable actions upon biodiversity. Again this is not a 'stand alone' problem but part of the defuturing and relational character of structural unsustainability. One wonders why these dangers go by with so little questioning. Does the dominant way they are defined instrumentally feed the assumption they can be solved by technology? Is it because some seem to be distant that it is assumed that people of the future will have the knowledge to deal with them? One area, however, where there is growing debate is how existing and emergent worldly circumstances are actually changing not just the environments of our existence but also the very essence of what we are as beings.[8]

In the light of these remarks, consider this: between 1936 and 1938 in a dangerous moment in the career of Martin Heidegger, and the beginning of one of the most dangerous moments of the twentieth century, he wrote his

---

[7] Elizabeth Kolbert (2014), *The Sixth Extinction: An Unnatural History*, New York: Henry Holt.
[8] See, for example, Stefan Herbrechter (2013), *Posthumanism: A Critical Analysis*, London: Bloomsbury.

Beiträge zur Philosophie (von Ereignis), and while viewed as his most important work after *Sein und Zeit (Being and Time)*, it was not published until 1989 (the centennial of his birth); the English translation, *Contributions to Philosophy (From Enowning)*, appeared in 1999. The following text is taken from this work as a means to reflect upon how 'making' (and also remaking) can be viewed against the backdrop of the kind of dangers that now need to be understood:

> Everything 'is made' and 'can be made' if one only musters the 'will' for it. But this 'will' is precisely what has already placed and in advance reduced what might be possible and above all necessary – this is already mistaken ahead of time and left outside any questioning. For this will, which makes everything, has already subscribed to machination, the interpretation of beings as re-presentable and re-presented.[9]

Two qualifications frame what Heidegger says here and direct how we should read it: the first is that humanity exists in '*the epoch of the total lack of questioning*', and second 'everything has already subscribed to machination' (a condition of everything becoming instrumentalized).[10]

What Heidegger is saying, and what it means in relation to the making of the disaster of extinction (for us), is that philosophy took a turn with Plato that continued throughout Western metaphysics that was based on a productivist mode of thought (the world as structure able to be remodelled by human beings). Thus what this knowledge sought to disclose was instrumental thought as enabling (world) making in its most extended sense (the making of ideas, science, technology and form) as a directed reign of knowledge in absolute dominance. This thinking is 'machination' at its extreme, and it has been present from the very birth of the modern Western mind. Questioning hereafter thus became almost completely bonded to 'how to make' and was thus viewed by Heidegger as the end of questioning at its most fundamental level – which is the level at which the question of why is paramount.

So in saying 'Everything "is made" and "can be made" if one only musters the "will" for it', Heidegger is effectively stating the potential of human beings. But he then goes on to point out that this 'will' is precisely what has already been emplaced and so, in advance, reduces what might be possible and above all is necessary. In saying this, the instrumentalism of machination is exposed as integral to a will that delimits what could be made. As such, it constituted a

---

[9] Martin Heidegger (1999), *Contributions to Philosophy (From Enowning)* (trans. Parvis Emad and Kenneth Maly), Bloomington, IN: Indiana University Press, p. 76.
[10] On 'machination' I am indebted to the insight of Brad Elliot Stone (2003), 'What is Machination?' Chapter Two of PhD dissertation, *Dominions and Domains*, University of Memphis, Memphis, TN.

mistake that travelled out into the future, which excluded and 'banned', that fundamental questioning of 'why make' that would have enabled a questioning and opened the possibility of another and essentially necessary making.

The result of this (still continuing) trajectory of construction is an actual deformation of making. As a consequence, what appears to be made is in fact an unmaking: a breaking of the world of essential dependence by the making of an antithetical world within it (making weapons of mass destruction is a crude illustration of the point). Thus a future is made that effectively defutures.

The discourse of sustainability, and all that is offered under its aegis, has yet to learn this. At present it still remains lodged in the very instrumentalism of unmaking and so folds back into the foundation of the problems it presents itself as working to resolve. Architecture is deeply embedded in this situation. What it creates always travels towards decay and eventual death – often after only a short duration of time; and infrequently over a long time. It is also a destroyer: every building leaves a trail of destruction in its wake. The trail can be small, but often it is not. One of the greatest material crimes here is the vast expenditure of non-renewable natural resources and the accumulation of a vast amount of embodied energy in structures that capital has destined to have a short life.

The danger of the unmaking of the world of our dependence by the world of our construction, with the city as its paramount attainment, goes mostly unseen. What is visible is the fast disaster. This can be seen in specific disaster events that happen very quickly, such as extreme weather events resulting in high numbers of human casualties. The destruction of rainforests, the melting of sea ice because of global warming, sea level rises, the salination of wetlands and the loss of biodiversity, all lack obvious visual markers for most people. But then beyond these dangers there is the possibility of going past a tipping point that triggers a fast and total collapse of the entire global system, including the industrial system. As the Earthinsight report of NASA's Goddard Space Center study cited in its introduction: 'there is a clear prospect of a collapse in coming decades of industrial civilization due to unsustainable resource exploitation'.[11] Some reports have gone so far as to say this could happen within the next two decades.

Slow disasters feed the fast disasters – problems coming from the generation of power by the burning of fossil fuel being an obvious example. What is not so readily recognized is the staged process of slow disasters. Cities like Jakarta in the newly industrializing nation of Indonesia tell this story.

Greater Jakarta has a growing population heading towards 30 million. As a delta city it is at the confluence of thirteen rivers. It gets major and regular

---

[11] Nafeez, 'Nasa-funded Study'.

floods. These have been made worse from the run-off created by the clearing of the hills behind the city. Besides being at risk from sea level rises, the destruction of the mangroves, which once lined the foreshore, has increased the impact of storm surges. Jakarta is a slow disaster in process. Actions taken in its 'development' have layered risk upon risk. People already often die due to the extreme weather events it experiences. Slowly over the coming century, and beyond, the sea will claim the city. Meanwhile, a major cyclonic event or an earthquake could pre-empt this slower demise. Little stands between the city and its fate. The sea wall 'protecting' the city makes the point. It has been allowed to fall into disrepair. This inaction went alongside other short-sighted measures, like the clearing of the hillsides for development, which set up a potential for other urban ecological, social and economic disasters together with a systems *breakdown*.[12] If these events happen, and are severe, then there is the possibility of a total urban *collapse*. Thereafter there would be a partial or total *abandonment* of the city (rapid or staged). So is Jakarta doomed? Perhaps. The more rampant the development, the more the informal sector of the city is ignored, the more consumption continues unchecked, the more the danger grows.

The world is full of such fated cities in denial of their fate. These cities are terminal. They are likely to die before water drowns them. In many cases that death will come as soon as the value of property disintegrates – on this, Miami could well be one place to watch.

Obviously, there will be attempts to rescue some of these cities. If enough money is spent, some time for some cities will be bought – but the likelihood is that most attempts will fail. Very significant abandonments of parts of cities, or entire cities, will happen. At the same time, new kinds of conglomerate cities will form, especially within megaregions, thereby creating what effectively will be new city-states. Other new city forms will also arrive. But the imperative to save and revitalize huge numbers of existing cities will be of enormous importance. Here is where metrofitting will have its day. At this point it is important to again re-emphasize that metrofitting is not just about simply repairing what already exists. Rather, it goes to actually transforming the city via remaking it in mind and matter. So such change is not just about repair and the structure and scale of the fabric of the city, its functional operation and economy. It is also about the reconstruction of the social and cultural nature of the city and its psychological landscape, its environment of work and semiological presence (its life as a sign).[13]

---

[12] The loss of plants and trees and the introduction of hard landscape dramatically increases the volume of water from storm run-off flowing into the city.

[13] One that comes to mind is the now famous Torre David tower block in Caracas. Although they had no electrical power, many of the 3,000 homeless people who moved in walked hundreds and

As will increasingly become clear, forms of remaking within metrofitting, whatever their practical expression, are always to be political, social and cultural. More than this, whatever is being remade equally implies the remaking of time (especially as the time-space of the city as event). If metrofitting is to gain any traction, it requires to be seen within such general, as well as in more specific, contexts.

The notion of 'the end times', the future as apocalyptic, the coming of zombies, has become intrinsic to popular culture: it is the stuff of movies, television, video games, novels, popular music and as such has spawned sub-cultures. Ecological disasters – actual and expected – are now one of the staples of the media, movies and novels. Environmental problems are now elemental to education from grade one to post-doctoral. In the contextual ambiguity of this milieu there is the huge gap between dystopic projections and the presentation of instrumentalized problems to be met with pragmatic solutions. This situation can be characterized as the schism between the depths of the unsustainable and the superficiality of 'sustainability' (as mostly an instrumental form of responsive action). Besides the 'logic' of sustainability underpinning the sustaining of the unsustainable, the economy of industrial civilization and thus the dominant politico-social status quo, *fails to comprehend that unsustainability is essentially grounded in us*, in our very being (our ontology). We humans, as makers of a world-within-the world, were destined to create the unsustainable, but modernity supercharged this propensity. Yet the cause of *the problem* – our ontology – is almost totally overlooked. When placed alongside the still growing global symptoms of unsustainability (not least global hyper-consumerism mobilized as to power continual economic growth), almost all proposed actions claimed to be sustainable are token.

This is not to say that water treatment plants, renewable energy systems, 'green buildings' and so on should not be created, or that they do not improve specific conditions. But they do not overcome the fundamental problem (us), rather they function within 'the logic of the mind' that is the problem. Within this logic, a great deal of what is presented as a problem assumes the need to create a solution. Whereas so much of what threatens is beyond our means

hundreds of stairs of this almost fifty-storey block on a daily basis. What was created in the end was a vertical village coming out of the abandonment of a building that was conceived to be quite otherwise. With some certainty one can say that there will be many more buildings like Torre David in the future. Such structures invite innovation: like from the recovery of ancient and medieval mechanics to transport materials and maybe people up the vertical face of the building. Here is a technology of ropes, chains, pulleys, weights, human-powered winches, slings, counter-weights, hoists, jibs – much of this technology has modern forms (especially from sailing and climbing). Combined with a huge amount of available labour power, a new imaginary could be created. The point to be emphasized about such thinking is that it is not offered and claimed as a solution but rather as a starting point. See McGuirk, *Radical Cities*. The sad postscript is that in 2014 the city removed the people and the building was demolished.

to solve. For example, no matter what we now do, sea levels will continue to rise for centuries and the impact of the loss of biodiversity to date is not going to be reversed. Moreover, nobody has any idea what the intermediate impacts of these problems will be. Will key links in food chains be broken? Will some species of animals or insects arrive in plague proportions? Will huge pandemics be triggered? Who knows?

Certainly the call for human beings to reduce their destructive impact upon their world of dependence has to be made far more effectively than it has been to date (otherwise a possible ecological 'corrective' collapse will occur and large numbers of Earth's species will not survive).

In the face of the deepening condition of unsustainability and the impossibility of solving many unstoppable defuturing processes, our species' 'survival will largely depend upon the degree to which it can adapt. Adaptation is the essence of metrofitting the city as an environment of material, socio-political, economic and cultural human existence. Again it cannot be reduced to purely instrumental action to sustain the status quo if it is to have any efficacy.

City of fear

Cities have always carried some connotation of fear, be it legitimate and grounded or perceived (both of which are directive of action). Here is the fear of dark places, the mob, criminal gangs and the deranged, but now something has changed.

In 1951, Ernst Jünger remarked that 'fear is symptomatic of our times'[14] – his context: the shadow cast by both the inhumanity of the Holocaust and the atomic bombing of Japan. During the Cold War this fear was amplified by the omnipresent threat of global nuclear annihilation. Now, in the present age of absolutely insecure futures, fear has become a deeply embedded and unsettling structural element of the human psyche. In some respects, the more informed one becomes the more there is to fear. This situation suggests a new psychology is in formation – one relative to the proximity to danger.

Against the backdrop of the acknowledged massive challenges to humanity, with the myriad dangers that travel with it, it is clear that fear itself has become instrumentalized. And this masks what needs to be the guiding concern in our facing fundamental dangers of our time. For instance, 'the fear of the everyday' now translates to 'health and safety at work' and especially to laws dealing with any exposure of the young to the dangers of drugs, pornography and paedophiles. The measure of this fear is that parents are becoming ever more

---

[14] Ernst Jünger (2013 [1951]), *The Forest Passage* (trans. Thomas Friese), New York: Telos Publishing, p. 27.

protective. Hereafter, homes become a zone of protection, the street a place of danger and fear a feedstock of neuroses. Then there is race, street and gun violence, and the rise of the city as a dominant site of conflict, including proliferating asymmetrical warfare. It's easy to dismiss such observations in the living room of a house in North Shore Sydney, a comfortable apartment in downtown Oslo, a townhouse in Singapore, or on a quiet street in Oxford, but not so easy if you live in informal Caracas, on the South Side of Chicago, in shell-scarred Ramallah or in the ruin of Homs.

As Urick Beck has sought to make clear for many years through his numerous publications, we all now live in a 'risk society'.[15] From crossing a bridge after a flood, to major investment decisions and the dangers posed by taking students on a field trip, everything in highly developed nations has become subject to a risk assessment. Meanwhile, for 'the rest' danger and fear is something else: it may be marked by a handgun in your car's glove box, life in a gated community or a bulldozer coming down your street towards your informally constructed shack, a visit to a hospital with almost no money to pay for treatment, or a bomb on a bus.

Having said all this, and having paid heed to Jünger's comment, what is actually being described is not new. Rather, it is the current manifestation of what Friedrich Nietzsche called nihilism.[16] Subsequent events have vindicated his conclusion that what modernity did was to render subjects helpless before the forces to which they were exposed. Neither wars, nor revolutions, nor least of all capitalism have slowed the dynamics of destruction of the world of human dependence enacted by the world of human creation (with the city at its epicentre).

Nihilism is the underpinning character of unsettlement – this in both its conscious form (concern for the self as inseparable from concern for the future) and its unconscious form (the lack of care for the self or the future accompanied by the negation of time by hedonism). The nihilistic life is one where aversive action can be taken to improve one's immediate conditions, but without any sense that anything can be done about underlying causes. Such action is fatalistic and a resignation to helplessness so often covered over by the pursuit of pleasure and distraction. Dominantly this life is lived in 'the city of panic' as characterized by Paul Virilio.[17]

Global and local fear converges on the 'city of panic'. The apparent speed of action taken to reach any destination, any goal, is in some sense an attempted

[15] See, for example, Ulrich Beck (1999), *World Risk Society*, Cambridge: Polity Press.
[16] On nihilism, see Friedrich Nietzsche (1968 [1901]), *Will to Power* (trans. Walter Kaufmann and R. J. Hollingwood), New York: Vantage Books, pp. 9–82; and Tony Fry (2012), 'Nietzsche on Nihilism', in *Becoming Human by Design*, London: Berg, pp. 25–32.
[17] Virilio, *City of Panic*.

speeding out of a panic that knows the city to be a disaster. The city continually arrives globally as a fast disaster, this as it constantly becomes a target in war, with an attack that can come from the air, the ground or both. In this age where war and terror do not stay in place, any city, anywhere, can become a designated target. Confirmation of this is provided by surveillance technology as it has become omnipresent in everyday life everywhere. The imaged strives to hold panic in place. The entire world is scanned from the sky; no matter how secure one might feel, there is no place that is assuredly safe. Gated suburbs (be they in the richest or poorest nations), with security compounds, CCTV cameras, infrared and movement sensors, armed guards, watch towers, steel doors, guard dogs, checkpoints, are all semiotic markers of the 'city of panic'. Security has actually become integral to our lifeworld, and because of this a mostly illusory basis of safety. As said, and as we all existentially know, some cities are far more dangerous than others. In the worst, thousands die each year from gun violence – currently in the USA it's ninety people a day.

2

Understanding the city as a designing event

This chapter introduces and poses a question central to the book: what do cities actually design? Clearly the question implies a change in how design and cities are perceived – one that moves from just viewing the city as incrementally designed and constructed over time to equally seeing it as a designing event in itself. Two qualifications are now required: the first is to explain the circular relation between the designed and designing; and the second to exposit what is meant in this context by 'event'.

The design of the city is a continual process from its moment of conception to the everyday major and minor designed additions made to it during the course of its existence by design – by professionals and by the people living in it who add to its material and social fabric. These actions, of course, interact with each other in both positive and negative ways to improve or, without intent, harm the city aesthetically, operationally, economically, environmentally, socially or culturally. A straightforward example here is traffic management, which if done well makes the city better at an operational level, but if done badly obviously has the opposite effect. Either way, at the most general, the more traffic the more the (urban) environment suffers. The designing of the city does not reduce purely to its phenomenal forms but clearly extends to the prefiguration of the forms of ways of life, conduct in the public sphere, sensibilities, social relations, and the economic cultural practices of its population. In this context, whatever is designed goes on designing modes of worldly engagement, use and user actions. So it follows that the ontology of the urban subject is designed in large part by the ongoing ontologically designing nature of the elements of the city.[1]

---

[1] These dynamic relations between the city, the subject, ontology and design reflect the more general mutually animatory exchange between the proximity of being and things whereby the engagement of the one by the other expresses the essence of the things and a perpetual process of transformation. A consideration of 'the thing' has become a significant object of contemporary philosophical enquiry (in contrast to the Kantian view of 'the-thing-in-itself'). Martin Heidegger's essay on 'The Thing' ('Das Ding', 1950) has been especially influential – see *Poetry, Language, Thought* (trans. Albert Hofstadter), New York: Harper & Row (1971).

All of what has just been described when gathered together brings us to an understanding that the city is not just a place but equally is an event. In fact, the city is a conflation of both (it is a place as event/event as place). However, it, and its designing, is not contained by these relations, so it is not automatous – climate and natural events, trade, migration, war and so on clearly rupture its specificity, articulate it to the elsewhere and have huge impacts.

Moreover, what is now being seen in the present epoch is the city turning away from itself – at the same time it increasingly becomes an epicentre of 'unsettlement' and a place of passage (this rather than just remaining the largest locus of settlement). With the aim of gaining a better understanding of metrofitting in this process, the city as event, and how to think the city as unsettled by its changing metabolic conditions will be explored.

The event

Why be concerned about 'thinking (the) event(s)' in its plurality? The most basic answer is because the dominant ways of our mode of being as event have to change (due to the auto-destructive consequences of how we live), in order that 'we' continue to be as a species. While one can say that in the variable unsustainability in which we exist, there is already an absolute demand for 'us' to change; in 'reality' we cannot change unless 'the event of our coming into being' changes. From the perspective of volunteerism, this imperative seems to be a double-bind, but if 'the thing' (in this case the city metrofitted) is understood in the context of the dynamic of ontological designing, no appeal to a conscious subject is needed. In grasping this the importance of design dramatically increases.

Philosophically, one can start by recognizing:

- our existence is punctuated by 'the event of our being' and 'our being as constituted within particular events';

- the notion 'event' here is not just a way to register a temporal condition reflecting city as a place and object of constant animation embedded in the very structures of language and action;

- the temporality and causality of 'events' are determinants of the worlds of our existence. As such, ontologically they are both *a cause* and are *the caused*. Similarly, they can be both designed and designing.

Certainly there is no consensual philosophical understanding of exactly what events actually are. Difference proliferates as the discursive contexts within which they are viewed change. It is also the case that how an event is viewed changes according to the particular epistemology through which it is viewed.[2] To acknowledge this places thinking the event back at the birth of classical thought and questions of what exists (the event of), how and why. However, our concerns here are not with retracing the philosophical steps back to this past but with dealing with understanding the contemporary event. This can be registered as having two moments, the first prefiguring the second.

The key first registration of this moment can be taken from what Alfred North Whitehead stated in *Process and Reality* (1929): '. . . the actual world is built up of actual occasions';[3] thereafter he uses the term 'event' to name these occasions.[4] This moment is equally echoed in works by Martin Heidegger, as in *Beiträge zur Philosophie* (*Contributions to Philosophy (From Enowning)*), written between 1936 and 1938, and in *Das Ereignis (The Event)*, 1941–1942.[5] Notwithstanding their differences, Whitehead's 'organic philosophy of becoming' resonated with Heidegger's notion of 'event toward the beginning' via an 'appropriative event' (*Ereignis* being one translation of this concept).

Moment two situates the event among the concerns of Continental Philosophy. This is perhaps best represented by a contested understanding of the event between Gilles Deleuze, who drew a great deal from Whitehead (in 'What is the Event'), and Alain Badiou ('The Event in Deleuze').[6] Unquestionably, philosophy has a lot to say about 'event' but rather than digressing into a labyrinthine engagement, our concern remains directed towards bringing it to an understanding of the agency of design and the city. As should now be apparent, the issue of what an event is cannot be divided from the knowledge by which it is defined and elaborated. Obviously this suggests that in order to comprehend how to understand and engage (the) event beyond the familiar, and more specifically, how it can be understood as a transformative event, it has to be named. 'Metrofitting' is it so named. Thus it is presented not merely as a process but rather is brought to the city as: the naming of a transformative element of the city as event. As this it can be seen as: a synthesis of word, narrative, action, happening, extension plus technical engagements. By implication, it defies reductive definition. It is a bringing together, that which

---

[2] Here we are reminded of Plato's remark that 'we see with our mind not our eyes' – this as eyes are simply instruments that facilitate sight.

[3] Alfred North Whitehead (1978 [1929]), *Process and Reality*, New York: Free Press.

[4] Ibid., p. 73.

[5] Heidegger, *Contributions to Philosophy (From Enowning)*; Martin Heidegger (2013), *The Event* (trans. Richard Rojcewitz), Bloomington, IN: Indiana University Press.

[6] Gilles Deleuze (1992), 'What is the Event', from the *The Fold, Leibniz and the Baroque* (trans. Tom Colney), Minneapolis, MN: University of Minnesota Press, and Alain Badiou (2007), 'The Event in Deleuze', *Parrhesia*, No. 2, pp. 37–44.

individually and collectively animates. It is a process of reciprocal appropriation (*Ereignis*)[7] – every thing draws on another thing. None of this happens of itself: it is always situated. This means that as process, the event is also political.

As Alain Badiou makes clear, process is political so long as 'its material is collective'.[8] His understanding of collective is not as 'a numerical concept' but rather 'the vehicle for a virtual summoning of all'[9] – which is to say it is 'a bringing together and a comprehending'. By bonding *Ereignis* (the appropriative event) to process, as Heidegger explained, appropriation is shown to belong to 'the event'.[10] Badiou's understanding of summoning can be read as just another way of comprehending appropriation (so both could be said to be integral to understanding *Ereignis*).

Events of course are not discrete, they exist as chains and flow: they are transitive, conjunctural and disjunctural. From the perspective of the city, it is important to comprehend the object/event relation that ontological design exposes. Object-things are events insofar as they act in an animatory way (Heidegger calls it 'thinging'). The essence of things does not lie within them but exists in their performative attributes – the knife cuts, the mower mows, the aeroplane flies, and traditionally the city animates all that is gathered within it (but times are changing). So designed objects (which include cities), as eventing events go on designing via their ontological agency. This is the case irrespective of whether the object is material or immaterial (for instance, messages have material causal consequences).

Whitehead, and Deleuze after him, both state, as Graham Livesey remarks, that the place of '. . . the creation of new events is both affirmative and productive'.[11] But events in themselves do not have a reducible value. They can be good or bad, regressive or progressive, positive or negative. As argued elsewhere, design, as an ontologically designing event, can both future or defuture.[12] This comment connects to a problem in the ways 'becoming and creation' are presented by Whitehead, Deleuze and others. As indicated at the start of the book, creation is dialectally indivisible from destruction. Thus whatever becomes (comes into being) is always an arising out of, displacement, negation, and the destruction, be it of idea, meaning, process or matter. Planet

---

[7] In these two remarks, Badiou, 'The Event in Deleuze', p. 37 and Heidegger on *Ereignis* converge.
[8] Alain Badiou (2005), *Metapolitics* (trans. Jason Barker), London: Verso, p. 141.
[9] Ibid.
[10] This understanding is central to the fundamental proposition underpinning Heidegger's *The Event*.
[11] Graham Livesey, '(2010), 'Deleuze, Whitehead, the Event, and the Contemporary City' [https://whiteheadresearch.org/occasions/conferences/event-and-decision/papers/Graham%20Livesey_Final%20Draft.pdf], p. 14.
[12] Tony Fry (2009), *Design Futuring: Sustainability, Ethics and New Practice*, Oxford: Berg.

Earth arose out of destruction (the 'big bang), the spherical planet by the displacement of the notion that it was flat, the human via a negation of the animal it was, the made world at the cost of the destruction of the natural, and so the dialectic rolls on. The failure to give sufficient attention to the ever presence of destruction is in fact one of the main reasons why we humans are so unsustainable. We are blinded by the pleasures and rewards of creation and ignore the costs.

Event is not merely 'life' – organic becoming – for what comes to be and what destroys are also things that have been brought into being. Event is what is drawn into, is appropriated by, and is expropriated from a continual process of change. Nothing stands still. Certainly meaning can never be anchored in stasis. It is brought to things. Language as event (is event) is always in change.

Badiou says that 'The event is neither past nor future. It makes us present to the present.'[13] After Walter Benjamin, one can say: the only event is 'now' – the *ur-time* of the everlasting now. But 'now' is not a constant moment – the now of now is an event of speed. Change – climatic, technological, geopolitical, urban – is continually accelerating.

Ungrounding the event of the city

The city is caught up in this event of speed, as an event. The city is a change-event as well as a place-event. It is the locus of the becoming, arrival and departure of matter, commodities, meaning, information, capital, people: everything functions within a synthetic metabolism. Cities exist as always between what they were and what they are becoming. By degree, this means they exist as a process of betweenness – notwithstanding appearances, nothing is fixed. Everything is betwixt energy and movement, construction and destruction, care and neglect, preservation and transformation, futuring and defuturing. To realize this is to realize the multifarious forms of their ontological designing of being and beings. Re-emphasizing: cities design ontologies that design cities, not in the sense of their conceptualization via a prefigurative master plan, but rather by the ways people appropriate from the city those things they use to shape (design) their everyday lives that in turn and *en masse* end up designing key elements of the city.

To understand cities in this way renders the perceived divisions of their material substrate and their economic, social, cultural and political superstructure obsolete, as well as urban politics in its current institutional

---

[13] Badiou, 'The Event in Deleuze', p. 39.

form. To say this is to recognize that 'The essence of politics is not the plurality of opinion' but rather '. . . the prescription of a possibility in rupture with what exists'.[14]

Change unifies difference in the city as event; once it did this slowly, but now increasingly quickly. Every city is *en route* to its destiny. Every city, as event, has a birth, a life and a death – but their time is not as ours. A concern with architecture here confuses: there was the city before architecture (as a discourse). Expanding just the category 'architecture' will neither save the city or architecture itself. In the face of growing urban complexity, the disruption and coming destruction of many cities, and the continued assent of the informal, *the practice of architecture and its discursive order(ing) will fail/has failed as it stands before these coming forces of transformation.* It is not that it will cease to exist, but rather it will become (and for much of the world has become) irrelevant. Architecture as art marks this irrelevance most overtly.

Emmanuel Levinas pointed out that: 'The event of dwelling exceeds knowing.'[15] One can rewrite this and say 'the event of being exceeds knowing'; this expresses nothing more nor less than putting the arrogance of privilege in its place. Our (human and animal) being is not only incommensurate with our knowledge but is the very thing that is most important of all to understand, but it escapes us – 'we' do not know how to dwell (some cultures have forgotten this, some never learnt it, and then there are a very few others that have retained a trace). But now what is arriving is a displacement of a sense of dwelling, and even of its very possibility. Dwelling, it will be remembered, is not simply a mode of being in place but a way of being formatively in the world in body, mind and spirit.[16] Dwelling is active not static.

Unsettlement returns

As indicated in the previous chapter, in our present age fear – actual, manufactured and imagined – has become an even more structural element of the human psyche. The more informed one becomes about 'the state of the world and changes in the nature of humanity', the more one fears the arrival of 'a future without a future'. While unlikely to be expressed in these terms, a sense of uncertainty about the future is widespread and the more one has a proximity to actual structural dangers (like sea level rises, resource pressures,

---

[14] Badiou, *Metapolitics*, p. 24.

[15] Emmanuel Levinas (1969), *Totality and Infinity* (trans. Alphonso Lingis), Pittsburgh, PA: Duquesne University Press, p. 153.

[16] Such an understanding is at the very core of Martin Heidegger's essay 'Building, Dwelling, Thinking', in *Poetry, Language, Thought*, pp. 143–162.

diminishing food security, war), the more one sees especially exposed 'people' being unsettled. It follows in fact that unsettlement is becoming/will increasingly become a pervasive human psychology. This condition does not arrive of itself; it is constructed and is inherently ambiguous in the way that knowledge of the human condition (and knowledge of changes of the human itself) is being placed in the context of an accumulative picture of the problematic state of the world. The intent of this knowledge may well be to inform and prompt action, but so frequently when it appears it actually negates the very possibility of acting. The scale of problems overwhelm, fear paralyses, and the subject feels helpless and completely without agency – such is the nature of nihilism.

Nihilism reveals itself as the underpinning of unsettlement, in both its conscious form (concern for the self as inseparable from concern for the future) and in its unconscious form (the lack of care for the self and the future accompanied by the negation of time by totally self-indulgent and self-harming action). So positioned, and restating, a nihilistic life is one where action is only taken to improve one's immediate circumstances, but without any sense that anything can be done about what caused them. It is fatalistic. Dominantly this life is lived in the city – the city of panic. Paul Virilio's characterization of the city of panic is not a city panicking. He does not conjure people running the streets in fear screaming, fighting to get out of the city by whatever means they can find, or looting supermarkets to stockpile food. Rather, it is a state of mind that knows that all that seems substantial, firm and certain is not. Panic is repressed not expressed, except when it surfaces and is felt as unsettlement. Panic thus ensues from the realization of a total loss of any ground that secures.

Unsettlement is carried by a feeling of foreboding – a foreboding about the arrival of 'natural', or 'human-induced', unwelcomed defuturing events (events here denote time rather than being) that are likely to arrive in the immediate or distant future no matter who 'you' or where 'you' are in the world. Unsettlement also begs to be thought not just as a description of the 'state of the world' or as a 'state of mind' (its psychology) but as the lived of lost settlement (living without having anywhere else to go). Thus in recognition there is nowhere they will be welcome, and as people 'of the camps' make clear, life so lived is without a future other than as the continuation of an abysmal present.

It needs to be understood that physically unsettled people: the internally displaced (IDPs), 'climate refugees', and refugees of war are categories that no longer stay clearly divided. Estimates suggest that 200 million people will be displaced by conflict and climate change by 2050 and that the current figure is almost 27 million per year.[17] This situation in itself would be a massive crisis, and one that could run for a century or more.

---

[17] Disasters displace over 26 million (http://www.unhcr.org/565c13c26.html), and refugees from Syria alone now number over 4.8 million.

To confront unsettlement is to fundamentally shift one's view of 'being-in-the-world'. Cities do not look secure, the prospect of more and larger informal sections exiting the city looks certain, mega-camps will arrive, militarized borders and barriers with be the norm. To be the unsettled will be to be unwanted anywhere: displacement is already being criminalized, borders are being closed. Looking at such projections – what can be done, when, how – metrofitting cannot claim to offer a solution, but it can confront such problems with a process of engagement.

This situation also exposes just how tenuous our 'grip on the world' actually is and how pathetically misplaced and inadequate 'business-as-usual' forms of urban development and object-based design 'solutions' actually are.

Unsettlement, as seen by the Syrian/European refugee crisis, confounds geography. The inundation of the delta region of Egypt will have consequences for the entire country; the displacement of the Cuban population of Southern Florida will have effects across the nation; the reduction in the volume and nutritional value of rice produced in Southeast Asia will have major regional impacts; and in view of the immigration policies of Australia and New Zealand, where will the many thousands of Pacific Islanders go in the not too distant future? Effectively, all the problems that converge to constitute unsettlement elevate 'normal' human insecurities to instal a dramatic and higher order of anxiety. As such, they present another and mostly overlooked expression of the unsustainable.

The causal conditions of unsettlement can come from a convergence of many forces and associated threats and are worth reviewing briefly. Obviously a changing climate, linked to rising sea levels and extreme weather events, is very significant (cyclones, tornados, storms, riverine floods, wind, heat, fire, hail), and will become increasingly so. Such problems themselves go on to generate food and water crises as well as trigger other 'natural hazards' like dust storms, landslides or desertification and the spread of vector-borne diseases. Large numbers of hungry and thirsty people displaced by war, or because their water supply and agricultural system has failed, and who are looking for sustenance, safety and shelter, may well cross borders uninvited in large numbers – such action can and does precipitate conflict.

As Earth's planetary resources become ever more depleted and thus stressed, geopolitical reconfigurations of the world will increasingly arrive. Some borders will be redrawn, and shifts in the power-balance between nations will occur. More nations may even degenerate into dysfunction and break-up. At the same time there will also be the rise of new politico-economic formations (the rise of megaregions and of globally disaggregating nations is already underway).

Besides all the more predictable biophysical and geopolitical issues, it is also very likely that many socio-cultural and psychological problems will arrive

– these coming from the breakdown of community, as well as dangerous clashes between secular societies and those based on faith (and between faiths). Social unrest from failed expectations of consumerist culture, large-scale technological systems' failure and inequity are already evident in Asia and Latin America.[18] All these problems are already arriving in nascent forms and are being telegraphed in the world's refugee camps.

Unsettlement will no doubt become an unfolding character of our age. The contradictions of national and global leadership are in fact what help to feed unsettlement (as seen in, for example, the contradiction of a commitment to continual global economic growth in a world with a growing global population, resource stress, still rising greenhouse gas emissions and structural climatic change and new forms of spatial injustice). There has to be another paradigm of worldly human occupation!

Of course it would be misleading (i) to give the impression that everyone is unsettled (for it requires, at worst, the arrival of a certain existential discomfort with the status quo, or, at best a level of awareness of contemporary defuturing circumstances), and (ii) to assume unsettlement is uniformly experienced. Globally there is a huge disparity between the 'concerned privileged' and the 'poor and desolate'. Unsettlement is, of course, especially evident in nations that are in conflict, in excluded and fragmented cultures, broken social structures, failing economic dynamics, dysfunctional collective psychologies, among growing modes of homelessness, and in the many disturbed minds that populate refugee and internment camps.

Some of what is being said here is not new and resonates with what is being said by many other people, be it in different ways. Part of the problem with unsettlement is that while a great deal of the problem is evident, at least instrumentally, its dynamic and seriousness is ignored in favour of short-term bandaid action. The appearance and arrival of major epoch-changing problems are met with deafness and blindness. Even what can appear as insight evidences naiveté; for example, here is Richard Sennett: 'So great are the changes required to alter humankind's dealings with the physical world that only this sense of self-displacement and estrangement can drive the actual practices of change and reduce our consuming desires.' Sennett then, with Eurocentric abandon concludes that, 'rather than confronting the self-destructive territory *we* have actually made' *we* strive to escape into 'idealised nature' [my emphasis].[19] 'We' are not 'the all'.

---

[18] This is an emergent situation in China. And in Venezuela in April 2016, for example, as widely reported by the international media (including the BBC and CNN), the national power system failed (the hydroelectric power supply was unable to operate due to drought) resulting in massive power blackouts, the working week being reduced to two days, a lack of food in the shops, and looting and riots.
[19] Richard Sennett (2008), *The Craftsman*, New Haven, CT: Yale University Press, p. 13.

Of course, neither messages nor purely instrumental actions are enough, hence the imperative of comprehensive processes such as metrofitting that sees the city as a designing event rather than just a structure and system to sustainably refashion.

Thinking towards a metabolic event

Understanding the city as event, as process, as the gathering of all designing, as life, as a metabolism, as a metabolic event is another kind of circling wherein the familiar returns as the unfamiliar.

A transformative engagement of the metabolism of the city by metrofitting of it would be an important task, but not on the basis of the reductive way this condition of exchange is understood. To make this clear, three explanatory moves are actually needed. The first is to present the dominant current understanding of the urban metabolism, the second is to present a historically grounded critique, and the third is to put forward a contemporary revised perspective of the metabolic.

Thinking the urban metabolically is not a new idea, but one whose explanatory efficacy has been diminished. This is immediately evident if one, for instance, contrasts the importance given to the idea by Marx, who viewed metabolism as a way to comprehend and explore the relations between nature and society, labour and history, with the approach of Abel Wolman – a key figure in establishing the study of metabolisms as a field of contemporary practice. Wolman employed the concept to make sense of problems of air and water quality in US cities.[20] In a global review of the field between 1965 (the year Wolman's study was first published) and 2009, around fifty articles that focused on twenty comprehensive scientific studies were looked at by Kennedy, Pinceti and Bunje.[21] What this review showed was just how limited the field of inquiry had remained. System determinants of the social and cultural factors of everyday life of urban populations were simply overlooked.

What their study revealed was that there were two major research methods in use. The first was the 'emergy' method that centred on flows and process with a specific focus on solar energy (in doing this a particular unit of measurement was created – the solar energy joule – and it was applied to all urban metabolic processes of exchange). Method two was 'material flow analysis' – an input/output model able to quantify waste and pollution. This

[20] Abel Wolman (1965), 'The Metabolism of Cities', *Scientific American*, Vol. 213, Issue 3, pp. 179–190.
[21] C. Kennedy, S. Pinceti and P. Bunje (2010), 'The Study of Urban Metabolism and its Application to Urban Planning and Design', *Environmental Pollution*, Vol. 159, Nos. 8/9, pp. 1965–1973.

was directed at the flow of materials into and out of cities. It aimed to mirror biological processes whereby nutrients are chemically transformed into energy that enables regenerative growth to sustain an organism. This process centred on a cycle from a nutrient input to its transformation, then to growth production and finally to the expulsion as reintegratable waste (animal and plant compounds that provide soil nutrition). A city does not fully mirror this process, because inputs completely exceed what is needed to sustain life and in many cases are ecologically harmful. Moreover, there is nothing in the city to limit the growth of 'the organism'. Not only can waste not be eliminated, or reintegrated, but in the current forms of cities the rate of production of inputs cannot be checked. Obviously rapid urbanization ever accelerates the production and control of waste. It can also be noted that no functional model exists that can enable a full metabolic integration via the waste management industry (even if it were to be 'cradle-to-cradle' – which is actually a reductionist concept closed to the relation of things within the animatory event). The waste management industry is effectively a marker of the failure of waste to be managed – a failure it has a vested interest in extending and to which, for example, landfill bears testament.

All of the thinking on waste and metabolic process gets nowhere near confronting the fundamental problem of the economy of desire that created the dynamic of consumerism/hyper-consumerism, with the city as the prime site of unchecked/encouraged consumption (a key expression of ever expanding unsustainability).

So let's now go back and look at what history left behind.

Karl Marx used the concept of *stoffwechsel* (variously translated as 'material interchange', 'material reaction', 'exchange of matter' and 'metabolism' – the latter used throughout the 1970 Penguin edition of *Capital*). The concept also appeared in a number of his other publications, but most notably in *A Contribution to Political Economy* (1859), and in his *Grundrisse* (1857–58), which was essentially his notebook towards capital.[22] Common across all his comments was the recognition that the concept of metabolism allows the identification of the dialectical relation between nature and society wherein both human beings and non-human beings are interactive agencies. Metabolism mediates this relation in particular, as Marx said, between 'man', labour and nature. Thus in his theory of value, including the use value of a commodity, there is always an appropriated natural element. He held this to be independently true within every form of society.[23] Marx's views were

---

[22] See Paul Hampton (2009), 'Marxism, Metabolism and Ecology', *Solidarity*, No. 156, July, pp. 20–27 [http://www.workersliberty.org/story/2009/07/30/john-bellamy-foster-marxism-metabolism-and-ecology].

[23] Ibid.

actually influenced by the scientific developments of the day. Specifically in terms of metabolism he made a number of references to Justus von Liebig, who wrote on chemistry and the negative transformation of modern agriculture. Writing on this topic in *Capital* Marx notes that it not only exploits the agricultural labourer but also robs the soil of nutrients.[24] More than this he also places this recognition of metabolic dysfunction in an urban context:

> Capitalist production collects populations together in great centres . . . on the one hand concentrates the historical motive power of society; on the other it disturbs the circulation of matter between man and soil, i.e., prevents the return to the soil of its elements consumed by man in the form of food and clothing.[25]

Marx goes on to call for '. . . a restoration of a system' that allows for the 'circulation of matter'.[26]

The observation made by Marx on these issues once provided material that fuelled a vigorous debate within Marxism and on ecology. Notwithstanding Marx's own concern being carried forward, not least by Frederick Engels, William Morris, Rosa Luxemburg and others, the issues of metabolics were cast aside. Yet in recent years the debate has been revived, especially by the controversial writing of John Bellamy Foster.[27]

Without suggesting that Marx's views can simply be imported into a model for contemporary action, they do provide an opening into a broader vision – one that goes beyond the outlined restrictive instrumental ways metabolic methods are being brought to the notion of sustainable cities. These methods, following Wolman, reduce the perspective to a waste stream management of material flows through the city. Not only is this perspective insufficient but it is also predicated upon a particular kind of city – one with a significant level of urban-developed and well-functioning infrastructure. Such a view thus excludes a vast number of cities in many continents. More than this, it also displays a disdain for detail. For instance, consider the following remarks by Frank Ackerman when commenting on waste: 'Waste management can be viewed from two distinct perspectives: either in terms of sanitation or of

---

[24] Karl Marx (1957 [1867]), *Capital*, Vol. 1 (trans. Samuel Moore and Edward Aveling), London: Lawrence & Wishart, pp. 474–475.
[25] Ibid., p. 74.
[26] Ibid.
[27] See, for example, John Bellamy Foster (2013), 'Marx and the Rift in the Universal Metabolism of Nature', *Monthly Review*, Vol. 65, Issue 07 [http://monthlyreview.org/2013/12/01/marx-rift-universal-metabolism-nature/].

materials recovery.'[28] These perspectives are obviously valid but there are many more than two.

Waste can be viewed via various systems: as an industry with a mixed record and, as said, as a vested interest in the production of waste; a local labour-intensive practice versus an industrialized one; as an industry that can be organized vertically, or horizontally with connections to urban farming; and as local business development. Just taking a technical view is inadequate. Likewise, the reduction of the urban metabolism to metrics is not enough, because it simply reduces the problem of waste to the remit of a management system. The issue is far more complex than this, for as we have seen, huge sections of cities with large informal settlements are beyond the scope and reach of this type of mode of management.[29]

Metrofitting, metabolism and event

To bring metrofitting to metabolism is to constitute an explicitly political event – so what would that look like?

Starting with the extant instrumental materials flow, a metrofitting model would work from a perspective of recoding the process by bringing creation and destruction into the picture, and in so doing a far more differentiated view of 'waste' would be created – one in which the cultural as well as the material would figure. The very category of waste would be interrogated. Moreover, it would mean looking at a restriction of flows whereby freedom by Sustainment starts to override market freedom with redistributive justice increasingly playing a part in directing routes of inputs and outputs. In other words, the notion of a metabolism cannot be simply treated as a 'system', rather it (already) requires recognition as a political problematic. Now it would be foolish to claim what has just been outlined is a solution. Instead it is posed as an elemental starting point to what needs to become ongoing metrofitting research bringing 'time', the dynamics of immaterial exchange, social ecology and an address to inequity all into the picture.

Time, of course, is implicit to the event – the event is change, and thus it is time. To reiterate, 'time is that in which events occur' (Aristotle). One can begin to think metabolic process in time from the recognition that it deals with whatever comes into being, rots away, decays or is totally consumed. In this

[28] Frank Ackerman (2005), 'Material Flows for a Sustainable City', *International Review for Environmental Strategies*, Vol. 5, No. 2, pp. 499–510.
[29] Stephanie Pinceti (2014), 'Urban Metabolism and the Nature of Sustainable Cities', Interview with Jon Christensen, *Huffington Post Green*, 15 September.

respect, the process links economic consumption to the very foundation of what is biologically consumed, as understood as the fully digested (in the same way the disease of consumption eats the body of its host away). Can it not now be claimed that the urban metabolic process is (a) disease?

Here, then, is the locus of the imperative to reconfigure the urban metabolism so it becomes contained and constrained by viable and complex functions of exchange. Unsurprisingly, this enormous challenge for metrofitting can only be contemplated and enacted within the context of city as event.

The city as event so engaged, and to resist speeding entropic arrest, needs to develop modes of social exchange based upon introduced social and intercultural relations. This will not happen by itself. Moreover, it will only happen if power itself is exchanged and a new relation between equity and understanding, the formal and the informal, is forged.

While still only an idea inviting exploration, what is clear is that such as activities cannot arrive as a grand or global scheme (like the under-thought, undercooked and gestural Rockefeller '100 resilient cities project', a project which, if taken seriously, would cost many tens of billions of dollars and focus just on cities of pressing need – which is certainly not the case in relation to the current project). In contrast, a starting point for the kind of exploration being advocated would perhaps be a small series of catalytic projects opening as 'action learning events' to learn, unlearn and relearn a fundamental understanding of the metabolic process in its relational and situated interconnectedness. Central to this action would be a traversing of the spaces of the city, the drawing of lines, the crossing of boundaries, the creation of borderland locations and the founding of knowledge that would enable interconnectivity.

3

What designs a city?

The city has been defined as a designing event. The obvious question now arrives: but what designs the city? What now follows is an identification of some of its designing force. One can claim this designing as a process, but clearly it is not orderly, uniform, systematic or universal – which is to say that every city is unique and always designed by more than those instrumental design practices such as architecture and planning that bring its materiality into existence. In development or decline, the designing process of the city is certainly never complete or reducible to just its built fabric, or divisible from continual flows of events. While the forces that design a city are always particular there are also commonalities, and a consideration of them takes us beyond the familiar discourses of urban design. Our focus will be especially on those contemporary transformative forces likely to deliver trauma to many cities and hundreds of millions of people. These events will inevitably alter how cities in general are perceived and designed in the future.

The primary concern of the question 'what designs a city' is not with the familiar but with the mostly unknown and so unfamiliar.

Design in a context of failed foresight

What has become increasingly apparent is that no matter the acclaimed qualities of a great deal of the world's cities, at the most fundamental level, so many transpire to have been fated in some way at their very moment of inception – this often by flawed location, design and planning decisions. To support this claim, let's look at the top ten of the most at-risk cities in the world as they evidence such failures of thought and knowledge in their formation and development. In doing this what will be registered are problems that need to be recognized now, some of which might be solved, adapted to or avoided in other cities in the future.[1]

---

[1] http://www.businessinsider.com.au/cities-most-at-risk-of-natural-disasters-2014-3?op=1#9-los-angeles-usa-2.

Historically, some of the most serious environmental situations threatening many cities stem from them being inappropriately located on flood plains, deltas, on earthquake fault lines and so on. In many cases, risks were not initially recognized, but in others economic expediency outweighed known dangers. Moreover, what often started out as a small settlement grew organically into a large urban centre with substantial built fabric – the city simply arrived incrementally without questioning its geography or having an overall vision or plan.

With the current availability of climatic and geo-technical data the kind of pragmatic, logistical and economic reasons that resulted in the inappropriate location of cities would now be viewed as totally unacceptable. This is not to say badly located cities are not, and will not, be built in the future. Money has the ability to override ethics and calculated risk.

Here, then, are the ten cities whose fate is sealed by climate change and other impacts that will arrive at an unknown point in perhaps the not too distant future. As will be seen, thinking about these cities raises a cluster of critical questions linking back to past design and those defuturing decisions based on expediency that clearly demonstrated a failure to grasp the consequences of building a city in an inappropriate location. Consideration will also be given to the still mostly overlooked issue of spatial injustice (grounded in inequity), and the huge need for adaptation and relocation – all these issues are central to the agenda of metrofitting.

The top ten

City number one is the Tokyo-Yokohama regional urban nexus. It has a population of 57 million people plus – it has the highest concentration of risk in the world with eighty per cent of the population exposed to an active earthquake fault-line with an especially high associated tsunami risk. Manila arrives as number two: it has a greater population by area of almost 30 million at risk of earthquake and flood. China's Pearl River Delta is number three and contains five cities with a population of over 37 million people – it is exposed to the highest risk of flooding from storm surges in the world, as well as to cyclonic events. The Osaka-Kobe complex in Japan is fourth, and with a population of 32 million is at risk from earthquakes and tsunamis. Number five is Jakarta – a city which is forty per cent below sea level – with a population of 27 million people at risk from earthquakes. It suffers serious floods regularly. Nagoya has a population of 22 million people who are exposed to earthquakes and tsunamis – it is number six. Number seven is Kolkata (Calcutta), with a population of over 17 million people; it is at risk from floods, cyclones, storm surges and tsunamis. Shanghai, which is exposed to floods and typhoons, is number eight – it has a population of 16½ million people. Los Angeles is number nine and is located in one of the most earthquake-prone locations in the world – almost 17 million people live there. Finally, Tehran shares the same situation as Los Angeles. It has a population of over 15½ million people. These ten cities have a combined population of over 276 million people. Three of these cities are also in the global top twenty of those listed by the OECD as having populations exposed to climate change-related future sea level rises.

What a focus on these megacity forms of risk overlooks are the vast numbers of villages, towns and small cities globally that are extremely exposed. By taking them into account, a dramatic picture emerges which suggests that the global population at risk exceeds half a billion.

So what has really designed the city?

This question is posed essentially but not, as said, instrumentally. The starting point for considering the question is not with architecture, planning, urban design or developers but with a conjunctural assemblage that becomes gathered together and then *brought to it* as place. As this observation is unpacked, its significance will become clearer.

The designing event of the city is not linear or arrested historically. The designing of the city cannot be divided from what the city designs. At the very moment we characterize the consequence of this designing as 'urban life', the designing of the city and designing by the city encircle each other. People gather and constitute a space, which they occupy, whereby it becomes a proto-urban place. Gathering triggers the process. All this exists before the actual 'designing' of the city becomes apparent, so it cannot be placed in a narrative history of its formation (as is exemplified by Lewis Mumford's *The City in History*). The nature of the gathering, as expressed by needs, capabilities, collective knowledge and potentialities, while coming before discernible evidence of designing is directive of what is designed. The sociality of this event morphs: ideas get projected as intent, determinants arrive and are thought to be understood, and the familiar and unfamiliar interplay. Thereafter, patterns of social relations, topographically transcribed, become fused with the dialogue of placement in space. Thinking in place, building in space and dwelling all constitute an environment of meaning. The sum of these prefigurative practices works against any notion of architecture and planning/urban design being the foundational designing of the city, rather they emerge out of it. In pointing this out, one is simply drawing attention to those ontological conditions of being-in-the world wherein a convergence of forces, subjects and circumstances of place constitute events that in themselves form particular ontologies that direct these designing events. To better understand cities, the currently dominant ways of thinking about their design has given way to the unfamiliar and relationally complex. Our aim, then, is to start to uncover some of this complexity. Clearly there is a significant instrumental dimension to this complexity, but as our basic and briefly outlined examples will show, what determines change far exceeds a reductive description of its agency. The agency of the forces and events of change is always conjunctural and relational – listing these forces belies this complexity.

Logistics and resource proximity

Navigable rivers able to bring a marketable resource from the place of extraction or cultivation to a deep harbour and thus able to accommodate large ships can be, and frequently have been, seen as a logistical designing event. A city will arrive once such activities start to unfold with a sufficient dynamic. Historically, the city thus foundationally arrives with the establishment of an infrastructure of trade. This means the city and much of its form were determined long before any *applied notion* of designing commenced. Events layer upon events, intent upon intent (the ontological expression of design). Crucially this logic was generative of a pragmatism that overcame immediate problems while so often neglecting to think about what determinates of the future have been created. The lesson of the misplaced cities through short-term expediency, as accompanied by the overlooking of the future, has created consequences still mostly to be learnt. Extreme examples exist that make the point.[2]

More overt and speedier economic imperatives can and do bring directive logistical events into being. A market arrives – it could be for almost any commodity: coal, iron, timber, wool, live animals, grain, sugar, cotton, etc. Demand means its production dramatically increases in a short space of time. Quickly storage, transport distribution, housing, commercial businesses all arrive. The development of these facilities, together with the growth of a labour force, become the authoring events directing the designing of what ends up being projected as the designed city.

Climatic and environment factors

The availability of good and evenly distributed rainfall, good grazing land, and a climate conducive to farming animals or growing particular kinds of

---

[2] One of these examples is the new capital of Egypt – see *The Guardian* [http://www.theguardian.com/cities/2015/mar/16/new-cairo-egypt-plans-capital-city-desert].

crops – grapes, olives, wheat, potatoes, apples, citrus and so on – all prompted settlement, commerce and urban development. Likewise, so did an abundance of minerals in particular places act to generate the rise and development of extractive industries, and thereafter a working population was able to create and extend a local economy. The creation of cities was not only designed out of the rise of an economy in hospitable environments but equally often in climatically harsh environmental conditions where wealth-producing resources were often located. In contrast, the use of the natural environment was also able to be valorized, and so turned into a commodity – the environmental experience provided by a commercial tourist venture (like a snowfield, hot spring, or coral reef). Here again are designing events that fed/feed the formation and development of another kind of city.

Political ideologies/idealism/utopianism/egoism and revolution

Historical events – such as a plague, colonial conquest, war or the discovery of a valuable mineral – create a symbolic, as well as material, impetus directing transformations of a city. Its history is not just its past but part of the designing event of its future. The city does not exist without having this symbolic power. In this context it can, and does, get appropriated by individuals, regimes, industries and states to express their power and/or to impose a vision. Here the city can become deployed as a stage upon which to project the past, a future, a dream or a nightmare: Paris and the rise of the Republic, Magnitogorsk and the rise of the Soviet Union, Brasilia and the rise of modern Brazil are a few of a myriad examples.

While symbolic practices generative of events can, and do, have very large, different and contradictory directive impacts on the design of cities (positive or negative), they always act to inscribe an identity at odds with the reality of place.

Economic events

As is widely known, there are now many large cities in China with a population of many millions that just a few decades ago were just small towns: all of this due to the nation's rapid (now slowing) economic development. In contrast, with the arrival of the post-industrial economy in the West combined with the coming of the 'global economic crisis' of the early twenty-first century, many developed countries experienced economic contraction, especially in areas of older industries. In the USA in particular, many cities shrank dramatically, losing a third or even a half of their population.

The key point to be reiterated here is that cities are designed by events from without as well as from within. Effectively they all contain conduits through which designing events flow, not least from capital, people, geopolitics and pathogens.

Conflict

Clearly, conflict is a dramatic event that has serious impacts upon cities. The city under siege, the city rendered to ruins, the Phoenix rising out of the ashes: events of conflict touch cities in numerous ways and often for a long time. Conflict has been a major designing event from the inception of cities. The destruction of a city is always more than just an attack on the lives of its population, for it is also an attack upon spirit, civilization and even the very essence of being human. Such events do not travel in one direction because they are also destructive of the destroyer, for they also render them homeless in a profound sense. The world-within-the-world they destroy is equally their own world.

The complete destruction of unprotected cities from the air went beyond the historic conquest and occupation of cities. It has dissolved any distinction between war and terror.[3] Thus all conflict in the late modern world is nothing but terror. Moreover, with the proliferation of terrorism, every city everywhere now exists as an actual or potential target. Although levels of risk vary, and for many cities are low, what this has nonetheless meant is that in our age all cities become militarized. The fear of an imminent attack upon the city is now inscribed into the event of the city itself – the eye of surveillance in the air and on the ground remains ever watchful. It is chilling to discover that there are expectations by war planning strategists that many future wars will be fought in megacities.[4] Another source of conflict comes with the expectation, as earlier mentioned, that large numbers of people will cross borders looking for food and water and will be repelled by force. The European, Middle Eastern and global refugee crisis folds into this scenario, and as military historian Gwynne Dyer has shown, increasingly such action has the potential to spark wars.[5]

---

[3] See Peter Sloterdijk (2009), *Terror from the Air*, New York: Semiotext(e).
[4] Strategic Studies Group (2014), *Megacities and United States Army: Preparing for a Complex and Uncertain Future* [https://www.army.mil/e2/c/downloads/351235.pdf].
[5] Gwynne Dyer (2008), *Climate Wars*, Melbourne, VIC: Scribe.

Fear, the control of space and bio-politics

From the earliest times of human settlement to the present, events that engender fear have acted to design cities – as with the fear of invasion by an enemy of the other race, culture, political ideology or religion. Gates, walls, towers, checkpoints, normal uniformed police, paramilitary police, secret police – these are all markers of this fear. It is also expressed in the ways space is controlled – this based on the premise that there are people and places (especially government and financial) that have to be protected from without and within. Urban populations and transient people are more and more being viewed bio-politically. What this means is that people become reified and treated simply as a mass of bodies to be managed by techno-mechanical means in highly structured, designed environments where no choices exist. Choice is removed by both 'hard' and 'soft' means: fences, walls, gates, enclosed spaces with guard dogs and facilities requiring keypads, key card or biometric entry, and then by private security contractors, police, plus paramilitary and military forces.

Religion

Almost all faiths, religious structures and events have also acted to design the form and life of cities, this within the city as constituted as event – a place of pilgrimage, a centre of worship, a centre of religious learning, the home of precious religious artefacts of the faith, and as the symbolic locus of the miraculous. For all these reasons, such cities have a material and ethereal relation to the followers of a particular faith. There is now an increasing divide between the cities of theocratic societies and secular society, and this division folds back into conflict, as so much of the present and past history of especially the Middle East and Indian sub-continent affirms.

Beyond history: what will now design the city?

The example forces outlined above are merely illustrations of a vast milieu of complex and symptomatic designing events. This designing is evident in many other different ways, including: the power of the agency of reason (especially in the form of the grid); the imposition of a politico-aesthetic ideal (like the modern movement in architecture); and, more recently, the notion of the creative class (creating 'the creative city'). However, new futural city designing events are equally now arriving, such as climate migration and adaptation; the management of huge, and increasing, numbers of refugees; new technologies and skills; and the commodification of spaces and edifices of culture.

On current trends, many of the present and imminent city designing events identified are going to have an increasing impact over coming centuries. Obviously the unexpected will also arrive. But there is a clear expectation that climate change, in its relational diversity, will be at the fore of future and futuring events – it will have enormous directive consequences and impacts, this no matter what mitigation measures are now taken. This is assured by the length of the life of greenhouse gases in the atmosphere, the time it takes for deep-sea ocean temperatures (the planet's thermostat) to change, and the fact that processes have now been triggered which cannot be stopped (including the widely reported melting of the glaciers of the West Antarctic). Certainly sea level rises will slowly redefine the world's coastlines, and huge numbers of villages, towns and cities will be lost, among them some of the currently most important cities on the planet. Additionally, the level of global warming, with its associated increases in temperatures, reductions in fresh water and linked ability to produce food, will make some areas of the world uninhabitable. The proposed actions (like the reduction target, mitigation measures and adaptation strategies agreed in Paris in December 2015) are not only weak but have no means whereby the 195 signatories can be forced to comply. These measures are ineffectual and do not confront the complexity or urgency of the problem. The claim is they represent a starting point, while *de facto* they mark action which is too little and too late.

There is a growing consensus among informed perspectives in and beyond the sciences that the political leaders of the world are not confronting the mega-causal problem of the planet (the consequences of anthropocentrism) with anything like sufficient understanding, seriousness or rigour. Meanwhile, capital remains bonded to business-as-usual and as usual sees crisis as an economic opportunity. Correspondingly public awareness is low. These remarks are not doomsaying but realism – there cannot be viable action in the contexts outlined without an understanding of the extent and complexity of defuturing problems.

The abandonment of cities and other settlements because of severe climate impacts, related economic collapse and violence is going to create a massive and unprecedented population of people on the move, often without anywhere where they will be made welcome – as is seen, for example, in the Middle East, Burma, Bangladesh, North and East Africa. These comments are not speculative: the process has already started. Camps for the displaced will continue to be created everywhere; informal construction will proliferate on a currently unimaginable scale. Many existing camps are already becoming informal cities, and they will exist for a very long time. There will also likely be 'nomadic cities of passage' to which the displaced people will travel, pass through and change. This situation will create a huge crisis for NGOs and governments. The already existing management of refugee camps demands immediate and urgent action. They beg to be viewed futurally and seen as providing a basis for learning how to deal with coming and greater displacement problems. Currently the political and human failure to deal with this problem evidences chronophobia, and the eyes of politicians and policy makers cannot focus beyond the short-term pragmatic agenda.

As ever, major efforts will be made to protect wealth – the massive rise of gated communities in Africa and Latin America already indicates the rate and scale of this action. And as we shall see in a later chapter, there is increasing concentration of wealth in megaregions. All this portends new kinds of global divisions between the rich and the poor within cities, and between cities inside and outside the megaregions.

Many cities will certainly fracture under the pressures resulting from what they will be exposed to. As a consequence, wastelands of the destroyed and abandoned will increase dramatically. Likewise, new urban environments beyond gated compounds will be created, as will hyper-protected built environments of corporations and governments (corporations are already in this business), and private armies will form (again this is happening). Likewise, and in time, cities of the artificial are likely to be created, via environmental and conflict-defensive architecture (especially in megaregions) – more on this later. In contrast, as has been learnt from Cuba, urban foodscapes will be recognized as an economic and food security necessity – again they will become widespread. Again, these observations are not wild leaps of fancy but simply extrapolations of existing trends.

Metrofitting: the space is everywhere

Everything commented on so far in this chapter feeds into what has to become the agenda of metrofitting.

The present and future consequences of climate change have particular geopolitical implications, especially in altering the power structures of the world we know. The process has already started. For example, China has bought land in Africa to gain increased food security and there are competing territorial claims by a number of nations wishing to extract mineral resources from beneath the sea as the polar sea ice melts. Already there are nations, such as Fiji, unable to meet the costs incurred by large-scale, high-impact extreme weather events. Moreover, territorial abandonment has started, especially from many Pacific islands.

Increasingly, how the world has been mapped geopolitically is at odds with how it now is. Climate change is adding to this disjuncture. The 'old world order', as based on a Eurocentrically formulated international law (*jus publicum Europaeum*), has fallen, and a coherent new order has failed to arrive, while at the same time global power blocs are reconfiguring (not least China and Russia). Concurrently, regions like the Middle East remain extremely unstable. What now underscores this observation is, in fact, that the published map of the world (be it in print or online) does not correspond with the geopolitical landscape. In this context, Robert Kaplan's book, *The Revenge of Geography* has been especially contentious.

The book is a mixture of reactionary conservatism and provocative insights gained from a close reading of contemporary geopolitics.[6] However, many of his insights are undone by an argument replete with nostalgia for nineteenth-century cartographical patriarchal authoritarianism. What Kaplan's viewpoint suggests is that if only the maps were put right by 'a few good men', then the world would be in good shape (literally). Not only does this position evacuate the vast social, political, cultural and economic complexity and turmoil of the contemporary world but also even at the level of cartography it makes no sense. Effectively, representations of sovereignty no longer completely map onto national borders – the ownership of parts of Africa by China, the fragmentation of nations like Syria, Libya and Iraq, and the start of the abandonment of Pacific island nations all confirm this view.

Likewise, events of the past are now converging with those coming from the future. From the past one can cite the politico-cultural damage that resulted from the Congo conference of Berlin in 1883, which carved up Africa paying no heed to natural borders (Kaplan's obsession), topography or tribal geography. What it established were spatial and cultural divisions, inequity and sources of conflict that continue to the present day. To believe all this can be put right by a simple remapping exercise is pure fantasy. What violence destroyed cannot be recovered, and even if a reconfiguration of natural geographic borders was a good idea, there is no available political mechanism able to implement such change. Fragmentation likewise cannot be undone – as the failure of Pan-Africanism has affirmed.

As for the future, an epoch of change is underway that will place all visual representation of the world in a continuous state of flux. What will

---

[6] Robert D. Kaplan (2012), *The Revenge of Geography: What the Map Tells Us about Coming Conflict and the Battle Against Fate*, New York: Random House. As the reviews indicated, the book was viewed to be controversial – see, for example, Juliet Fall (2013), 'The Revenge of Geography by Robert Kaplan', *Society and Space* [http://societyandspace.org/2013/06/27/revenge-of-geography-by-robert-kaplan-reviewed-by-juliet-fall/], and Anne-Marie Slaughter (2012), 'Power Shifts: "The Revenge of Geography" by Robert D. Kaplan', *The New York Times*, 5 October [http://www.nytimes.com/2012/10/07/books/review/the-revenge-of-geography-by-robert-d-kaplan.html].

result from the geopolitical reconfiguration between the East and the West? What will the future national borders of the Middle East or of the Russian Federation look like? How many nations will cease to exist as a result of climate change? How radical will be the reconfiguration of the world's coastline be? In response to such questions, the only certainty is uncertainty. A closer look at what is happening geopolitically in the world confirms this assessment.

Consider, for instance, China. It is increasingly moving into reconfigured geopolitical space, and not just as mentioned in Africa but in the way it is repositioning itself in the South and East China Seas by expanding its navy and building airstrips on islands contentiously claimed to be Chinese territory. Such action has resulted in heightened tensions with its regional neighbours, in particular Taiwan, Vietnam, the Philippines and Australia, and also with the USA, which is strengthening its defence alliances and regional military presence.

Russia has shown itself to have expansionary ambitions, and not just in Eastern Europe but also in the Middle East and Latin America. And then there are the various problematic border relations in the world, many of which are becoming increasingly dangerous, including: Afghanistan/Pakistan; India/Pakistan; Israel/Gaza; Israel/Syria, Syria/Iraq; USA/Mexico; Venezuela/Colombia; India/Bangladesh; Cambodia/Thailand; Sudan/Southern Sudan; North/South Korea; Russia/Ukraine. All of these relations are not only complex but run counter to the rhetorical claims of globalization. In a failed world order, the relations between global power blocs become increasingly volatile, and although there is a global economy it does not function within any real politically or culturally unifying force. Europe is weaker, and the problems and conflicts of the Middle East will run for decades and beyond, with the influence of the USA in the region having diminished (for the good or the bad) as a result of its failed interventions in Iraq and Afghanistan. Meanwhile, as said, tensions in Asia are increasing, and economic divisions in Africa between stagnating and prospering economies are growing. Added to all of this is the evident weakness and continued loss of authority of the United Nations. Thus not only are there numerous and growing global geopolitical problems but the already weak means to address and resolve them seem to be becoming increasingly ineffective. Clearly, and repeating again, climate change is and will make this situation worse. Here one notes the fence dividing India/Bangladesh and the militarization of that border, the keeping out of refugees by nations building fences in Central Europe, the looming high impact of climate change on the economies and populations of African nations in particular, and the global prospect of a mass exodus of 'climate refugees'. These are just some of the worsening global trends and they are certainly a cause for serious concern, with the fate of cities deeply implicated.

More specifically, there are many cities located in areas in, or near to, areas of conflict, In fact cities are ever more becoming sites of conflict and acts of terror. As already mentioned, these developments are causing the militarization of cities globally. Furthermore, all cities, to a greater or lesser extent, are being touched by climate change, and will become more so in the future. And then more generally, every city is structurally implicated in an unsustainable metabolism (via its economy and population's way of life). Some cities are making a modest effort to instrumentally advance sustainable practices, but many others are only making token efforts, or not acting at all. To date, none are setting out to fundamentally transform how their populations live and work.

From what has been said, it follows that all cities, by degree, are broken and in need of repair – this is not to reinstate their past but to cope with the future. This action, as it folds into metrofitting, goes as much to the micro-issues of the domestic and to the everyday as it does to the scale of the urban and beyond. Consumerism connects all these levels of engagement.

Without question consumerism feeds anthropogenic global warming, not least by inscribing populations into unsupportable and unsustainable modes of production, and the utilization of non-renewable materials that advance cultures of excess. Structurally unsustainable, consumption continues to be globalized apace. This would not be a problem if consumption were integral to an urban metabolism that actually consumed – but this is clearly not the case. Unsustainable consumerism rather than being a means to redress global inequity, in fact does the reverse. Gradually in the short term, but rapidly in the mid and long term, it speeds defuturing, which puts everyone, especially the poor, at risk.

Globally the city remains an attractor to ever more people in their belief that this is where they will gain the benefits of the modernized world. So framed, the dynamic of urbanization gained ever more momentum as a magnetic force. Rapid urbanization became, and is, a massive problem, as the number of people arriving completely outstripped/outstrips any ability of many cities to accommodate them. Consequently, the informal areas of these cities have grown dramatically. As a designing event, this process has ontologically relocated these people's sense of being-in-the-world. In this context, it transforms their perception of space, the nature of their desires and the structure of their everyday life (including the challenge of how to survive economically).

Over fifty years ago, Lewis Mumford wondered if 'the city will disappear, or will the planet turn into a vast urban hive?' In large part, the answer to his question has arrived: there are now cities with populations as vast as those of medium-sized nations. Some mega and large cities are heading towards mergers to create a fusion between city and megaregion. In fact, this process has already started. Meanwhile, rural populations everywhere are shrinking.

Again, bringing the longer-term prospect of climate change into the picture, it may well be that at even at current levels of warming, significant areas of the planet outside cities will become wastelands and life in very many cities will become far more environmentally challenging. Meanwhile, it is worth repeating that the demand for food will continue to escalate as the global population grows. Against this backdrop the industrialization of agriculture faces huge challenges of long-term sustainability and supply. So to answer Mumford, many cities have become hives, the city as he knew it is in many respects disappearing, and urbanization has overtaken the city to create urban conglomerations that are only cities in name.

Ontological space

There is no relation to space outside our being-in-the-world in a located sense – it has no ontological signification for us outside this condition of our being situated. As Heidegger made clear: there is no 'us' and space for together we dwell.[7] Other than in the abstract, as many thinkers across many cultures have made clear, the one cannot exist without the other. All understanding of space comes from us, which also implies that it is more than we all (in our difference) understand.

Space opens for us, and therein it is in this opening that we dwell in place. It has always been so. In this respect, occupation implies making and dwelling. It therefore follows that we never experience space as unlocated, as world-space. This means it designs directionally. So while we act in space, the space in which we act is directive of our actions. And more than this, our being-in-the-world is a constant relational and transformative dynamic between the near the far, and the felt as engaged and experienced. It is in this setting that our lived relations to the city and its metabolism are constituted as future directive actions in and upon space. What needs to be understood here is that space is numbered among the 'urphanomene' – indicating it is perceived as originary. As such, 'it' is something that for us has always existed and has been elemental to how and what we perceive and experience.[8] Yet the word 'space' is actually a surrogate for that groundless nothingness in which objects exist. This is to say that space only becomes present by virtue of objects in it, be they objects in the classroom, the stars in the heavens or the walls of a room.

Order is another example. Much of what Carl Schmitt's work sought to expose was the tension existing between the ontological indeterminacy of a firm ground of order and the establishment of such a ground (which could not

---

[7] Heidegger, *Poetry, Language, Thought*, p. 156.
[8] François Raffoul (2012), Book Review: 'The Event of Space: Andrew J. Mitchell, *Heidegger Among the Sculptors: Body, Space, and the Art of Dwelling*', *Gatherings: The Heidegger Circle Annual*, Vol. 2, p. 91.

be spatial and only be political, for order is a no-thing that cannot exist independently from disorder – if it were not for the one the other could not exist or be named).

Space and order, of course, were literally brought together in the grid, but only by an applied prefiguration of reason that reified space as an object of sight. However, this applied prefiguration was not deemed to be reason but order (which is to say order was respectively claimed by the discourse of reason).

Grids are not new. They are to be found as the basis of urban design even in the ancient world in China, Egypt and what is now Pakistan.[9] Not only did they represent the rationalization of physical space but they also portended the rise of geometry and acted as a fundamental 'figure' in the foundational discourse of reason. It is thus not surprising that two of the places where streets were first organized in a grid pattern were Giza (the village in Egypt that housed workers during the building of the pyramids around 2500 BCE) and Babylon (rebuilt in 1700 BCE). Both Egypt and Babylon have of course been acknowledged as the birthplace of geometry.[10]

City planning based on the grid was fostered by Alexander and applied across the Greek empire. As a planning form of the city, the grid was adopted even more expansively by the Romans who made it standard across their empire – this standard was based on a unit of measurement (the 'castra') used for every level of construction right up to the city itself. Thereafter, it became part of the general repertoire of city design that was to become global. At times grids were used irrationally; they became applied without thought, not least when topography was ignored.[11] They also marked the most programmatic application of all design schemas of striated space.

Metrofitting spaced

Unmaking, clearing and making (via remaking or the creation of the new) are all practices that can produce new meaning (with or without visible change), as with community ownership of place, or the positing of spiritual value with

---

[9] Hannah Higgins (2009), *The Grid Book*, Cambridge, MA: MIT Press.

[10] The first Greek philosopher, Thales, took knowledge of geometry from Egypt to Greece. Thales is regarded as the first Greek philosopher because he countered the mythological knowledge of the world of Homer and Hesiod with rational accounts. He gained the ability to do this from the time he spent at the Temple of Waset (now part of Luxor). He became a significant influence on Anaximander's thinking, whom was in turn one of the teachers of Pythagoras. Not only did Pythagoras accompany Alexander to Egypt but he also studied in Babylon.

[11] For a full account of the history of the grid, see Higgins, *The Grid Book*.

the created materiality. They are all the product of specific acts of unmaking, clearing and making, as a bringing of place into the placement, that allows the meaning – worldly, spiritual and sacred – of extant humans to arrive. Metrofitting as a fundamental engagement with the urban goes not just to the material fabric of the city but also to its 'dark places', the fear that the city holds, and the forms of urban sickness that are found in polluted spaces, contaminated land, prisons, asylums and the cancerous excess of landfill. The metabolic unbalance and bias of the city towards destruction and 'hygiene' are evident in the pathological spaces of biophysical and socio-psychological breakdown. The homeless, discarded and dispossessed, travel ahead of the city, in the company of what is broken, as registrations of those internal factors directing its fate.

Our journey now is towards a borderland zone wherein striated space (noted as the divided and controlled – be it physically or in law) is undone as it becomes a zone of overflow. A politics of bypass forms in such a zone.[12] So often neglected, such a zone is the means by which 'the city' (authority) can state that space so deemed is 'not our concern', for it is outside our control[13] – while all the while viewing it as a form of this abomination, as it grows and breeds, with fear (the *cordon sanitaire*, like the one that existed between Old Delhi and New Delhi, represents an extreme example of this space). The uncontrolled, the aberrant, the 'informal' – as the feared is so variously named.[14]

From his position of being a celebrated post-urban architect, Rem Koolhaas viewed Lagos from a helicopter. The vast dystopic spectre of the informal city as a pattern that exposed a dynamic functioning dysfunction vindicated his post-urban perspective – which has received praise, brickbats and sound critical appraisal.[15] His romantic formalism equally abstracted this city as image (in one of his interviews on Lagos he talked of 300 images on which he intended to write). For him raw creativity and ingenuity in the struggle for survival are conflated. Then there are the aerial images that he comments rendered 'the everyday flow of pain (and pleasures) into the abstraction of the pattern'.[16] The fact that out of his visits to Lagos, with and without his Harvard study group, Koolhaas has produced four unpublished books (*de facto* four

[12] Ravi Sundarram (2010), 'Imaging Urban Breakdown', in Gyan Prakash (ed.), *Noir Urbanisms*, pp. 245, 255.
[13] Felipe Hernades, Peter Kellett and Lea K. Allen (2010), *Rethinking the Informal City*, New York: Berghahn Books.
[14] Vyjayanthi Rao (2012), 'Slum as Theory', in C. Greig Crysler, Stephen Cairns and Hilde Heynen (eds), *The SAGE Handbook of Architectural Theory*, London: Sage, pp. 671–686.
[15] See, for example, Laurent Fourchard (2010), 'Lagos, Koolhaas and Partisan Politics in Nigeria', *International Journal of Urban and Regional Research*, Vol. 35, No. 1, pp. 40–56.
[16] Sundarram, 'Imaging Urban Breakdown', in Gyan Prakash (ed.), *Noir Urbanisms*, p. 242.

versions of the same book) marks his lack of resolution of thought and contradictions. Insight, confusion and idiosyncratic theorization (not least of modernity and globalization) characterize Koolhass's views of Lagos and its informal economy and urban fabric. Reaching for a greater grasp of complexity he never quite arrives, his perspective extends to Africa itself.[17] Whatever critical engagement – including of the 'free market' – he deploys, it seems to sit within an uncritical relation to globalization. But then in contrast, he sees conflict inherent within it that naturalizes the relation of mainstream development (including the relation of the architect to developers and the state). Yes, there are solutions to extrapolate but this does not mean the patterns Koolhass sees and hermeneutically constructs are a self-correcting auto-solution. *Gelassenheit* is not the answer, neither is 'development' nor the bulldozer of urban planning. If an answer is to arrive, it cannot be devoid of a liberatory politics in which social, spatial and economic transformations are directively present.

The informal city arrives/is arriving with the decline of the infrastructure of many cities: continually 'the formal' gains informal 'attachments'.[18] Meanwhile, totally informal cities are arriving – be they called refugee camps, boat-people detention centres, or reclaimed areas of abandoned cities. The picture presented by the far left, social democrats and far right equally reduces the informal population to a circumstantially created single class, whereas the reality is quite different – its socio-cultural difference can be very marked, both socially and visually, with an underclass at one extreme, and poorly paid and educated young professionals at the other. Likewise, the borderlands between the formal and the informal can be equally indistinct. When bringing the concept of metrofitting to these contexts (for metrofitting can draw no distinction between the formal and the informal) there has to be an understanding that change cannot arrive as external imposition. The whole issue of intervention is in fact not something extraneous to the metrofit agenda but an issue of central concern. Intervention cannot in any way be imposed: it can only be created through cooperative relations with the

---

[17] First, is the issue of understanding Lagos not as an isolate but part of both the difference within Africa and as part of a common historical trajectory? As the 2015 International Monetary Fund Report noted, by 2035 it has been estimated that Africa will have more people entering the workforce than the sum of the rest of the world combined. It has a population that will have quadrupled by the end of the century. But equally it has a vast store of human and natural resources combined with a huge level of inequity and corruption plus many conflicting geopolitical and theological forces competing for power and influence. Second, one cannot comprehend Africa without an understanding of colonialism as the 'underside of modernity' having created the imperative of decoloniality that globalization strives to override – see Walter Mignolo (2011), *The Darker Side of Western Modernity: Global Futures, Decolonial Options*, Durham, NC: Duke University Press.

[18] Ibid.

capabilities and creative nous of communities of need. Non-interventionist modes of intervention based on a viable relation of exchange should be viewed and treated as major challenges, in their own right. There is certainly no place for the cultural myopia and professional arrogance of architects displayed in statements like this:

> Engagement with informal housing offers alternative models with respect to the autonomy of architecture's creative agency, as well as its authority with respect to form and program.[19]

The contribution architects can make in redressing 'the problem' is negligible. Those actions that are currently being made are gestural, token and frequently patronizing. Moreover, whatever the good intentions, the insufficiency of architectural knowledge is continually being demonstrated. To put the scale of the informal sector in context, consider this: UN Habitat reported that eighty-five per cent of all new housing globally is informal. In Africa, more recent figures note that it exceeds ninety per cent. In many cities in Latin America, the figure is around seventy per cent.[20] Architects would do well to view this area as an opportunity to unlearn and relearn architecture, especially in terms of what it actually means to be creative in 'shock' environments where the scale of the problem is overwhelming both in a quantitative sense and in relation to existential dramas. For example, just a few remarks on Delhi will make clear that the informal sector constitutes a 'shock-city' within a city wherein the material and psycho-social foundation of everyday life are assaulted by shocks on a continuous basis.

The National Capital Region of Delhi has a population of the order of 40 million people, in which informal settlements are included. In a condition of metabolic overload, dysfunction establishes a form of political urbanism that arrives on the street to help make some kind of operative life possible. This effectively means a political urbanism arrives as a counter to, or supplement of, the inadequacies of the formal institutional political order. In such a city, the life of a very significant segment of the population is lived in a perpetual state of emergency in spaces of 'ecological collapse'.[21] The shock of life in such a city comes from the operational speed of capitalism, violence and the

---

[19] Cairns and Jacobs, *Buildings Must Die*, p. 187.

[20] UN Habitat (2007), *Cities Without Slums*, Nairobi: UN Habitat, and Jim Meikle (2011), 'Note on: Informal Construction', International Comparison Program, 5th Technical Advisory Group Meeting, 18–19 April, Washington, DC [http://siteresources.worldbank.org/ICPINT/Resources/270056-1255977007108/6483550-1257349667891/01.02_ICP-TAG04_ConstructionNote.pdf], p. 4.

[21] Sundarram, 'Imaging Urban Breakdown', in Gyan Prakash (ed.), *Noir Urbanisms*, p. 247.

media-sphere kinetically impacting with the everyday struggle for survival of millions of people in conditions of dysfunction (traffic, utility service failure, infrastructure breakdown that privilege can bypass). It has the worst air of any city on the planet. Here crisis is the underside of Western modernity, a normative destructive force extending out into the future. As for the rising middle class, the ambition is to cast off a problem deemed impossible rather than strive to find ways to solve it.

Here metrofitting comes not with answers but with the need to learn. It is another way to begin.

4

The city, humanity and time

Consideration will now be given to ancient, pre-modern and colonial cities, but why? Do they have any significance to issues of remaking cities and to metrofitting? The answer has to be 'yes'.

Our starting point is to acknowledge that to remake cities one has to understand how they were originally made (the founding moment of the materialization of their design) and what this history reveals about the nature of contemporary cities. How colonial cities need to be understood historically and futurally will be especially considered. In doing this, and across geographies of difference, what will become clear is that many contemporary cities are still touched by the darker side of this history, as fragmentary ontological forms of the afterlife of colonialism continue to arrive inter-generationally.

In the first place there was Uruk

As acknowledged earlier, the Southern Mesopotamia Sumerian cities of Uruk and to its south Ur were among the first cities ever constructed. Babylon, to the north, did not arrive for almost another 2,000 years.[1] The critical issue here is not the veracity of truth claims but the significance of the narrative of an ancient city's formation.

Over a period of about 700 years, Uruk developed from agricultural villages established some 8,000 years ago on what was then the banks of the Euphrates River.[2] Uruk rose to become a powerful city-state and regional force for

---

[1] On this history, see Petr Charvát, Zainab Bahrani and Marc Van de Mieroop (2008), *Mesopotamia Before History*, London: Routledge; Harriet E. W. Crawford (2004), *Sumer and the Sumerians,* Cambridge: Cambridge University Press; William Hayes, M.B. Rowton and Frank H. Stubbings (1964), *Chronology: Egypt, Western Asia, Aegean Bronze Age*, Cambridge: Cambridge University Press; Lewis Mumford (1961), *The City in History*, London: Penguin Books; and Mitchell S. Rothman (2001), *Uruk, Mesopotamia and its Neighbors*, Santa Fe, NM: School of American Research Press.
[2] Subsequently over time the course of the river changed.

urbanization. The region itself became of major importance agriculturally and economically, especially through the domestication of einkorn and other grains.

The walled city of Uruk was said to eventually have accommodated a population of around 80,000 people, making it perhaps the largest city in the world at the time. Accounts suggest that by 2700 BCE it was ruled by King Gilgamesh (of the legendary Epic of Gilgamesh fame). Archaeological evidence has shown that the city was complex and had areas of well-planned narrow streets, public spaces with temple complexes and one or more ziggurats.[3] Most remarkably, the city had a system of canals that linked irrigation systems to the Euphrates. When the path of the Euphrates River changed the city was abandoned.

Ur was equally complex. Archaeological studies have revealed that the city was conceived to support regional economic activity together with providing a place of defence and worship for a growing community. Research on the city's built structures indicates that they were positioned in relation to each other within a symbolic schema. There is also evidence that much of the decoration on these buildings was also symbolic. However, exactly how the profane and the sacred were understood by the city's population is not clear, neither are there any exact chronologies of its development. So while archaeology and historical research based on ancient inscriptions and texts (remembering the birth of the first cities overlapped with the birth of writing) enabled a lot of knowledge to be uncovered (some of which is contested), there is still a great deal that is unknown. Of what is known, there is a continual danger of hermeneutic back loading (for example, a contemporary understanding of 'the sacred' may have nothing in common with ideas of how the symbolic function of images and objects were understood in the ancient past). Even so, what is evident is that the development of cities cannot be ordered to an evolutionary *telos.* Uruk and Ur were not only far more advanced than many cities that arrived much later, but even more significant they were also created without referential forms other than those in village settlements, or obviously any historically established formal sense of design.

So said, there are features of the design of many ancient cities that appear to be firmly lodged in now arcane functions that were then directive of their life. The city as cemetery is one example, wherein the accommodation of the dead was a major directive feature of a city's urban form and its everyday life. Yet in contrast, dealing with large numbers of the dead, and the memory of them, may equally be influential on the future form of many cities. Conversely, the dead may also have carried disease, resulting in cities being abandoned. Lewis Mumford's view that 'urban life spans the historic space between the

---

[3] Mumford, *The City in History,* p. 91 points out that this spatial organization is very similar to the walled cities of Northern Africa still standing.

earliest burial ground' and 'the Necropolis' could well take on new significance in our age when the risk of pandemics is increasing.[4]

Clearly there are also features of ancient cities that are present in cities of today that will also travel out into the future. In particular, and notwithstanding issues of readability, the structure of the city has always in some form mirrored structural forms of power: the temple, the city wall and gate, and the city square are a few of the more obvious examples. Expressions of power, of course, took on an explicit form with the Greek notion of *polis*, wherein the political subject (the member of the exclusive political community that excluded women and slaves) and the space of politics (the materialized forms of the city-state) were deemed to be one, with the citizen emergent (ontologically) out of the objective conditions of the ethos of political community. The *polis* was a condition of transparency – a politics of public life and a stage upon which everyday life was lived. Which is to say the *polis* cannot be reduced to the purely material form of the city.[5]

Without question, while the *polis* is not recoverable as such, what can be created is a 'political community' gathered in a built environment that is centred on establishing a quality of life that counters hyper-consumerism. So considered, the 'political community' has to be viewed within the ethos of metrofitting, but not idealized as a utopian construct. Remaking the city and remaking the/its political community cannot be separated from one another as a futural imperative. Both are going to become increasingly important in meeting the challenges of the future. Responding to this imperative, and linking it to the project of the Sustainment, suggests the importance of the city has to substantially increase.

Yet the very concept of 'city' is not secure: there are now many signs of change that support this statement. Consider, for example, the perpetually temporary city reconfigured out of camps, cultures of the displaced, communities in passage and the stateless who will never belong to the state in which they live. Such neo-nomadism certainly begs the reinvention of what a camp is and the forms of a dematerialized everyday life. The very foundational principle of nomadic life – that you only own what you are able to carry – invites being viewed with new significance. Then there is the city as a mobile political and cultural structure: a way of life that is neither nomadism as it was, nor settlement as it is. Emergent environmental and geopolitical circumstances are almost certainly going to dictate new forms of the city.

Remarks made on 'the camp' and the nomadic obviously gain salience because of the hundreds of millions of people who will be displaced in the next

---

[4] Mumford, *The City in History*, p. 15.
[5] On the *polis*, see Thomas R. Martin (2013), *Ancient Greece*, New Haven, CT: Yale University Press.

century and a half. The extent to which these people become (or not) a problem directly goes to defining and creating an appropriate political community able to create an affirmative politics of movement. What this might look like and how it can be created is elemental to the agenda of metrofitting, remaking and resilience. Certainly at present there is an absolute global failure to recognize, let alone contemplate dealing with, the scale of this problem. Moreover, what this problem exposes is an amplified human condition that has extended over millennia: the tension between settled and unsettled populations wherein war was waged on the nomadic. Like so many of the serious problems of the present it is, by default, thrown into the future for those yet to confront it in a moment of unavoidability. This occurs along with many other futural problems that are ignored, neglected or are simply unable to be recognized.

It is already clear, for instance, that the cost of future catastrophic dysfunction (compound systems' failures) and environmental impacts will be astronomical and well beyond the means of governments. This observation immediately brings us back to the crucial importance of a political community and the creation of an ethic of dwelling appropriate to the age and the absolute necessity of adaptation.

Responses like the return to, and proliferation of, the compound, the walled city and the militarization of the city, all have to be viewed as such examples of unwelcomed recoveries from the past (the city wall, the moat, the castle). These spaces are seen by the privileged as innovations in response to the insecurity they feel, as well as the means to withdraw from what they deem to be unsavoury. Such action goes exactly to the point made on the need for a political community able to form and direct a social ecology of support, and sufficient redirective power, to begin to reconfigure modes of human earthly urban habitation. Metrofitting invites being viewed as one means (knowledge, theory, methods, ideas, practices) to facilitate this action. Currently it is a nascent project and ambition. Getting it understood and recognized as significant is the immediate task – one indivisible from getting the idea and politics of the Sustainment acknowledged as a prerequisite of human existence.

Colonial cities, the colonial matrix and the future

Establishing recognition of the growing importance of non-European cities is implicit to thinking about the relation between political community, social ecology and metrofitting. They are the largest, at most risk and most seriously challenged cities in the world. At the same time, the possibilities and problems of these the cities of Asia, Africa and Latin America are not going to stay in place. Certainly if current unsustainable trends continue, their problems and populations are going to become uncontained and overflow. What Rem Koolhaas took to be energy and creativity is not only contradictory but finely balanced within the dialectic of Sustainment. Slippage into destruction and disaster can happen in an instant.

In his influential book *Global Cities*, Anthony King wrote: 'Colonial Cities can be viewed as the forerunners of what the contemporary capitalist world city would eventually become.'[6] This prospect has become closer over the recent past as the international labour market has become more fluid, as migration has continued, as refugee numbers have increased and as many industrial cities were left to their post-industrial fate of shrinkage and decline. It is also clear that any sense of there being any real transition of colonialism to post-colonialism has been illusory and ungrounded. What has become evident is that all that has happened is that the nature of colonialism changed. While modernity and colonization have always been of time and space – and as Walter Mignolo has remarked, both became the pillars of Western civilization – what this union has progressively done is to appropriate and fuse technology and knowledge to constitute a new instrumental ontological domain of colonization. Carried by globalization, the geography of colonialism is of the everywhere.

What is also evident is that the city, as a speed machine, accelerates the passage of what is created within it to its destruction – this under the direction of a continually renewed ontologically designing domain in which people learn, work and play. In one direction what is created is the hyper-real city of rapid development and capital growth, and in the other direction a rapid withdrawal, wherein the colonial city projected by Anthony King arrives. These two cities of inclusion and exclusion, the formal and informal simply mirror the relation of modernity and colonialism as they bleed into each other in the era of Western global expansion. Progress and regress are thus not only two faces of the epistemology of the new colonial matrix but again, as we shall see, are traversed by enduring features of the old in the new.

The colonial matrix was founded upon a Christian theological construction of an order that acted to define difference according to its values of civilization, race and humanity. This became transposed into a secular regime of knowledge directed by philosophy and science, while still retaining a normative measure of humanity according to a Eurocentric designation of what it was to be civilized. The power of control of the colonial matrix was configured by Western epistemology and directively projected at: the management of the economy, the structures of authority (not least the law), the specification and regulation

---

[6] Anthony King (1990), *Global Cities*, London: Routledge, p. 38.

of racial classification, gendered sexuality, knowledge and how subjectivities were constituted.[7] It acted in the name of God and reason and strove to progressively exercise complete power over everyday life.

Cities were created, viewed and managed within the violent enframing of this matrix. What it created was on the basis of the destruction of all that the colonized were or had been. Moreover, it unknowingly imposed conditions that, as is now clear, cannot be sustained. In this setting, the city was viewed and designed as a structure of the control of bodies and space – prefiguring what is now understood as bio-politics. This all in the name of function, and the ordering of things and bodies to appear, operate and progress in their proper place under the direction of reason.

What has just been said is not mere conjecture. Clear evidence exists, the Spanish 'Laws of the Indies' being a extremely good example, one worth selectively citing.[8] These laws were promulgated by King Phillip II in 1573 and consisted of 148 ordinances that were directive of the location, building and populating of settlements of two types: military towns (*presidios*) and civilian towns (*pueblos*). Effectively they combined design and planning regulations with instructions on the development and direction of colonized and colonizing communities of 'the newly discovered populations of the Indies and their pacification'. Effectively anything that could be regulated was. What this process marked was phase two of the colonization of the Americas – the arrival of the order of civilization after the period of wholesale slaughter.

Ordinances 1–14 went to the establishment of settlements – here is number 3, which is a short example:

Having made, within the confines of the province, a discovery by land, pacified it [and] subjected it to our obedience, find an appropriate site to be settled by Spaniards – and if not, [arrange] for vassal Indians to be secure.

Ordinances 15–31 instruct the Spanish on:

. . . the formal issues of encountering, greeting, teaching and punishing the native Indian population.

All the rest of the ordinances (32–148) govern city life and planning, including action for colonizers to move out to 'populate adjacent areas discovered for the

---

[7] See Walter Mignolo (2011), *The Darker Side of Western Modernity: Global Futures, Decolonial Options*, Durham, NC: Duke University Press, pp. 8–20.

[8] The English translation cited is by Axel Mundigo and Dora Crouch (1977), 'The City Planning Ordinances of the Laws of the Indies Revisited. Part 1: Their Philosophy and Implications', *The Town Planning Review*, Vol. 48, pp. 247–268 (with permission). Translation of ordinances 92, 102–107 by Ramon Trias.

first time'. Location is also a big issue, both inland and coastal, in relation to climate, water, soil quality and farming. However, the main rationale for colonial settlement is specified in ordinance 36, which was to 'preach the gospels' to the Indians for this was 'the principal objective for which we mandate that these discoveries and settlements be made'. The specific details of the make-up of the settlement are exact and centred on sub-divisions of thirty households, each having a specified lot size and with a particular number of domestic animals for every sub-division. All land uses were required to be surveyed and marked out, the form of governance detailed and the designation of required official administrative positions made. Many ordinances addressed the layout of the settlement and stated that 'the main plaza is to be the starting point of the town' (ordinance 112). The grid of the town, the width of streets, all emanated from the plaza as its key reference point – it had to be of a minimum and maximum size in ratio to the scale of the town. What all the detail added up to (and there is a lot of it) was an expression of power, order, control and reason that in turn manifested the idealized structure of the mind of Western modernity. But overarching all of this was the function of religion, which was not just about bringing God to the Godless. It was about making Indians – who were initially classified as 'uncivilised and without God' and as such slaughtered as animals – into humans.[9] The intent of colonization was absolute.

The instrumentalism of contemporary (epistemological) colonialism was prefigured by the subordination of bodies to technological systems[10] – in this the bodies of the colonial matrix, as in the Laws of the Indies, were treated as moveable machine parts, as disposable labour power and as units of designed function over which the incorporated human beings had no control. Timothy Mitchell gives a number of illuminating examples in his book *Colonising Egypt*. The growing of cotton for the European market was one such example. Rural peasants had their places in the field carefully marked out and they had

> . . . their duty or quota exactly specified and their performance continuously monitored and reported . . . the 'general system of dependence and subordination' was more fully elaborated in a sixty-page booklet issued in December 1829 . . . which described how peasants were to work in the fields, the crops they were to cultivate, their confinement to the village, and the duties of those who were to guard and supervise them . . . it included at the end fifty-five paragraphs stipulating in hierarchical detail the punishment for over seventy separate failures of duty by peasants and supervisors.[11]

---

[9] The initial genocidal destruction post 1492 was based on a designation that indigenous people were not human.

[10] Epistemological colonialism is effectively the retained agency of the globalization of the rational mind of the Enlightenment carried by modernity as it has devalued and erased indigenous knowledge.

[11] Timothy Mitchell (1988), *Colonising Egypt*, Berkeley, CA: University of California Press, pp. 40–41.

Here, then, is a different time and place but a commonality of ground with that of the Americas with the colonization of subjects constituted as a life negated. The consequence of ordered violence against dehumanized human beings in the past is still active in the present. Its afterlife retains the ability to direct the lifeworld of people in the former cotton growing regions of Egypt: it is inscribed in the landscape, and in values, memories and traces that mark social relations within the community and between it and the local state.

Decoloniality in this context requires acts of delinking everyday thinking that has been *enframed* (imposed to hold the subject in place) together with acts of 'epistemological disobedience' that refuse to think in compliance with the imposed order of mind. Obviously, this is a hard and painful process of liberation.

As the city was no mere backdrop to the colonial regime but was structurally part of it, it follows that it has to be deeply implicated in its undoing. Organized as a geography of power: it was an ordering in which the subaltern subject was positioned in the space of the environment, an everyday lifeworld, and social placement. It was also a domain of de-severance where a proximity to that which was made close did not in any way mean it was near. One graphic example of this was that during the 1950s, workers recruited from the Caribbean to fill labour shortages in Britain often described their sea voyage to the country as 'going home'.

In the shadow of such a history, how then do we view contemporary cities? The advanced city has numerous inscribed epistemological structures (technologies, compliance codes, standards, operational regulations, byelaws, ordinances and so on). It has aesthetic hierarchies of form and instruments of power that the state and corporation mobilize; its social structure is indivisible from inscribed spatial power and the division of economic and cultural capital; all its services are fully controlled and regulated; and now overlooking everything is an ever more sophisticated system of surveillance. The policing, control and management of urban life rests, as discussed, upon the city of fear. Chaos, civil disorder, crime, violence, terrorism, disease, are all present for citizens of privilege but mostly held in check by the combined forces of control. For most citizens in such cities, peace rides on the back of repression – it has been made normality, and when questioned it is proclaimed to be the price to pay for peace and safety.

But for so many cities, fear coming out of the colonial city still arrives in urban daily life. It is of the here and the everywhere. It comes from the both the near and far. It's what Franz Fanon called 'the return of the repressed', be it now in a myriad of confused, angry and corrupted incarnations that mostly blur sight of the passage of fear from any historical path or any simple understanding of causality. Injustice, poverty, ignorance, resentment, desire, revenge, confusion, ambition, dysfunction mix together in numerous blends in the minds of the colonized – this to nourish the generation and reception of fear. Here is the fear of dark places, dehumanization, life behind the wall, the brutality of paramilitary police, the violence and corruption of overcrowded prisons, gang-life, power-hungry maniac politicians, and frightened parents. In this setting, it is clear that what colonialism breaks cannot return as whole. Hunger, need and desire energetically embrace what globalization and development offer. But it comes at a price and the debt bond is just another form of colonial bondage. At best, all that can be retrieved via decoloniality are damaged but valued fragments of memories and decontextualized stories whose trace can be carried in the ruin of the city. Erasures are read as signifiers of loss, and the marks of a silenced past. We are all destroyed by the destruction of our past, but the colonized are the most destroyed.

What metrofitting now looks to be here is as much a matter of mending mind and memory as it is of material repair(ed). As such, it brings the Sustainment to a borderland between loss and a socio-spatial just mode of being-in-the-world. The scale of this undertaking is vast and daunting, yet in reality there is no *affirmative* choice other than a (re)making in the betweenness of traces of the pre-colonial and the arrival of neo-colonizing globalism. Justice, equity, identity and a voice versus ethnocide and ecocide all meet at the crossroads where the energy to create a future meets its fate. Metrofitting, in all its possible forms of created difference, has to be made elemental to such remaking in place.

In this scenario, there is no room for the romanticism of the likes of Rem Koolhass and the imagery to which he is attracted but does not see.

Space, power and the colonial city

As seen, in contradiction, colonial cities were frequently well planned – they worked well to realize their negative objectives. As they 'developed', there were three overwhelming issues that directed such planning: race, disease and sex.

The concern with race translated into racial segregation. This action being legitimized on the basis of a designated racial inferiority of the colonialized, which in turn eventually became theoretically undergirded by the claims of eugenics. In its colonial mission, eugenics was in truth 'scientific racism' deployed to prove, for example, that African races had the lowest ranking of human intelligence. The British and Germans especially embraced this kind of thinking. As such, it was employed to give colonial powers the freedom to plan and build colonial cities on the basis of 'racially informed principles'. Designated 'inferior races' were structurally designed out of cities by land and property values, the confiscation and rezoning of land, and the throwing up of a screen of legal complexity. Long after eugenics had been shown to be scientifically flawed and to have no genetic basis, the racial structuring of cities lived on. Of course, action based on racial prejudice did not require a biological foundation. For instance, expressing a widely held cultural view in an interview in the *Madagascar Tribune* in 1924, a French architect said he supported racial segregation because it was appropriate for 'those who cannot or will not live by European Standards'.[12]

As Franz Fanon made clear in *Wretched of the Earth* in 1963, and as others have subsequently reiterated,[13] the level of discrimination and the acts of segregation were oppressive forms of mental (and at times physical) violence against the indigenous population at large that did substantial psychological damage. The justification for segregation was, of course, that it would 'improve living standards and protect cultural values in the city'.[14] The reality for the colonized, however, was the absolute reverse of this goal. Culturally, economically and environmentally the quality of their lives was appalling and the negative impact, especially upon the young, was huge. Paul Ugbaojah's study of the youth of Lagos in the 1920s made this very clear and also indicated how the determinant conditions of the time still have had consequences for the present.[15] Stealing, gambling, delinquency, drugs, prostitution and violence were rife, and therefore had (and still have) devastating results on the lives of families.

What these conditions meant was that not only was disease a designated pathology of many colonial cities, but it also arrived as a metaphor applied to characterize the social and economic 'sickness' of people, who were not only exposed to all the negative consequences of widespread deviant behaviour but also lived in vermin-infested slums.[16]

Colonial life totally destroyed tribal life and with it its social structure, values and foundation of authority, all of which had sustained people for millennia. The referential order in which people had lived was completely erased. The only options in life under the variable harshness of colonial rule was complete compliance, and with it an absolute loss (at least visually) of identity and dignity. Any form of non-compliance was regarded as deviance and punished. Between these two options there was no cultural space in which anything from the past could arrive or survive – yet, be it only as traces, fragments from the other world did.

---

[12] Franz Fanon (1963), *The Wretched of the Earth*. New York: Grove Press; Ambe J. Njoh (2008), 'Colonial Philosophies, Urban Space, and Racial Segregation in British and French Colonial Africa', *Journal of Black Studies*, Vol. 38, No. 4, p. 585.

[13] Ibid., p. 516.

[14] Ibid., p. 587.

[15] Paul K.N. Ugbaojah (2008), 'Culture-Conflict and Delinquency: A Case Study of Colonial Lagos', *ERAS*, Edition 10, November [http://artsonline.monash.edu.au/eras/files/2014/02/ugboajah-article.pdf]

[16] Robert Peckham (2011), 'Diseasing the City: Colonial Noir and the Ruins of Modernity', *Fast Capitalism*, No. 8/1 [http://www.uta.edu/huma/agger/fastcapitalism/8_1/peckham8_1.html].

Not only was discrimination and spatial segregation of the colonized claimed to be justified on the basis of their lack of an appropriate (European) way of life, but also that such people were also seen and treated as vectors of disease. There is a very large literature of especially town planning across the colonized world documenting the extent of segregation on this ground. Within this history it is unsurprising that a constructed fear of disease, literal and metaphoric, occupied a very significant place in this literature. As well as this, the culture of the colonized was equally feared. They were considered as mentally and culturally depraved. Music and dance were considered especially abhorrent (drumming was the most reviled, and in some places was banned completely[17]). Such prejudice underscored a less explicitly expressed cultural pathology and justification for segregation: 'the fear of white women of the lust of black men'. What this fear did was to create a perception that not only viewed black men as uncivilized but nearer to animals than white men.[18] In contrast, for the colonizers segregation rested upon their culture and political ideology distinguishing itself in every way possible from the 'backward' and 'uncivilized' mores of the colonized.

Besides the organization of urban space in colonial cities being discriminatory and based on crude racial prejudice, it was also directly linked to assumptions about sanitation as linked to disease, this especially in Africa – a continent projected in popular media as a wild and exotic land yet full of savages, disease and death.[19]

Doctors were complicit in the use of disease as a basis for segregation. The fear and fact of disease was actually used to legitimize some of the most draconian of the planning rules.[20] One example is the adoption of segregation policy in Freetown, Sierra Leone, by the British in 1901. It was undertaken in significant part on the basis of medical advice that asserted that 'natives' were 'vectors of the deadly malaria disease'. This fear was taken to a new height when there was an outbreak of bubonic plague in Lagos at the turn of the century.[21]

While the focus of much that has been said so far has been related to Latin America and Africa, the form and inhuman conduct of colonialism was global. To make this clear, and reinforce the connection between the designed form of the colonial city and the conduct of the colonial power, the Indian city of Delhi invites consideration. To do this Stephen Legg's excellent book *Space of*

---

[17] Njoh, 'Colonial Philosophies', p. 594.
[18] Ibid.
[19] Liora Bigon (2012), 'A History of Urban Planning and Infectious Diseases: Colonial Senegal in the Early Twentieth Century', *Urban Studies Research*, Vol. 2012, Article ID 589758 [https://www.hindawi.com/journals/usr/2012/589758/], p. 2.
[20] Ibid.
[21] Njoh, 'Colonial Philosophies', pp. 589–590.

Colonialism will be drawn upon, while at the same time connections to the colonial experience already outlined will be made.[22]

At the 'proposal' of Viceroy Harding, and with the approval of the King, the British 'moved' the capital of India from Calcutta to Delhi. They did this because they viewed the political radicalism and revolutionary nature of the province of Bengal, in which Calcutta was located, as a threat to the stability of the nation.[23] Government was to be housed in New Delhi, but between 1912 and 1926 it was accommodated in Old Delhi while the new incarnation of the city was being constructed. The chief designer of New Delhi was the British architect Edwin Lutyens. His design objective was to create 'a unique hybridisation between the imperial and the modern' that embraced the newly emergent practice of 'town planning'.[24] The symbolic start to the project was made in 1911 when the foundation stone was laid. It would be another twenty years before New Delhi was actually completed. Thereafter, it was projected as a global aesthetic 'showcase' of British sovereign and imperial power. Two absolute design regimes were applied with total control and authority. The conceptual substrate of the plan was the grid. It ruled every physical element at every scale from the urban form to the layout of homes and offices.[25] More than this, it was also applied beyond the spatial to the ordering of the operational social structure (including between races).[26] Layered onto the grid was an aesthetic statement of the imperial-modern. Effectively the style acted to partially mask the extremity of the design of striated space. This strategy can actually be read as a double movement whereby imperial power was being forcefully reasserted structurally while the immediate appearance created was of progress and good taste. Colonialism was en route to becoming modernized – retrospectively, this to withstand the demise of empire.

To make sense of New Delhi one has to see just how dramatic the class division between the old and the new was. Old Delhi has a rich and complex history spanning almost 5,000 years. But in 1857 a large part of the city was destroyed during the Indian Mutiny. Between 1648 and 1857 Old Delhi had functioned as the capital of the Mughal Empire. Spatially, experientially and

---

[22] Stephen Legg (2007), *Spaces of Colonialism: Delhi's Urban Governmentalities*, Oxford: Blackwell. Legg's argument itself substantially draws on Michel Foucault as reference (p. 237), but with an awareness of the Eurocentrism of his perspective.

[23] Legg, *Spaces of Colonialism*, p. 28.

[24] Ibid., p. 29.

[25] Legg details the specification of a prestigious bungalow that was at the top of a scale whereby location, plot size, building size and layout were all specified within an overall schema. The actual bungalow he details (for a senior official) consisted of a hall, dining room, living room, six bedrooms and bathrooms, two dressing rooms, two garages, three stables and thirteen servants quarters (one presumes it had a kitchen, but this is not listed). In contrast, the lowest of the low had a one-room home in a terrace. Legg, *Spaces of Colonialism*, p. 48.

[26] Ibid., pp. 48–51.

culturally it was and remained dense and complex. So what the creation of New Delhi set out to do was to establish a very clear and material statement dividing the worlds of the old and the new. Clear divisions were to be made between the organically formed and the logically imposed, the old values and the new structures of power, and colonial and colonized cultures. To understand the relation between the old and the new parts of the city, it is important to recognize that they did not directly interface with each other but were kept apart by a wide *cordon sanitaire*.

This cordon was created as a structural pathological separation. It was about obstructing the passage of contaminants and disease as well maintaining a division of race that kept Europeans and the Indian masses apart. It was also an obstacle to block organic waste flowing from Old Delhi into the New. As such, it was partially successful (although night soil did get dumped there). As for disease, there was a great fear of tuberculosis that killed enormous numbers of people in India. However, it was not the first disease to cross the cordon into New Delhi – this happened in 1931 with the arrival of a strain of meningitis from which two people died.

Notwithstanding the vast contrast between the splendour of New Delhi, the cotton fields of Egypt and the early colonial settlements of the Americas, they all shared the same designed political projects: the placement of bodies in space where every body had its assigned place in 'the order of things' so that fear, disease and deviance were contained and therefore could pose no danger.

Metrofitting: a reconnecting

What has hopefully been made clear is that colonialism is not arrested in the past but remains alive in the present in new and less visible ways. The suffering and global cultural damage colonialism inflicted is beyond calculation, and the geopolitical, social, economic and psychological problems it created live on in many of the geopolitical issues of the planet. In so many ways in so many places, it still writes much of the life of the city. This can be seen in the social division of labour, inequity and the spatial distribution, location and economic status (or lack of it) of migrants and refugees. But then there is the unseen of broken cultures, spirits, memories and minds in a world in which racism still exists, often wearing a new mask.

Now what is starting to arrive is a wave of dispossessed humanity that will become ever larger as climate change bites deeper and violence (not least prompted by its impacts) continues. How, then, will broken lives and broken cities (in the conditions of overtly visible dysfunction and hidden and visible concealment) fuse? Can they be constructively brought together? There are clues to the answer in the modesty, the simple lives and the cultural bricolage that colonized peoples so often managed to make in the space of deprivation (and continue to do so in many informal settlements). Such qualities and abilities are certainly more futural than those of hyper-consumers.

Even if the means existed (and some do, but not in well recognized forms), there can be no externally imposed solutions. Additionally, solutions and adaptation can but come out of the broken (in its human and urban/environmental forms). And as already recognized, the spaces of the broken already provide some lessons to learn from (not least those of the social cohesion of many 'slums' and informal settlements). What potentially metrofitting can offer is: analytic methods, ideas and practices able to be dialogically created and situationally appropriated, and while to have real agency this action requires critical mass, the process has already started.

5

Urban imperatives in the face of change

Unquestionably, the challenges cities will face in the future are going to be complex, huge and in some cases dangerous. They are beyond the means of any one organization, particular practice or profession to adequately engage and overcome. It follows that to address the scale of these coming challenges, they have to worked on collectively – this by a gathering of thought, knowledge, energy and people. Even so there can be no presumption that action taken will equate to the delivery of solutions to deep and structural problems, for as is becoming clear, humanity will just have to learn to live with many of them. Certainly the days when utopian urban models were imagined, shaped, represented and then applied to cities by architects, urban designers and planners are long over – but some dream on.[1]

This chapter will examine some of the complexity of these challenges by exploring a number of relationally connected determinants that are now becoming increasingly evident. It does this against a backdrop of coming pressures from the planet moving towards a human population of ten billion plus by the end of this century. On present trends, the impact of these people will continue to be amplified by ever increasing numbers of consumers and levels of 'consumption'. Likewise, it needs to be recognized that the larger this population, the more people will be exposed to actual or possible disasters (climatic, natural and the un-natural). Within this unfolding context, questions of the now constant growth of megaregions and megacities will be examined, especially from the perspectives of social exclusion, and the dangers of conflict coming from an emergent overlap between geopolitical

---

[1] This role is still being argued. See, for example, Brian McGrath and Grahame Shane (2012), 'Introduction: Metropolis, Megalopolis and Metacity', in C. Greig Crysler, Stephen Cairns and Hilde Heynen (eds), *The SAGE Handbook of Architectural Theory*, London: Sage, pp. 641–655. High-profile architects, architectural groups, architect-created models for cities and architectural projects will not overcome the challenges and associated problems cities face. Order cannot overtake the speed of disorder.

reconfigurations, tensions in and between national populations and climate change. These situations clearly and directly link to issues like global inequity, food security, mass migration, natural resource stress, and environmental degradation. Our narrative starts by looking at megaregions and then moves to consider megacities. It will acknowledge how cities are becoming the key interfaces with identified emerging global dangers and how this situation can potentially create conflict between the formal/informal divisions within many large cities. As will be seen a little later, this prospect is graphically illustrated by a report published by the US Army Strategic Studies Group in June 2014 that indicated that wars of the future would likely be fought in megacities.

Megaregions: the inside and the outside

Megaregions are a geo-economic indicator of shifts in national economies. As such, they mark a new economic formation and space of convergence between capital, technology, managerial process and administration. They are also indicators of the rise of ideological structures that are generative of 'post national political institutions' (in fact, megaregions have the potential to bring the very economic and political viability of nations into question).

The formation of megaregions, along with megacities, marks an emergent form of city-states and trans-city-states that arrives out of an industrial-urban complex with economic interests centring on one or several strategically significant market thematics, including: energy, industrialized agriculture, electronics, telecommunications, biotechnology and so on. Besides the process being a pragmatic fusion of interests, it indicates that urbanization has decoupled itself from the city to constitute a larger domain of ordered striated space. In this development there is a progression towards regions of growing relative autonomy that add to and accelerate the weakening of the state(s). What this produces is a reduction of economic viability to the proximate cities outside the megaregion (by drawing off their intellectual capital, skill pool and collective disposable income) as well as a reduction in the revenue base of the state (as many of the multinational corporations that set up within megaregions have elaborate financial and tax arrangements that mean they pay low or no tax to host nations). These are not new insights.[2] Such developments can be seen as producing zones of inclusion and exclusion now for several decades, but the scale and dynamic is growing. This is to say that megaregions now create a zone of opportunity and privilege, and

---

[2] See, for example, Virilio, *City of Panic*, p. 93.

thereafter strand and abandon a population outside their borders. In these regions of exclusion, the size of underclasses increases, capital investment declines, and the state (now with a reduced tax base) has to face the growing costs of increased environmental and climatic impacts, while being faced with dealing with greater and linked social, food and national security challenges. Obviously, this general characterization of change unfolds in far more nuanced ways within specific geographic and socio-political circumstances.

Another dimension of megaregions in particular is the economic power and technological capability they are already acquiring to provide a defence to *some* of the coming environmental impacts (especially those megaregions specializing in environmental technologies). At the same time, this development also represents a hyper-concentration of capital assets and people, which makes them very vulnerable, especially if hit by powerful extreme weather events that are beyond their defensive means. For example, the Pearl River Delta cities of Shenzhen and Guangzhou are within the largest and richest megaregion in China, as it extends from these cities across to Shanghai. However, these delta cities are very exposed to flooding from even a modest sea level rise of one metre or less. This is because the combination of the narrowing of the delta adjacent to these cities and the back-pressure from the three river systems flowing into it, together with the possibility of storm surges, increases risks from flood events that could be in the order of several metres.

The Pearl River Delta situation is not unique. Many megaregions and megacities are also located in delta regions. Historically, this is because these were places where the fertile flood plains, the logistics of river systems, the creation of ports and the growth of trade, all combined to establish large and vibrant economically important cities. At the same time their location now means that with a climate becoming more hostile they are increasingly at risk from coastal flooding, cyclonic events, storm surges and tsunamis. The level of investment in these regions is of course enormous, which means that assets exposed to risks are equally huge. The impact of the loss of these assets would obviously not just be limited to the megaregion but have massive follow-on consequences for many financial markets globally.

The arrival and ascent of megaregions contributes to, and makes more complex, the situation that now pertains after the fall of the old world order and the failure of a new one to arrive. In this context, they are regarded as 'primary geographic units for integration' in whatever partial post world order actually arrives[3] – this because in many cases, as said, they are overtaking the economic power of nations. While currently accommodating less that twenty

---

[3] See Karen Lang and Arthur Nelson (2009), 'Defining Megapolitan Regions', in Catherine L. Ross (ed.), *Megaregions: Planning for Global Competitiveness*, Washington, DC: Island Press, p. 110.

per cent of the global population (currently growing at 134 million per year), megaregions generate nearly seventy per cent of global economic output.[4]

Megacities

Globally, the number of megacities is projected to double to about eighty in the next decade and a half. The largest are all in Asia (with Tokyo topping the list with a population of over 38 million people). Delhi, with a population of 28 million, makes it the fourth largest megacity in the world – it has actually increased the size of its population by forty per cent in the last decade.[5] However, Mumbai is expected shortly to overtake Delhi, and will become home to over 30 million. The UN estimated that within a decade a new kind of megacity will arrive with much poorer populations – cities like Lima (Peru), Kinshasa (Democratic Republic of Congo) and Tianjin (China) indicate this trend. There is also a whole cluster of cities currently with populations of 8 million en route to becoming megacities by 2030.[6] The developmental momentum of this scale of urbanization represents a massive land-grab and in many ways represents a new order of urban sprawl.

What continually begs to be emphasized is that this process of rapid urbanization is like nothing that has ever happened before. It is completely without control; is dramatically adding to the informal sector; creating a likely condition of future conflict; has massive and still very poorly understood consequences for global food security; is in large part driven by the commodity semiotics of capital, and is having many impacts on rural culture and economy. One can claim that the combined elements of this situation are not well understood by anyone. Additionally, urbanization is having very serious consequences for the internal structure of cities and how they are now viewed geopolitically and strategically. To this end, consideration is now to be given to how these developments again fuel fear and with what consequences.

These issues are not incidental to the agenda of urban metrofitting, but are at its core. Broken environments are not just a feature of old cities in decay but are equally a feature of the informal areas and stressed metabolism of many new and expanding cities, as is often visibly evident in mountains of waste. Remaking cities against this backdrop can be viewed as a task on an immeasurable scale, and one with an unavoidable destiny if this planet is to accommodate the size of

---

[4] Richard Florida (2012), 'Introduction', in *Megaregions*, New York: Island Press, p. xviii.
[5] Paul Webster and Jason Burke (2012), 'How the Rise of the Megacity is Changing the Way We Live', *The Guardian*, 21 January [https://www.theguardian.com/society/2012/jan/21/rise-megacity-live].
[6] Joel Kotkin and Wendell Cox (2013), 'The World's Fastest-growing Megacities', *Forbes*, 4 August [http://www.forbes.com/sites/joelkotkin/2013/04/08/the-worlds-fastest-growing-megacities/#5605a3a224cd].

population it is expected to have. Such a challenge extends out into the future at a scale perhaps equal to the rise and development of cities themselves. With certainty one can say that the unsustainability of our collective mode of earthly habitation cannot continue if we as a species are to have a future. In this respect, remaking is not a matter of choice. However, it is equally clear that humanity does not have even short-term instrumental answers to the emergent conditions of urbanization – solar panels, recycling bins, improved public transport systems and the like add up to no more than trying to stop a speeding juggernaut with the front brake of a bicycle. Currently, what is now being attempted to be sustained (the paradigm of the economic *status quo*) is totally unsustainable. Cities, as a main locus of human habitation, are on a destructive trajectory towards making our species homeless. Remaking cities is thus indivisible from a remaking of humanity's dominant mode of earthly habitation.

Questions of fear, questions of defence

For many people, especially in the more unstable nations of the world, fear of violence and fear of a hostile environment are on a convergent path leading to a deepening fear of the future. The reaction to this is often to hide, be it by withdrawing into a state of repression, hiding behind walls, constructing fences or 'going armed'.

For a number of decades now, fear of actual or possible violent home invasion has prompted the comparatively wealthy in many parts of the world to live behind walls and gated compounds protected by security staff or, at the extreme, within fortified compounds. Around the world this trend has escalated to the extent that huge numbers of compounds have been, or are being, built – some to house tens of thousands of people. These post-urban spaces of inclusion/exclusion will certainly increase as planetary problems grow.

The arrival of the environmental and social impacts of climate change is altering how the problem is pictured, although the depth and seriousness of such change has yet to arrive in popular consciousness – it is a void to be filled.[7] As the scientific and sociological evidence makes absolutely clear, there is little recognition that:

---

[7] Following the preoccupation of Hegel and Heidegger with the ontological relation of 'being and nothing', where in order for something to be there has to be non-being (nothing), Sartre brings this to the issue of consciousness (Part 1, Chapters 1 and 2 of *Being and Nothingness* (trans. Hazel E. Barnes), New York: Washington Square Press, 1993) where a nothingness of consciousness denotes a lack of identity. This void thus becomes seen as the condition of possibility for consciousness, and thus identity, which as Heidegger points out, is the very basis upon which Being and the human being can be thought. Martin Heidegger (1969 [1957]), *Identity and Difference* (trans. Joan Stambaugh), Chicago, IL: University of Chicago Press, p. 11.

- existing mitigation action and greenhouse gas emissions' reduction targets are totally insufficient;

- even if mitigation action is effective, because of the long atmospheric life of greenhouse gases and the slow speed of change of deep ocean temperatures (which function as Earth's thermostat), the problem will be around for at least several hundred years; and

- governments are not confronting and communicating to their populations the known consequences of climate change that will unfold over time.

Known environmental impacts can be divided into those for which no defence is possible (where adaptive action is essential), and those where the threats of damage by extreme weather events can be reduced (by making infrastructure, public services and utilities more resilient and by constructing 'protective architecture' for critical facilities such as power stations, water treatment plants, hospitals and fire stations – the cost of such action being prohibitive for many nations).

No matter what is done, very large numbers of people are going to be displaced, especially in those countries at highest risk, often the poorest. Moreover, as acknowledged, large numbers of people crossing borders uninvited looking for food and water will be met with a hostile and violent reception. Likewise, significant numbers of people coming from devastated cities will come to others looking for sustenance and shelter, with the possibility this 'invasion' will cause civil unrest.

Another likely response will be that the creation of defensive environments and architecture will proliferate and extend the protective capability of gated communities against climate impacts and incursions by displaced people. As can be seen in a recent overview,[8] the literature on this area is very underdeveloped and has advanced little since Teresa Caldeira's much cited book *City of Walls* published a decade and a half ago.[9] But, as history suggests, as the privileged feel more threatened such developments will occur.

What Caldeira's work on the defensive architecture of São Paulo drew attention to is some of the coming dangers that can be expected in the future. She made clear that São Paulo was a city where protective barriers, fences and heavy-duty security were all responses to fear, insecurity and violence that became features of everyday life for its population.[10] The violence that

---

[8] Seth A. Okyere, Seth O. Mensah and Matthew Abunyewah (2014), 'Back to the Future? Caldeira's Fortified Enclaves and the Consequences for Contemporary Developing Cities', *International Journal of Humanities and Social Studies*, Vol. 2, No. 6, pp. 66–71.

[9] Teresa P.R. Caldeira (2000), *City of Walls: Crime, Segregation and Citizenship in São Paulo*, Berkeley, CA: University of California Press.

[10] Okyere *et al.*, 'Back to the Future?', p. 68.

prompted the action was extreme. A report from James Holston provides a chilling example:

> . . . gang-cartels (called 'comandos') organised massive prison rebellions, during which they denounced hell-hole conditions of state imprisonment, demanded justice, killed their rivals. Their organizations spread to the poorest neighbourhoods where they ran both drug cartels and supplied social services that the state neglected. Beginning in May 2006, the *Primeiro Comando da Capital* (PCC) repeatedly paralysed the City of São Paulo, attacking police stations, government buildings, banks, buses and prisons. The result of this insurrection was that around two hundred police, guards, suspected gang members and innocent bystanders were killed, as well as the City being paralysed.[11]

Besides being responsible for these deaths, the PPC destroyed buses, burned down banks, tortured, mutilated and decapitated the bodies of rival gang members, which they then burned. In such a context, Virilio's notion of the 'city of panic' is no mere evocative metaphor of contemporary urbanism but a literal description of an actual urban reality.

However, what is said about São Paulo can equally be said about other cities in Latin American countries, including Venezuela and Colombia, as well as in other parts of the world, as seen more recently and graphically in the Middle East. Events of violence create fear, and this in turn has a design and psychological consequence well beyond the event's location. Added to this situation has been the wider fear of terrorist attacks being a real prospect in cities that are far from those specific sites of conflict that spawned the terrorist organizations. And then there is the proliferation of asymmetrical warfare being fought in urban environments.

Because terrorism mobilizes fear as a weapon, its actions are never just site-specific – they are always about generating fear of an attack elsewhere. While this prospect links back to earlier comments on megacities and future wars, it also feeds a general and growing sense of unsettlement just about everywhere. Danger is now deemed to be totally mobile and so can arrive anywhere at any time. As a result, the city is becoming ever more concerned with security and so becoming increasingly militarized – some of this is visible but a great deal goes unseen.[12]

One form of this invisibility centres on 'big data' assembled from movement tracking, credit card transaction monitoring, street CCTV, drone and satellite

[11] James Holston (2008), *Insurgent Citizenship: Disjunctions of Democracy and Modernity in Brazil*, Princeton, NJ: Princeton University Press, p. iv.
[12] Tony Fry (2014), *City Futures in the Age of a Changing Climate*, London: Routledge, pp. 159–162.

surveillance, movement and audio sensors, email message scanning and so on. Intelligence data gathered on possible 'targets' also expands the very category 'target'. Moreover, fortified spaces are now not just domestic or military but are integrated into the very fabric of the city: security-controlled office blocks, malls with security technology and a team of armed security guards, and high-security zones around and in government building complexes. More than this, many embassies, legal institutions and defence organizations not only have all been designed or retrofitted to have a defensive capability, but also with a capability to repel attack.

At the other extreme, military hardware is also increasing its presence in cities (although mostly kept 'undercover', at least in the cities of the industrialized nations). This includes everything from armoured personnel carriers, air defence missiles to bomb disposal robots, drones, and long-range sniper and assault rifles. Likewise, the ability to quickly and completely lock-down a city, or at least its central business district, where security moves from invisible to visible is now a well-rehearsed action that can, and often has, altered the relations between the military, the police, paramilitary police and private security organizations. As an aside, one should remember that most armies in the world do not exist to fight wars with external aggressors but to maintain 'order' within their own nation.

The megacity battleground in the age of unwinnable wars

In terms of conflict, the current age is like no other. None of the wars currently being fought have been formally declared – they are all asymmetrical. The major battlegrounds are now urban. Humanity now lives in a fully weaponized world. Aircraft, trains, trucks, cars, motorcycles, buildings, garden fertilizers, letters and parcels, gas bottles, and above all, the explosive-loaded human body: these are just some of the more obvious examples of 'weapons to hand'. More than this, once 'the enemy' had a face and was coded as a clearly identifiable sign (via a uniform). We could see and recognize a difference of appearance. Now it's no longer the case: an enemy might look like us, they might not; they might be in a distant land or in our midst. It now takes very little for a single act, like a siege in a city building, the arrival of a paramilitary police unit, gunfire and a few deaths to unsettle an entire nation.

The prospect of conflict in cities, at its most extreme, is seen in registration of future wars occurring in megacities. The already mentioned publication – 'Megacities and United States Army'[13] – makes this very clear. It reports on a

---

[13] Strategic Studies Group, *Megacities and United States Army*.

one-year project by a specially formed US Army team published in June 2014. The report is predicated upon the expectation that megacities are likely to become combat zones, and it recognizes that:

> Megacities are a unique environment that the US Army does not fully understand . . . It is inevitable that at some point the United States Army will be asked to operate in a megacity and currently the Army is ill prepared to do so.[14]

Two months prior to this report, the Modernisation and Strategic Planning Division of the Directorate of Future Land Warfare of the Australian Army published its *Future Land Warfare Report*.[15] It also recognizes that for the Australian Army in the future 'operating in high density urban terrain will no longer be a discretionary activity . . . and will require the Army to better understand the way cities are designed and how they work (the "metabolism" of cities)'.[16] The report also underscores climatic factors such as food security and the fact that by 2030 half the population of the world could be suffering from a reduced supply of fresh water.[17] In contrast to the US Army report, this report has a far more conceptual and technological focus. It looks specifically at the role of robotics, digital technologies and cyber warfare, while also recognizing that the role of the soldier has to, and will, change. This change might include 'cognitive enhancement', 'exosuits' (which amplify the body's skeletal-muscular capabilities) and the use of 'long-lasting stimulants'.[18]

Both reports recognize that megacities are rapidly becoming the epicentre of human activity and as such it is very likely that they will generate 'friction' that will prompt future military intervention. At the same time, the reports acknowledge that the scale involved – both in terms of the size of the population and geographically – makes all prior spatial methods of containing and dealing with conflict within cities impossible. They also recognize that not only are the number of megacities growing rapidly but also many of them are located in what the report authors regard as unstable parts of the world. The

---

[14] Ibid., p. 3.
[15] Directorate of Future Land Warfare (2014), *Future Land Warfare Report 2014*. Canberra, ACT: Directorate of Future Land Warfare [http://www.army.gov.au/ /media/Army/Our%20future/ Publications/Key/FLWR_Web_B5_Final.pdf].
[16] Ibid., p. 4. Indicating its perspective was regional (Asia Pacific), the report stated that the population centres it would intervene in 'are likely to be urban areas in close proximity to the coast'. In confirmation of this, the Australian Navy has just commissioned (November 2014) *HMAS Canberra*, the first of two amphibious assault ships – which will be the largest ships in the Australian Navy. These can carry eight helicopters, heavy equipment (armour and artillery) and 2,000 troops.
[17] Ibid., p. 9.
[18] Ibid.

assessment is therefore that risks are increasing and to ignore this is 'to ignore the future'.[19] From an intelligence perspective, and on the basis of what has already been learnt from conflict in cities, megacities can expect to be seen by groups that threaten as both zones of opportunity and as safe havens. Thus they can be regarded as 'fraught with strategic risk'.[20]

What the US report also recognizes is a gap in the existing way the army understands large cities. Apparently they are not 'treated as units of analysis for intelligence collection or featured in planning scenarios'.[21] Thus the report acknowledges that this situation needs to be resolved and that large cities should now be viewed and treated as such 'units of analysis'.[22] What this actually means is gathering far more detailed information than is the conventional practice to, for example, produce checklists of targets identified from existing methods of reconnaissance.[23] Here, then, is another example of a coming invisible militarization of the city.

The US Army report sets out to acknowledge megacities as complex systems that are not reducible to a specific form. But it then undercuts this understanding by suggesting that each city needs to be appreciated as a whole.[24] What is not comprehended is that there is no 'whole' because complex systems do not necessarily articulate with each other and many of the relations assumed to be systems do not function as such because they exist in a condition of dysfunction – they are broken. It is thus inappropriate to try to group megacities into topologies that totalize them (three types of totalization are presented: the moderate integrated, the loosely integrated and the fully integrated[25]) – such thinking gets nowhere near the actual complexity. Interestingly, using a totally different classificatory triadic model, architects have made the same mistake.[26]

It is important to understand that there are no viable positions available to objectify the complexity of a megacity. This means the army's strategic perspective will likely continue to crudely abstract its observations. In many ways, there is no difference between viewing a city-state (megacity) of 30 million people and viewing a small nation (some megacities are as large as,

---

[19] 'Strategic Studies Group, *Megacities and the United States Army,* Megacities and United States Army Report', p. 4.

[20] Ibid., p. 5.

[21] Ibid., p. 8.

[22] Ibid., p.

[23] Ibid., p. 10.

[24] Ibid.

[25] Ibid., p. 13.

[26] McGrath and Shane, 'Introduction: Metropolis, Megalopolis and Metacity', in C. Greig Crysler, Stephen Cairns and Hilde Heynen (eds), *The SAGE Handbook of Architectural Theory*, London: Sage, pp. 641–655.

or larger than, small nations geographically, economically and certainly in terms of population). Moreover, many of the functioning systems of the city – technical, social and economic – are not contained by the city, as some are distributed. Moreover, many differences cannot be seen: many things and people do not stay in place. There is no primary object of hermeneutic inquiry.

The US Army Report talks about the city depending on systems of 'finite capacity', which, if pushed past their tipping point, will render the city 'incapable of meeting the needs of its population'.[27] These cites don't have a finite capacity any longer – the rate of (in)flux of people and the level of metabolic overload means that 'normality' is a condition of failure unable to meet the needs of its population. In cities like Lagos, Cairo and Mexico City, the tipping point into dysfunction was passed long ago. Also, many such cities have no civil entities striving to meet those needs. In the majority of cases, the population of these cities consists of the privileged, the included masses and the abandoned. No matter the regime in power, what it predominantly sets out to do is to meet the needs of those sectors of the population that can maintain some degree of social and economic function for designated constituencies of interest to which the regime is aligned. As for the rest (be they formal or informal), they are left to survive as best they can. In many cases, the informal economy provides a partial contra-system of governance in association with radical organizations providing services to establish 'an army of followers' – such generalization clearly takes on very different forms in different cities. However, the trend is widespread and is a significant factor in the existence of structural instability. So while the report authors understand that the rate of growth of megacities outstrips their 'capacity of governance', they do not seem to realize that this creates a dysfunctional situation beyond the system's means of operation and control.[28] This again undercuts any notion of the city as a whole. It should also be noted that most as well as the largest megacities will be in Asia, Latin America and Africa rather than in the old industrialized nations. Megacities are effectively environments of multiple realities each with its own city within a city. In fact, the level of fragmentation of megacities negates the very idea of the city. Yet there is a ghost of a city existing in a complex urbanizing topology of formations and deformations, possibilities and impossibilities, convergences and divergences, not as presented here as a set of neat binaries but rather as islands of momentary function and as an environment of exclusion and confusion. By implication, megacities (as city-states in their own right, or as building blocks of

---

[27] Strategic Studies Group, *Megacities and the United States Army,* 'Megacities and United States Army Report', p.12.
[28] Ibid.

megaregions) are just as politically fractured and contested as nations. As the US Army should have learnt by now, in the complexity of asymmetrical warfare there is never an absolutely clear picture of who exactly are your friends and enemies. Combat in a megacity would add another layer of complexity to this situation merely because of the huge diversity of identities and cultural differences.

   While the US report makes a few passing references to climate change, it shows little recognition of just how exposed some of the largest cities in the world are to its impacts and to (un)natural disasters. Recent NASA data makes the loss of some of the world's delta region megacities absolutely certain, including those in the Pearl River Delta, Bay of Bengal and Java Sea. This process has already started. And as will be remembered, the largest of all megacities, Tokyo, with a population heading towards 40 million, is the city at highest risk on the planet. It is doubtful if any state has the ability to manage the displacement of the high volume of people resulting from a destroyed megacity. The likelihood is that millions of people will head to other cities seeking food, water and shelter. There is every chance in these circumstances that violence would occur, with limited ability to distinguish between protagonists. This prospect is in contrast to an example given in the US Army report, where a scenario is outlined of hostile actors attacking the city in sufficient force to destroy or drive out the local population.[29] In the case of a completely destroyed city, survivors would simply be trying to survive.

   Against this backdrop there are three other conflict scenarios that beg to be recognized: the eruption of violence from a group, or groups, of considerable size that are disadvantaged and finding it difficult to survive in the deteriorating circumstances of a deeply dysfunctional megacity; violence resulting from a contest for resources (especially food and water) post a disaster; and violence as a large mass of displaced people arrives from rural areas as a result of their area having been devastated by an extreme weather event resulting in total failure of the agricultural system.

   Not only are megacities not resilient, but they cannot be made so. They are of an unmanageable scale and create a need for resources that few nations can meet. The idea of resilience is currently being overplayed and under-delivered (one wonders if it is really little more than a token action feeding a counter-narrative to an emergent psychology of climate change fear).

   A good deal of the rhetoric of resilience is directed as a means to increase the ability of local infrastructure to withstand and recover from a disaster. This rather than the creation of a community's ability to prefiguratively reduce its ecological impact and cope with whatever disasters arrive. There is no

---

[29] Ibid., pp. 12–13.

resilience without the viability and vitality of community. On this point what should be noted is that the strongest communities within megacities are often found within their informal populations. But equally they are also likely to be the hardest hit because they occupy the most vulnerable of environments and are the most unprotected. It should be added that without the resources necessary to sustain everyday life, there is no resilience. The existence/provision of resources is thus not only a critical factor in the creating of the possibility of resilience but also a crucial factor in preventing post-disaster violence.

Again it is worth emphasizing that rather than trying to see the city as a complex whole, what has to be comprehended is its fragmentation and difference, its fracture zones and lines of division.[30] This situation requires another kind of mapping.

Bringing the issues of megacity war and resilience together, what begs consideration is a planned pre-emptive humanitarian strike when disaster looks unavoidable, but long before the situation has reached the critical stage of immediate mass evacuation. Such action implies engineers, medics and military labour power all working in partnership with communities to train people in rescue methods, first aid and the means of material recovery. It also begs creating preventative environments, secure resources and establishing emergency water supplies, energy and sanitation services. The Australian Land Warfare Report went a small way to recognizing this need.[31] But these suggestions are crude and undercooked. They would require a lot of research and planning to have even a small possibility of dis-arming conflict in a megacity. Again such action is outside the remit of metrofitting.

The geopolitical drift

The notion that it is possible to create a strategy that will prevent many of the kinds of global problems *en route* is totally unrealistic. There are going to be disasters, and some will be of a megacity scale. In this context, a large part of the metrofitting agenda is simply about learning how to think about cities in

---

[30] In contrast, the Australian *Future Land Warfare Report* (Directorate of Future Land Warfare, 2014) recognized that: '. . . urban environments absorb larger numbers of land forces than operations in any other type of terrain. For this reason, operations must be focussed on discrete zones within urban and peri-urban areas, rather than seeking to achieve control over entire cities or regional towns. This presumes understanding of a given urban area's design and metabolism, and must be underpinned by highly effective intelligence, surveillance and reconnaissance', p. 9.

[31] 'Operating in large cities within civilian populations will also require armies to engage with a much broader range of organizations that deliver security and social services than has previously been the case.' Ibid., p. 10.

another way so that the capacity to adapt and/or respond to the coming situations is increased. Doing this runs counter to two dominant qualities of how the future is viewed 'within' the *status quo* of global hyper-consumerist globalism. So many of the issues that will determine humankind's ability to deal with a fraught future are not being confronted. Governments marginalize much of the scientific knowledge given to them and the science community overlooks the importance of social and cultural understanding and action (which the humanities have failed to develop sufficiently). All perspectives fail to develop an adequate politics able to seriously challenge the inertia of the political *status quo.*

Likewise, issues are not being understood in time (in the medium and with urgency). Short-term perspectives rule, as does 'chronophobia': the fear of time and the illusion of permanence. An assumption has been created that there is time (when in many respects it is already too late) and that science and technology will find the means to secure humanity's salvation. It will not be so. Everything needs to be thought in time – this is something essential to learn. Acting in time (that is, in the medium and with a sense of urgency) is essential.

It is sobering to consider that by the end of the century (which is no time at all), if current trends continue, there will be over ten billion people on this planet, a grab for resources, many hundreds of megacities together with climate change impacts that will certainly be far more serious than is presently being communicated. The prospects are frightening.

Putting the importance of metrofitting into this context, it begs to be seen and developed as a non-idealistic, non-utopian and formless alternative to urban implosion (from dysfunction) and urban explosion (from population pressures and a state of perpetual urban war).

6

New imaginaries and the city

As has been made abundantly clear, metrofitting of cities is not simply posed here as an instrumental technofix. It requires a far more complex, rigorous and imaginative confrontation of the issues of how our species can be futurally sustained in urban environments. By implication, this means making leaps of mind beyond current forms of contemporary urban life, but in ways that are not utopian or phantasmagorical. Before moving on to related questions of design, it is worth giving some consideration to the conceptual implications of this observation.

There is something wrong out there!

The more complex the material, cultural and mental world of human construction, the more problematic a universalized hegemonic and ocularcentric Eurocentrism, with its dominant way of knowing, becomes.[1] This issue directly affects our concern with the complex city, how it is seen, able to be known and imagined to be other than how it now is. To address this epistemological issue appropriately, we need to come to it via a digression.

As was learnt from Marshall McLuhan, and as Jean Baudrillard reiterated, the screen was not, and is not, a surface where images of reality appear but rather was, and is, part of the real. But in recent years something has changed: 'we' are no longer purely a viewer but equally have become the viewed. We oscillate between screens, this as the seer and the seen (via the omnipresent eye of the surveillance camera).

So much of the world, our world, now arrives mediated by, and on, the screens of smartphones, tablets, laptops, desktop computers, TVs and cinema. What arrives and is engaged is a mixture of the invited and uninvited

---

[1] Two particular mechanisms of universalization beg acknowledgement: the globalization of reason and epistemological colonialism. These issues are of course major concerns of decolonial and post-colonial studies.

image that shapes our desires, perhaps our work and certainly our pleasure. No matter if you are rich or poor, the screen is omnipresent. Yet for all this, what of the world do we see? Who actually watches the world? These questions are not about looking but about critical observation (vision with intent to knowingly see).

Undeniably there are problems: what we know (the knowledge that gives us our hermeneutic capability) in the complexity of the complex worlds in which we live never coincides with the nature of change in the world. Knowledge is therefore often 'out of joint'. This is because much of what drives change – like desire, taste, fear, excess, scarcity, public opinion or environmental reconfiguration, science and emergent technologies – is not directly visible as such, but specificities to which historically constituted abstract knowledge (categories and concepts) is brought. Sight/sound/thought and the seen and the heard thus exist in this condition of growing temporal disjuncture – and thus to the ways knowledge has become out of joint. Climate change again provides a good example.

We see and experience climatic events but knowledge of the seen is increasingly being mediated by an awareness of climate change. However, few of us have access to the most recent and most developed understanding being produced by climate science. Thus there is a disjuncture between our interpretation of seen climate events and how a more informed scientific perspective would see them. Even so, change still remains ahead of what climate science can report; this practice is in fact both enabled and delimited by the historical data and upon which its models depend. Then, at another level, as Niklas Luhmann showed, and as second-order cybernetics affirms, systems cannot be observed from a position external to them (thus it is the climate scientists who construct and hermeneutically occupy the system models that they then use as a basis to plot and interpret data).[2] The problem of observation that second-order cybernetics addresses is registered via the notion of the 'observation of observation'.[3] Effectively, nothing observed is independent from the anthropocentric knowledge brought to it, the subject and presence. What the system represents belongs to the system not to the represented.

The next problem is that, notwithstanding the proliferation of screens: we view the world from what we know and from where we are. My place in the world in not yours: thus existentially the world is viewed (in all its appearances) via a subjective, mostly ethnocentric and conjuncturally inflected lens of being-in-place (itself a complex fusion of geography, culture, memory and discourse).

[2] Niklas Luhmann (1989), *Ecological Communication* (trans. John Bednarz, Jr.), Chicago, IL: The University of Chicago Press, pp. 22–27.
[3] Ibid.

The reality of what we see, including on screens, spans representations of what immediately appears before us and is judged to be real. But the appearance of things conceals (façades hide, beauty can mask, and aesthetics so often deceive). Our hermeneutic capability is ever tested. Knowingly and unknowingly we continually see that which cannot be truly known beyond mere appearance. Unfortunately, the true status of what is seen does not declare itself, so we find ourselves ever turning to the representational play of memory of the seen, ideas, knowledge, language, and representational intertextuality. Yet while sight is always part of a moving mix, what is seen is so often taken to be, and treated as, the obvious.

If too much weight is placed on an object, it breaks. In the screen-world of late-modern life there is a huge overload of imagery. At no other time in human existence has this situation existed. The barrage of images is relentless. The city has become a site of visual saturation. In so many ways, the weight of images has broken (as well as transformed) the power of imagination. The broken imagination (the imagination of unrestrained appropriation, eclecticism and assemblage) is driving the ever-faster redundancy of the manufactured image. As such, misreading its truth claims is part of our broken world (the world of defuturing unsustainability). The largely uncritical way in which the digital has been embraced (not least by 'progressive' architects) is adding to the problem of the speeding redundancy of information and the image.

Buildings as image

Transposed to the economy of built structures, a ridiculous situation has arisen whereby the more sophisticated building technology has become, the shorter the design life of structures and the faster their turnover (economically and thus literally). Such structures make a material statement on chronophobia – they fake an appearance of permanence. Effectively, under the direction of developers, and enabled by interconnected markets, built structures in the 'fast economies' have become part of the waste-stream of consumerism. In such a semiosphere, no image can be sustained in time. To destroy the built image is to destroy its materiality (as the development industry knows full well). So here is what surely needs to be the main concern of 'sustainable architecture': to confront and engage rather than mostly create one-off 'green buildings' for mostly unsustainable organizations and lifestyles. Here, then, is another imperative that makes responding to the need for metrofitting urgent and important. Countering the produced redundancy of the image of the built form is surely a metrofitting imperative!

Of course, the Sustainment requires images to be created. But these need to be within a contextual frame that allows them to be seen as relationally connected in place and time – this not to arrest how change is seen but rather to retain the possibility of its metabolic management. In so saying, the use of information/data begs to be recast.

Where the kind of thinking just rehearsed leads is recognizing that a negative ontological designing of the screen, and the onslaught of images it projects, has become a force of imagination's colonization. The nature of imagination has changed at best, ironically and in significant part, into a practice of recycling from a visual memory and constituting bricolage out of which 'the imagined' is then drawn. At worst, imagination is being erased in the instrumentalization of intelligence that underpins professional practices and technologies as governed by the marketplace, seen, for example, in the ability of design software to generate endless iterations of a thematic visual form. These views on imagination, and the lack of it, are not conjecture. Evidence abounds. The fact that design schools run courses on 'creativity' – because of an education based on learning to comply (with the dominant paradigm) – is one instance of a cultural environment wherein imagination is destroyed. Likewise, it has been shown that in a saturated (visual) media environment, the ability of children to imagine declines.[4]

Where can thinkers of imagination take us now?

To begin to consider this question, a key qualification needs to be made: ethnocentrism creates a disposition to take culturally specific objects and modes of thought as if they were universal. So framed by this disposition, the West projected imagination as defined within Western epistemologies and so imposed its understanding without reservation. But there are and have been other ways of thinking about the nature of imagination. One that has endured is seen within Confucianism, wherein the production of aesthetic coherence was deemed more significant than logical relations of, say, form and content. What this does is to alter the configuration between reason and imagination.[5]

---

[4] What has happened in design and architectural education is that the idea of creativity retains its subjective agency but the capacity to be creative has become narrowed within a realm of the normative. This situation is manifest rhetorically – deviation from the norm is so often designated as 'thinking outside the box', whereas unrestrained creativity is not predicated on such referential difference. It stands outside the world as it is, not simply the box of convention. As is widely recognized, research on children and diminished imagination has been given public profile by Ken Robinson – see *Out of Our Minds: Learning to be Creative*, Oxford: Capstone, 2001.

[5] David L. Hall and Roger T. Ames (1995), *Anticipating China: Thinking Through the Narratives of Chinese and Western Culture*, New York: SUNY Press, p. 168.

In turn, this action shifts hermeneutic practices towards analogical procedures based on associational connotations and differences both by and beyond the image as a point of speculative departure.[6] Notwithstanding the efforts of modernity, the image and the imagined do not remain the same, and uniformly function, when moving from the one culture to the other. Clearly, there is also a literature on different understandings of imagination in other cultures, not least the Indian and Islamic, supporting this view.

The Chinese saw image as a clustering in which sensory experience, produced by Confucian thought, was gathered in order to be socially situated so as to prompt social memory and practice. As a result, imagination becomes indivisible from a communal experience.[7] The links that existed between the social, the relational and imagination that once informed Chinese worldviews were centred on ethical development rather than upon reason and economic advancement. Sadly, such a relation to the image now only has a residual trace in the present.

Exploring the idea and fact of imagination (be it briefly), and gaining a broader understanding of it, is not being viewed here as an end in itself, rather it is bonded to advancing cultural processes and practices for metrofitting that responds to a demand for another way of seeing and engaging the familiar in the remaking of cities. There is a rich vein of material to support this exploration. To illuminate: in his celebrated work on imagination, Richard Kearney outlines the ways its differences are characterized over three periods starting with premodern narratives from the Hebraic and Hellenic to the Medieval.[8] The narrative of his second period opens with Kant's notion of the transcendental imagination, which he took to be 'the source of its own truth'[9] and a 'divine flame within man'.[10] He then moved to focus on the existential imagination, with five thinkers highlighted: Kierkegaard, Nietzsche, Heidegger, Camus and Sartre. Out of this account two main observations are made: while human beings have the capacity to imagine their 'being-in-the-world' as it is or might be, they cannot go beyond the limit condition of death. Next there is the observation that while humanness can be imagined, as the example of the cyborg illustrates, this is not the same as trying to imagine a condition of not being human.

Postmodern narratives provide the basis of his third account. Imagination here is characterized as 'parodic', and (via Lacan, Althusser, Foucault, Barthes and Derrida) what is exposed in different ways is the inauthenticity of imagination. What the 'parodic' imagination registers is an extremely serious

---

[6] Ibid., p.125.
[7] Ibid.
[8] Richard Kearney (1988), *The Wake of Imagination*, Minneapolis, MN: University of Minnesota Press.
[9] Ibid., p. 155.
[10] Ibid., p. 159.

situation, one that has deepened since Kearney addressed the issue in 1988 centring on theoretical positions that characterized imagination and the imaginary as technological effect at the end of humanism over which the individual 'creative subject' has little control.[11] Obviously, this equates to the notion of the demise of imagination within the domain of consumerism, the hegemony of cultural technologies and the image-saturated environments of globalization as lived in urban everyday life. The technological colonization of the imagination is now very well advanced and travels with misplaced liberatory claims. In true Orwellian double-speak, the freedom of technology is asserted, whereas it is becoming seen as providing an absolute un-freedom of addictive dependence. As for creativity, especially in relation to imagery, technology has the ability, as said, to generate an unending stream of variation and difference. Thus 'creativity' has been reduced to a simulacrum. Against this bleak analysis, which stands on more than a decade and a half of rigorous analysis by substantial thinkers of varied stripes, one now asks the absolutely fundamental question: 'is imagination really dead?' If the answer is yes it is, then we all dwell in a condition of absolute nihilism and can do nothing about being carried into the defuturing darkness of unsustainability. But if the answer is no, then what has to be faced is that imagination has to be able to transcend 'the now', not withstanding that in many respects it has been laid to waste and can now only be found isolated (especially in marginal places and in the borderlands between the residues of the knowledge of indigenous cultures and the deconstructed basis of colonizing Western epistemology).

As characterized: the trajectory of humanity is one of profound unsustainability (be it called progress, development, globalization, consumerism or modernization). This situation makes demands on imagination as never before. In so saying, it could well be that the fate of humanity rests with somehow recovering from its forgotten, overlooked, denigrated and unrecognized places.

Of course, the creative class would have it otherwise as they roam the wastelands that hyper-reality projects as the spaces of desire found in the wealthy centres and corporate enclaves of all major global cities. Tragically, they are the most colonized of all classes. It is they who deliver 'creative' services and 'technological innovation' to the techno-capital nexus. In so doing, they unknowingly conceal with style the degree to which the 'divine flame within man' that was imagination has been extinguished.

The last part of Kearney's book has a literary and filmic perspective and in various way details accounts of end times. While the account is predominantly Eurocentric, it supports the argument that the present evidences a condition

---

[11] Kearney, *The Wake of Imagination*, p. 251.

of image saturation within which imagination is in crisis – with its nature and fate uncertain. Yet this may be the case, it is equally true, as indicated, that the critical circumstances of the human condition now require the ability to imagine another way of being more than at any other time in the existence of our species. If it is not possible to become other than we currently are, as creators *and* destroyers of our conditions of dependence, 'we' will not survive. The message can and should be bluntly stated: imagination has always been one of the key factors in the ability of human beings to survive, and notwithstanding the challenge that critical state presents, this will increasingly become the case.

A distinction now needs to be made between imagination as elemental to the human mind and its reification as idea. The claim that Aristotle 'discovered' imagination is false. All he did, which others perhaps did before him, was to disclose something that was already ontologically present but unnamed. More fundamentally, it is clear that the development of our hominoid forerunners and thereafter our species was directly linked to imagination. This is evident in the transformation of the stone into a tool (which required seeing a stone as having a quality beyond its appearance) and thereafter bringing what it was imagined to be able to become into existence. What it became was fundamentally prefigured by an idea of what could be. So at the start of this process, which began many hundreds of thousands of years before the arrival of *Homo sapiens*, an ape-like animal with stone in hand was just one tool-using animal among other such animals. But what this proto-human did was to gain the ability to see something in the world, as other than it appeared to be and then to create things from a process of mind that had never existed before with the aid of the stone tool. Artifice continued to develop over the entire span of human evolution, eventually creating the complex world-within-the-world in which 'we' all now exist. This process of observation, imagination, prefigured action (design), making – all went ahead of any reflective moment of analysis and classification.

The crucial break made by the Enlightenment for the West was to move beyond imagination deemed to be a gift of God and as essentially unknowable as an object of inquiry. In particular, for Descartes it was a force existing in an intermediary condition between mind and body.[12] Whereas for Spinoza the body constitutes the mind – they fused and were seen as one. The body, as function, was in fact a mystery that Spinoza believed could only be reached via the imagination.[13]

Knowledge of imagination seemed to surge forward through its engagement by Kant, Fichte and Hegel, but at the same time by it being treated as discrete

---

[12] See Desmond M. Clarke (2003), *Descartes's Theory of Mind*, Oxford: Clarendon Press.
[13] Yirmiyahu Yovel (ed.) (1994), *Spinoza on Knowledge and the Human Mind*, Leiden: E.J. Brill.

a categorical dislocation was produced. So while a recognition of its significance arrived as that 'which is first and original' (Hegel)[14] and 'that from which reason sprung' (Kant), it was not until Heidegger revisited and further elaborated the notion, which he did in his *The Problem of Metaphysics*, that imagination became recognized as a cognitive capacity at the very basis of understanding the sensible (as schemata – the retaining formation). Heidegger fully acknowledged the importance of Kant's exposition of transcendental imagination (as the means by which knowledge of the world is gained via the synthetic power of imagination – *einbildungkraft*), but at the same time he did not think that Kant had sufficiently developed what his own insight revealed.[15] Consequentially, Heidegger enhanced the idea via his own phenomenological interpretation, and in so doing he distanced himself from Kantian idealism.

Turning from imagination to the imaginary, Sartre outlines how image and imagination are elemental to mental life and are not just supplementary to thought but woven into it (and so constitute what is now understood as the semiosphere).[16] But more than this he also showed how imagination and life are not divided from each other, rather they exist directively in a continuous play (in the company of desire). It is by this play that he believed that the imaginary arrives in consciousness. He prefigures these remarks by presenting two types of awareness of the imaginary.[17] The first is the imaginary as an invention of mind that comes from mind. Second is seeing what is seen as other than it is (acknowledged above as an ability of the proto-human animal). Here mind prompts a counter-perception that somehow ruptures the indexical relation between object and idea.

Putting the claim of imagination destroyed before these two points would suggest a residual imagination is lodged in (our) animality and is intrinsic to what Heidegger called 'the care structure'[18] (the means by which (our) being survives), while the cognitive locus of imagination may have (dominantly) diminished to become merely technological effect at the end of humanism (the instrumental imagination). So, in sum, the future and fate of imagination can be said to rest with its trace, that which resides in its margins and perhaps a regenerative potentiality from animality. It is clear that the outcome of this massive topic of research entirely depends upon the place from whence it

---

[14] Cornelius Castoriadis (1997), *The World in Fragments*, Stanford, CA: Stanford University Press, p. 215.
[15] See Martin Heidegger (1990 [1929]), *Kant and the Problem of Metaphysics* (trans. Richard Taft), Bloomington, IN: Indiana University Press.
[16] Jean-Paul Sartre (1972), *The Psychology of Imagination*, London: Methuen, pp. 109–140.
[17] Ibid., p. xi.
[18] Martin Heidegger's notion of being-in-the-world situates *dasein's* everydayness in 'being absorbed in the world'; see Heidegger (1996 [1926]), *Being and Time* (trans. Joan Stambaugh), New York: SUNY University Press, pp. 292–304.

begins: this place is plural and contested. Thus imagination folds back into the domain of that complexity beyond the complex.

One of the mantras of our age of unsettlement is that 'we' (the entire human race) have to 'adapt or die'. However, to be able to adapt one has to be able to see and make things otherwise – adaptation thus demands imagination. More than this it is not simply a matter of pragmatically adapting the world around us but actually and more fundamentally recognizing adaptation also applies transformatively to us. Yet between past and current ways that the future is projected there is a whole history of failed dystopic imaginaries that were so often initially authored as utopias. It is into this enormous and critical task of imagination reconstituted that metrofitting is situated – as a practice this is actually the union of imagination and adaptation (seeing the same as otherwise). In this context, the words of Ernst Jünger still resonate: imagination is the 'basic force for the action'.[19]

No matter the form of imagination, it cannot be divided from the relational complexity of the sensory field – imagination not only requires being-in-the-world (even as a recoil) but feeds upon this world as a condition of necessity (at its most developed via perceptual mind and sense in the company of the agency of language and idea). *De facto*, our contemporary disaggregated understanding of these categories disables imaginative thinking. This view counters the reductive and ocularcentric construction of imagination, expressed as visual image, as it negates the importance of speech, sound, touch and smell.

At any given moment in time, normative thought designates that radical change to be impossible, yet history shows it is constantly attained. The impossible transpires to be relative to what we know at the time. In turn, what is known exists with the potential to embrace what Immanuel Kant called the 'transcendental imagination' (as it is able to bring something totally new into being out of a condition of limitation). The actualization of this potential requires the directive force of the need to transcend the specific conditions of limitation, be they of mind or matter.

Unquestionably there is now a massive need to overcome the huge forces of defuturing unwittingly liberated by unreflective human creativity (that is, imagining but without considering the consequences of bringing what is imagined into being). Failure to grasp the indivisible relation between creation and destruction (the dialectic of Sustainment) has been intrinsic to this propensity. Such generalizations have exceptions. Differences within and between cultures, and their economies, are significant – especially within those cultures that embrace rituals of destruction to expose a process of

---

[19] Jünger, *The Forest Passage*, p. 33.

regeneration (Shinto temple burning and rebuilding to underscore forest regeneration being one example).

Imagination, imaginaries and the city

To imagine (instrumentally) the future of cities requires consideration of a wide range of different geo-climatic and environmental conditions of possibility while acknowledging that some cities do not have a future in the mid to long term. It is already becoming increasingly clear that what a city is now is a plural entity, an insecure material condition, and changing category. Moreover, urbanization is no longer a formative process in the creation of cities but something that overtakes them. Likewise, new megacity-states are becoming forces of incorporation that can fuse several cities. Viewed from a longer frame of reference, one cannot assume the permanence of the city as currently understood. A form of earthly habitation beyond the city may arrive, remembering the world in which we now live was once completely beyond imagination. It is important to reiterate that we share the same situation of all human beings across all time and every civilization: we exist in a condition of delimited imagination (from the undeveloped to the damaged), but with as ever 'our' fate lodged in the proximate potential (one has to believe) it still retains.

Pragmatically, in emergent and future global climatic and geo-environmental circumstances materially and socio-culturally, there is an unavoidable need to transform much of 'what already is' within urban environments. Things have to become as other than they are. Even this instrumental task challenges the limits of existing knowledge, professional practice and political imaginations in a realization of just modest visions of transformation. Metrofitting names this process not as directed by a new imaginary but as a situation wherein the imperative for it becomes experientially and unavoidably encountered. It is only out of this work that a viable vision can emerge and *praxis* to bring it into being can be attained in given conditions of limitation.

Leadership in such tasks will not come out of the urban design and planning professions unless they themselves are unmade and remade so they may contribute to metrofitting as transformative ground creating new situated knowledge and action.

If the city is understood to be metabolic complexity, a site of assemblage, a multiplicity of realities and social interactions, rather than just built fabric and infrastructure, then the conditions exist for a possible exchange and transformation able to become the basis for starting metrofitting as process. By taking the city *as it is* as a starting point, it becomes possible to start to ask and attempt to answer why it has to be disassembled, reassembled and reanimated to become a futural environment in the face of unavoidable circumstantial imperatives. There is no pattern book to follow – process is the saddle, not form. Such a socially located exchange is essential to win support for a wider conversation: one able to lead to the transformations that are needed to meet some, if not all, of the challenges to be faced.

What all this implies is the obverse of a plan created by the few and then sold to, or imposed upon, the many. In contrast, metrofitting would draw the idea of the city out of the particular city in time and explore what needs to be done in public. The process will be slow and predicated upon inter-generational inculcation and the creation of a collective imagination (a selective assemblage). Such a process should start now!

'Imagine' a city with a created change community thinking future threats in an extremely plural way projected over 150 years and then identifying ways to respond to them without any certainty. The point here is not delivering solutions but transforming ontologies to enable the imaging of things futural, to cope with threats and deal with change in time (the medium and with urgency). Such action obviously has to be facilitated with a great amount of care, a lot of preparation, and a very clear understanding of why change is vital, plus time spent on a great deal of reflection. The conversations sparked have to be everywhere: in the media, in all educational institutions, workplaces, homes, in the political sphere and across every element of civil society and cultural life, and will run for decades. In other words, *the question of the future of the city in every respect has to become a structural element of everyday urban life.*

Currently, the nearest things to such an ongoing type of endless conversation are economics, institutional politics, sex, technology and sport (and in some cases religion). Effectively, the city becomes the concretized form of the future over-determined by a comprehension of the imperative. The quality of an outcome will take many decades, recognizing that the metrofitting of a city, as empowered by the conversation about the idea and its practices (now understood as the politics of the imperative), cannot be imposed or assured.

It follows that the first design task is to establish the social and organizational conditions of conversation. Central to this would be going beyond the longstanding fragmented ways in which cities became spaces of dislocated discourses (political, spiritual, cultural, economic, technological, environmental, design and planning). For this to happen, recognition of the seriousness of the situation, and the imperative to act, has to be made a collective of action (initially growing out of small groups). In this setting, displacement, unsettlement, a confrontation with the future as a locus of fear and adaptation, all provide key links between interrogating 'how things currently are' and a process of change able to feed a conversation centred on recognizing (i) imperatives, (ii) which of them could potentially be responded to and changed, and (iii) how to take effective informed collective action that is not just instrumental and short term. A conversation so understood implies a progression to a social environment wherein modest imaginaries can be encouraged, explored, developed with rigour and enacted in time (again as the medium and with urgency).

The entire approach outlined is counter to a creation of imaginaries of the city that conflate a crisis of critical distance with the whole history of utopias and dystopias. Addressing what to protect and how, remaking things as materially modest, creating socially and culturally rich space and activity deploying the remade as semiotically expressive of affirmative change (and as object of conversation and learning) – all these actions are possible openings in 'a situated modest imagination in action'. Additionally, adaptation is a vital object to be practically and imaginatively engaged in locally grounded ways, and while the 'to be adapted' is found everywhere in many cases, it has to be learnt to be seen in order to be recognized.

While what can be brought near and to hand is what is situationally immediate, *how the elsewhere is viewed also begs transformation*. While there are now many cities in the world that will not survive coastal flooding produced by increasing sea level rises, conflict, extreme weather impacts and other human-created disasters, dangers need to be brought to 'what is situationally immediate'![20] The conversation needs to be here, now and vocal.

It is also worthwhile identifying examples to critically examine. For instance, Detroit is a city cast as dystopic, whereas it has two dynamics that co-exist. One is degeneration and decline, the other is regeneration and recreation – both are at play at the same time. What the eventual result will be remains unclear, but it will be the consequence of this particular urban dialectic of place.

Staying with the USA, New York has a particular history of environmentally inspired futurist imagery, which will be considered in a moment, but first we note that in 2012 Hurricane Sandy put its future under notice. In the short term, there is a claimed technofix. In 2014, a Danish company won a contract to build a $335 million seawall around the city.[21] How effective such actions can be in the long term is an open question. It's not the only US city facing a big challenge. Miami is in the world's top-twenty at-risk cities. Sea level rises are already having negative impacts in Southern Florida. Eventually Miami will cease to be economically viable (this before total inundation), along with other

---

[20] The OECD has listed the twenty most at risk (this figure is to be taken indicatively – for every error there is a replacement). These cities include Mumbai, Shanghai, Lagos, Bangkok, Dhaka, Rangoon, Ho Chi Minh City, Jakarta and, of course, New York.
[21] http://www.theverge.com/2014/10/1/6874925/can-a-massive-seawall-save-new-york-from-flooding.

parts of the region. This will displace huge numbers of people, including a large number of Cuban-Americans. At the moment, there are 2 million plus Cubans living in the USA, seventy per cent of them in Florida.[22] The city of New York has a large number of Cubans, so it could be expected that several hundred thousand of the 1.4 million of the likely displaced in Florida will go there. Problems do not remain geographically discrete.

Without losing sight of Florida, here is another perspective on New York. In 1966, the US Department of Housing and Urban Development (HUD) commissioned Buckminster Fuller to design 'Triton Floating City' – the concept was initially for units to accommodate 3,500–6,000 people that could be scaled up for a total population of 90,000–105,000. The plan was to build a prototype in Chesapeake Bay. The idea rested on the argument that there was an enormous pressure on land use, while the sea, which covered two-thirds of the planet, could be economically exploited as a location for homes. The project never progressed, but there is every chance, in contemporary circumstances, that it will return in some form somewhere around the world. In fact, in a rather perverted form it already has.

In December 2013, *Business Insider*, along with other media, reported on the 'Freedom ship project' because it had been taken to the marketplace looking for investors.[23] The idea was to construct a floating city one kilometre long, twenty-five stories high, topped with a flight deck (making it a quasi-aircraft carrier). The proposal was for it to be built by a Florida company at a cost of ten billion dollars. Not, however, for 'internally displaced people' (IDPs) but for the rich (no doubt some from Florida). The vessel would be so large that it would be unable to dock anywhere in the world, which it would sail on a two-year rotation.

The floating city was not the only Buckminster Fuller futuring project. In 1960, he proposed, in collaboration with architect Shoji Sadao, to erect a giant dome over Midtown Manhattan.[24] The idea was that the dome would regulate weather and reduce air pollution, reduce cooling costs in summer and heating costs in the winter. This would mean that no buildings would require separate heating or cooling, this because the dome would provide a uniform temperature for everything within it.

The political leaderships of New York and Miami are at least partly aware of the problems *en route*. One would think an overall risk profile, strategic and action programme exists. If it does, it is not an object of public knowledge and

---

[22] US Census Bureau (2012), American Community Survey B03001.

[23] Adam Taylor (2013), 'Freedom Ship for the Super Rich', *Business Insider*, Australia, 4 December.

[24] Chu Hsiao-yun and Robert G. Trujillo (2009), *New Views on R. Buckminster Fuller*, Stanford, CA: Stanford University Press, pp. 135–136; and http://gothamist.com/2012/03/08/the_1960_plan_to_put_a_dome_over_mi.php 3/14.

discussion no doubt for one simple reason. Certainly in the short term, property values are given a higher value than futural action. Visionary, super-technology future-scape 'solutions' are maybe the only marketable option for capital to offset a huge property market loss. But it is totally at odds with the reality of predictable climatic, economic, social and cultural crisis. Crisis, of course, will arrive for numerous cities.

At its most basic and immediate, surely metrofitting can be viewed as a conversation that can break into the one-track myopic mindset of city governance (everywhere), and as such seen to be the counter discourse to making the *status quo* resilient.

7

Other worlds are coming

In contrast to the image projected by globalization, the direction of human futures will increasingly be plural not least because of the consequence of the globally differential and uneven impacts of environmental and geopolitical change diversifying life-worlds. Notwithstanding the challenges associated with revitalizing imagination, as previously made clear, this situation means that there is a need to develop far more geographically varied 'imaginaries' of human habitation. Rather than these imaginaries being disconnected from existing circumstances, they have to be created out of them. To recognize this is to grasp the global scale of the task of working to counter the current destructive and delimiting ways of world making. Building upon those ideas and actions central to metrofitting can be a significant contribution in rising to this challenge.

Destruction

A key to understanding worldly destruction is to comprehend that it has been elemental to the human condition. Our very coming into human being is an act of creation dependent upon the destruction of the dominance of our animality. As many thinkers, in numerous ways, have said, 'we are born an animal and are made a human'. The relation between creation and destruction (the dialectic of Sustainment) is not just implicit in our coming into being but is intrinsic to our actual mode of being-in-the-world itself as world makers.

As the abilities of human beings to materially create ever increased, and as the size of the human population grew constantly, so equally did the rate of destruction of the planet's finite resources. Within this situation of deepening unsustainability is the increasing damage to our planet's biophysical environment and climate. The socio-political and linked environmental impacts of climate change, together with resource stress and population pressures, are now adding to the risks of regional and global conflict. Notwithstanding the rhetoric and token action of 'sustainable development', the drive to create economic capital proceeds without taking account of, or responding to, the scale and consequences of this dynamic of destruction. It also needs to be understood that while technology can contribute to a positive response to this situation, historically it has amplified it, and mostly continues to do so.

The contradictory nature of human beings, as wilful creators and destroyers, provides the backdrop to the comments that now follow.

The culture of consumption, in its lack of a viable metabolism, is inherently destructive. So said, it is important to distinguish between regenerative 'vital nourishment' implicit in consumption ecologically understood versus the action of a metabolically dislocated economic category of consumption that 'feeds' those processes of continuous destruction that currently contribute to the structural unsustainability of human earthly habitation. This situation, understood here as 'defuturing', diminishes the conditions of dependence of our species and many other beings. At this point, it is worth reminding ourselves that there is no fundamental difference between the dominant economic and medical conditions of consumption: both eat away the very biophysical thing we humans depend upon – the body and the natural world.

If we are to survive as a species in any way that resembles what we now are, it is crucial that the implications (if not the language) of the dialectic of the Sustainment become directive of human thought and futural action. As Dietmar Kamper put it, '. . . it is time to realise that human knowledge (if it is to remain knowledge) has no other choice but to apprehend what it annihilates'.[1] Such knowledge comes with the creative potential of exposing the disjuncture between what Georges Bataille called the 'general economy', as it names the processes of exchange upon which all life depends, and the dislocated economy (the 'restricted economy' of existing capitalism), as it negates that upon which we all depend.[2]

Architecture is, of course, deeply embroiled in serving the 'restricted economy' and in so doing it supports the defuturing metabolism of cities, as they exist as a primary locus of production and consumption. However, architecture, architects and planners are not in command of the city. This is especially so in those parts of the world with cities with large informal sectors. Over recent decades, these dystopic elements of cities have become an ever more dominant and contradictory feature of rapid urbanisztion. People so often migrate to the city with expectations of finding opportunities and pleasures, but then they quickly find themselves living as members of an entrapped urban underclass. The 'world economic' ended the idea that these

[1] Dietmar Kamper, (1990), 'After Modernism: Outlines of an Aesthetics of Posthistory', *Theory, Culture and Society*, Vol. 7, No. 1, pp. 107–118'Thanacratic', *Theory, Culture and Society*, Vol 7, No1, Feb 1990.
[2] Georges Bataille (1988), *The Accursed Share* (trans. Robert Hurley), New York: Zone Books.

environments were harbingers of social mobility, and climate change is making this situation worse – this as even more people leave rural areas that have failing agricultural systems due to lack of rain, low soil moisture or salination of the water table by rising sea levels.

Along with this view, and in the prospect of a global population of ten billion people by the end of the century, urban and regional planning professor Barbara Norman has pointed out that to accommodate this number of people a new city needs to be built every five days.[3] Clearly, this is not going to happen. The problem is not simply solved by building more new cities. It also goes to the nature and transformed form of existing cities and how the rural should now be understood and engaged. Likewise, there will be an ongoing massive expansion of informal construction, especially in the poorest nations.[4] Two consequences are almost certain to follow: urban authorities will lose even more control of cities that have ever growing informal sectors; and climate change impacts will fuel civil unrest. In such defuturing conditions, other ways of thinking and acting are essential. Rethinking, and newly thinking, about sacrifice could well be one such example.

Sumptuary and spatial sacrifice can be constituted through acts of futuring self-interest to secure conditions of redistributive justice essential to advance equity globally. This would not totally reduce the prospect of conflict or defuturing environmental impacts but, if managed well, might be a way of the globally wealthy nations and communities 'buying' a more secure future. So positioned, sacrifice would not simply be lodged in seemingly morally altruistic acts of the profane but potentially be generative of the agency of a secularized sacred based on humanity's foundational conditions of survival (which are not merely biological and embraced by the concept of the Sustainment).

Understanding actions that recognize the survival of the species cannot be divided from countering the destructive force of unrestrained consumerism, while equally rebalancing the global ability to consume, are essential to establish geo-social justice. Cast in this way, sacrifice becomes part of a futural practice indivisibly linked to the advancements of universal common interests.

For this to happen there has to be a proliferating designing event that makes sacrifice a recognizable, replicable and widely imitated ceremonially inscribed practice. Such a designing event has to have a '. . . *procedure consisting of establishing a means of communication between the sacred and the profane worlds through the mediation of a victim, that is, of a thing that in the course of the ceremony is destroyed'*.[5]

---

[3] http://theconversation.com/cities-could-be-the-secret-to-fighting-climate-change-34915.
[4] Multiple UN Habitat reports this to vary between 60 and 95 per cent.
[5] Henri Hubert and Marcel Mauss (1964), *Sacrifice: Its Nature and Functions*, Chicago, IL: University of Chicago Press, p. 27. The victim is, of course, 'the unchecked consumer'.

Bringing the 'dialectic of Sustainment' and a designing event that ceremonially destroys the city of excess (the celebrated high-consumption cities of the restrictive economy) requires recognizing the remaking of the city stands upon its unmaking. The practice of metrofitting in this setting can simply be understood as the means by which the destruction of the dominant meaning of the city (the *thing*), by a designed profane defuturing event of ceremonial erasure, is supplemented by transformative material and immaterial actions to advance a condition of the Sustainment (the overarching project in which metrofitting is lodged). The very presence of the dystopic elements of so many cities is what provides the semiotic resource to erase the sign value of a city's dominant meaning. As a project, such action obviously begs strategically conceptualizing in the context of a specific city. There can be no uniform template.

The wasteland (the future and the unsustainable), the city that has been laid to waste (by war), the city that has been wasted (the post-industrial city), the city that wastes (every city) reveals that waste hides in the familiar. The designated image of waste is but a fraction of the whole. Commodity aesthetics conceal so much waste – the mass of this waste is waiting to happen in the very fabric and façade of the city: in warehouses, supermarkets, stores and in homes. While there is also a lot of material that is unambiguously waste, at the same time it also poses a very significant challenge for classification, not least because waste is as a much a cultural category as it is a material one. The difference between waste and resource can often be turned either way by cultural economic and technological intervention. Moreover, a lot of this waste is only notionally so contextually secure. Moved from one place to another, and semiotically transformed, things disposed of as waste (like steel cans, scrap iron, used bricks, animal manure, etc.) become revalorized as a resource.

At present, the process of industrial production, the culture of consumption, the environment of the city and the nature of the home combine to expose waste as an output of human activity spinning out of control. As urban populations grow, and many cities become ever more metabolically dysfunctional, problems of waste become very critical.

Mountains of waste are being created by landfill practices, and the waste management industry inappropriately reifies waste. Within the remit of metrofitting, the categories of waste require to be: culturally and economically recoded, perceptionally transformed, and directive of waste industry restructuring (so it can respond to a far more developed understanding of metabolic processes). Thereafter, and beyond such indicated reforms, three recovery streams of a 'new' waste industry need development: nutrient recovery (from putrescent material, animal and human liquids and solid expelled matter), materials recovery (from direct reuse of a reprocessing feed stock and as composite material feed stock or fuel) and energy (generated from bio-mass and high-temperature waste combustion).

All the technologies for such developments already exist. What is lacking, what demands design, is the semiotic and an organizational system, directed and able to overcome and incorporate the existing waste disposal and recycling industries. The point of this characterization is as much about an example of metrofitting being able to think 'general economy' advancement as well as about, and in relation to, waste.

Protection in the face of destruction

Protection against the destruction of the city cannot be reduced to just material actions. It is also a matter of governance, culture and spirit: all grounded in history and anthropocentric futural interests.

Within the Enlightenment there were two relevant positions towards the exercise of interests that can be represented by the perspectives of Thomas Hobbes and John Locke. Hobbes argued that the obligation of the subject to the 'Sovereign' existed so long as the 'Sovereign' provided protection of the subject.[6] If this was relinquished, then subjects have to protect themselves. 'The "Sovereign Monarch" cannot be extinguished by the act of another; yet the Obligations of the members may be removed.'[7] Whereas what Locke asserted was that if the Sovereign failed to 'protect life, liberty and property', then the people had the right to overthrow the state, as the primary function of government was the protection of property.[8] In both cases, freedom had to be sacrificed to gain whatever protection was proposed. The protection provided by contemporary governments was founded in this moment and then extended to cover: external and internal national security, biosecurity and public heath, a broad band of criminal and civil crime, risk to society, industry and businesses and more. But as the defuturing impacts of the unsustainable increase, the ability of government to continue to provide this protection diminishes. It is already very clear that many governments of non-industrialized and newly industrialized nations only have a very limited ability to provide comprehensive protection, and even this limited capability is becoming seriously diminished.

Cities can fall into ruins – some already have – but still partially function in this condition. In future decades, it will not be uncommon for cities at risk to

---

[6] Thomas Hobbes (1996 [1651]), *Leviathan*, Cambridge: Cambridge University Press, p. 153.
[7] Ibid., p. 230.
[8] John Locke ((2014 [1690]), *The Second Treatise of Civil Government*, §5, Adelaide, SA: ebooks@ Adelaide.

increasingly be totally or partially abandoned. Those cities with the means will attempt to stave off disaster – this with defensive technologies and architecture – but they will be the exception. But dominantly, as is already evident in Bangladesh and many other poorer countries, most measures will be taken by communities themselves. Action will be modest, this not just because the technology is unavailable (which it will be in many cases) but because the scale of the cost of dealing with coming environmental impacts (not to say the results of potential associated conflicts) will mostly be financially beyond the means of most nations. It is also doubtful if many governments will pre-emptively act before their coastlines start to be redefined or prior to significant disasters arriving. The implication of severe environmental, economic, practical and social problems en route is that they will be of such a scale that even if they are one or two hundred years away, action needs to commence now (not least to spread the costs). Getting the magnitude of this situation understood and engaged may well mean: conceptualizing, designing and planning action; raising vast amounts of revenue; moving hundreds of millions of people; building new cities for them (or providing construction materials); recreating local economies; establishing food security; and overcoming the trauma of entire urban populations. These tasks will combine to create a logistical project beyond anything in the entire history of humanity has ever done. What is almost certain is that the later responsive action is taken, the greater will be the disaster.

In contrast to those many cities under stress, as they face human and environmental crises with very limited resources, there will be the actions of the rich regions of the megaregions where protected cities will be created, some perhaps under a protective dome or other form of defensive architecture (obviously beyond the visions and technology of Buckminster Fuller). Such cities will be technically sustained by technologically advanced systems created by the industries within them. Already the most advanced renewable energy, water treatment, sewage management, biotech, new material and medical technology companies are in, or are planning to move to, megaregions. Rather than seeing such cities as utopian, or even desirable, one can expect they will be widely viewed as ambiguous. Putting the privileged into protective zones (environmental, food and security) will make divisions within and between nations and their societies even starker.

When the vast majority of humanity will exist outside these technospheres, in variable conditions of relative hardship, new dangers associated with such inequity will almost certainly arrive. It is now almost impossible to imagine the global economy and socio-political structure of such a world, except to say it is likely to be far more fractured and dangerous than 'now'. Again countering any simple utopia/dystopia binary, both situations will have dystopic features, and while the excluded will be exposed to greater risk one could expect a large amount of adaptive innovation to take place within these societies. What is happening in nations like Bangladesh would appear to confirm this view, as 'grass roots' adaptive action to sea level rises is being taken by communities themselves.

While extremes of dysfunction will occur, there is also the likelihood of substantial increases in forms of cooperation, sharing and commonality of purpose. Not of course in the context of a romantic bucolic idle, but in the harshness of a great deal of environmental turmoil, social and economic dysfunction and human suffering out of which, as the history of our species affirms, the ability to adapt to very changed worldly circumstances will and can be forged.

A conviviality: rediscovery and recreation

Ivan Illich published *Tools for Conviviality* in 1973. The book recognized many critical problems that now constitute the contemporary crisis: biological degradation prompting an environmental crisis, population pressures, global inequity, an economy acting as if resources were unlimited, technology running out of control deadening 'the human creative imagination'.[9] In response to this situation, he proposed to explore 'conviviality' as a term '. . . to designate the opposite of industrial productivity', stating he meant it 'to mean autonomous and creative intercourse among persons . . . with their environment'.[10] From a position critical of the destructive force of industrial society, and moving from the environmental to the personal, he proposed ways to redirect science and technology 'to endow human activity with unprecedented effectiveness'. This to 'permit the evolution of a life style and of a political system which gives priority to the *protection* [my emphasis], maximum use, and enjoyment of the one resource that is almost equally distributed among all people: personal energy under personal control'.[11]

What Illich has to say is insightful, recognizing for example that '[t]he industrial mode first degraded and later paralysed the nexus of productive relationships which co-exited in society'.[12] At the same time, he was also naïve in the light of the events that have passed in the decades since he penned his ideas. But notwithstanding the limits of his argument, the concept of conviviality begs revisiting and rethinking. Most significantly, his argument needs to be divested from its radical instrumentalism. In particular, while he

---

[9] Ivan Illich (1973), *Tools for Conviviality*, New York: Harper & Row, pp. 50–51.
[10] Ibid., p. 11.
[11] Ibid., p. 12.
[12] Ibid., p. 95.

went some way to recognize the ontological designing power of tools as they 'stamp' a commonality of environments, structures, work practices, personal relationships, and thereafter the difficulty of simply 'retooling society',[13] he also posited agency with the notion that a 'pluralism of limited tools and of convivial commonweals would of necessity encourage a diversity of life styles'. A little later he then asserted that: 'new tools would provide new options. Convivial tools rule out certain levels of power, compulsion and programming.'[14] While rejecting utopianism, and condemning industrially powered consumerism, what Illich puts forward is effectively a path to an anarchistic utopia based on 'alternative political arrangements' that would have the purpose of permitting all people to 'define the images of their own future'[15] – this in the recognition of the reconstruction of industrial society based upon 'a just distribution of unprecedented power'.[16] Key to all of this he believed was a convivial society *designed* [my emphasis] 'to allow all its members the most autonomous action by means of tools least controlled by others'.[17] Even more problematically he went on to say: 'Tools foster conviviality to the extent to which they can be easily used, by anybody, as often or as seldom as desired, for the accomplishment of a purpose chosen by the user.'[18]

All of these remarks by Illich presumed a particular relation to tools and technology that has now radically changed. Even the usage of the word 'tools' has changed. His understanding of them was actually outdated even at the time of writing. Fundamentally, he failed to sufficiently comprehend the extent to which we humans are not merely the users of tools with full control of them. Now so often humans have become an extension of tools and so used by them. This is to say, while 'we' design tools they also ontologically design us – it has always been so, but as tools have become ever more pervasive, intrinsic to everyday life and powerful, so equally has their ontological designing power.[19] Certainly, Illich recognized coming dangers: 'A tool can grow out of man's control, first to become his master and finally to become his executioner.'[20] Yet his observation here goes to the exception and is not used as a corrective to his idealistically posited hope with the tool (redirected) to become technically and socially extended as an agent able to construct a convivial society.

In the early decades of the twenty-first century, the perception of what tools are and do has changed, especially in popular culture. They are now

---

[13] Ibid., p. 16.
[14] Ibid., p. 17.
[15] Ibid., p. 13.
[16] Ibid.
[17] Ibid., p. 21.
[18] Ibid., p. 23.
[19] This issue is considered in length in my *Becoming Human By Design*.
[20] Illich, *Tools for Conviviality*, p. 91.

frequently seen not in mechanical and industrial terms but rather in the domain of electronic and information systems. Moreover, the concept of what a tool is has been generalized (some would say debased). In this context, a tool can now mean anything that effects change: from a dropdown menu item on a computer that allows changes to be made in a document, to 'applications' downloads on smart phones and computers. There is clearly less recognition of the techno-culture of pickaxes, front-end loaders, chainsaws, drill presses, lathes and arc welders by 'the masses' that constitute popular culture. 'Manual' craft skills are now on the margins of affluent societies and clean and soft hands have become *de rigueur*. Consequentially, so many skills that were once common across societies have declined (skills such as sewing, fitting a tap washer, cooking, growing vegetables, killing, plucking and drawing a chicken, replacing a pane of glass in a broken window, putting up bookshelves). Even more significant, the dominant relation to working in the electronic tool domain is to be totally atomized, totally individuated. Thus people cooperatively working together physically in so many settings has now almost disappeared. The factory machine shop, for instance, a place where once many people worked together cooperatively, is now one person in an office feeding instructional data to a robotic machine system, with another person on the shop floor employed to service the robots and maintain the materials inventory. Likewise, a farm employing ten workers working with basic agricultural machinery is now a single person operating sophisticated machinery, in many cases working under the direction of GPS guidance, soil sensors and downloaded web data. The point here is that the social relations of production wherein conviviality once existed (and could be developed) to a very large extent no longer exists. Moreover, the technologies that came with a tag of increased human freedom have now so often proved to have actually taken freedom away (via created dependence and the loss of any ability to control process). Tools now are more than ever deeply implicated in structures of power. They are task directive instruments of surveillance, mechanisms able to measure downtime, output and quality, evaluate and direct career performance and so on. So while the physical condition of work may have improved for many workers in advanced industrial societies (because heavy and dirty industries have robotized or moved to low-wage newly industrializing nations), workers are now more disposable, the working week over recent decades has got longer, and the workplace and the home have become connected. Life for many workers is thus now lived in a continuous flow of information and in a condition of being (formally or informally) on constant call.

On the basis of these remarks, the significance of the opening of conviviality as an object of inquiry by Illich is acknowledged, but his bonding it to tools (even with his qualification of what they are and do) is not seen to be sufficient. But neither is how his idea of conviviality has been appropriated by computer science adequate – this is mentioned especially in the context of the digital city as it is claimed to be an extension of the physical city.[21] So after indicating why this use of the concept is not embraced, another way that it can be brought to remaking the city will be put forward.

In her paper on conviviality for digital cities, Patrice Caire shifts the focus presented by Illich on the social to the computer and interaction while claiming the concept still retains an ethical value.[22] But in so doing her argument further embeds conviviality in the instrumental, this in particular as it is presented as a quality of relations enabled by an information web portal of a city that can provide 'conditions for social interactions' that facilitate the management of the internal regulation of social systems.[23] When brought to the digital city scenario by Caire, any critique of what Illich puts forward has no credibility at all, as the concept is reduced to merely 'user-friendly' means of information exchange across the administrative, business and entertainment exchange activities of a city. Moreover, conviviality is assumed to exist as an environmental isolate with subjects (outside the wider social milieu) moving between it and conditions of alienation. This could be assumed but cannot be put forward as *the* normative situation.

In contrast, there are three non-mutually exclusive ways conviviality can be developed in relation to remaking the city and metrofitting:

1   *Conviviality as a means of cultural extension.* This first example comes from Timor-Leste, where because of the tropical climate the working day in many rural villages starts early and finishes around lunchtime. In the afternoon, the village people sit around playing music, telling stories and amusing the children. Although extremely poor these people highly value this convivial way of life and the social structure that supports it. At the same time, whenever there is a major communal task to be done conviviality permeates the social relations of work. For instance, when a sacred house needs to be built, the entire village builds it: every one person having an assigned task. Stages of construction are punctuated with ceremonies where religion and pleasure merge. A similar ethos permeates life in many informal settlements where, as many commentators have remarked, 'community', mutual aid, sharing resources and social networks are all very strong, and goodwill and cooperation manifest in everyday life. Conviviality actually underpins the ability of such settlements to

---

[21] Patrice Caire (2007), 'A Critical Discussion on the Use of the Notion of Conviviality for Digital Cities', *Proceedings of Web Communities 2007*, Salamanca, Spain, February, pp. 193–200 [https://docs.google.com/file/d/0By6DOQr0Mz4JZHl1YXhvNnNxTU0/edit].
[22] Ibid., 2.1.2.
[23] Ibid., 2.2.

function. It undercuts them being written off as completely dystopic. It is also key to their future, for it can provide the social basis out of which environmental conditions can be improved. Such an example is not unique, though it is yet to be seen and developed in universal cultural differences within the contexts of conditions of exchange, based on a modesty of living and cultural change crucial for that global rebalancing able to establish economic and geo-social justice. Action of this kind is essential for the establishment of the Sustainment as it is linked to ways conviviality can be developed for and in the city.

2   *Conviviality as a social ethic that assists in the shift to a counter-consumerist way of life.* In order for it to be possible to attract people away from hyper-consumerism, something that is more desirable has to arrive. Effectively a quality economy has to be created able to displace a quantity economy. Conviviality has the potential to be such an attractor. This requires a generative process and a trigger that prompts and sustains such a creation. This constitutes a very different 'design as event' that challenges social relations of work so they actually become social (as illustrated by the Timor-Leste sacred house example). This transformation is also important for another reason. As environmental disasters threaten and arrive, the need for communities to be resilient dramatically increases. By implication, the community has to be able to organize itself so it can act preventively and reactively to disaster. The sociality of an ethos of conviviality is crucial in making this change. And then there is the third contribution.

3   *Conviviality as the basis of solidarity within the re-socialization of work.* Solidarity among the industrial working class in past centuries was extremely strong. Mineworkers, shipbuilders, steelworkers, dockworkers being some of the more evident examples – this solidarity permeated the social relations of everyday working life. It forged deep friendships and comradeship in the face of adversity and provided the means out of which working lives were improved in conditions of hostility coming from employers and the state. While the nature of the work created a great deal of alienation, the social relations of work made everyday working life possible. Modern work meant trading in the conviviality of labour, and the autonomy of the craft workers, all for higher wages. Henry Ford's introduction of the in-line assembly line and five dollar day (twice the average wage in 1913) in exchange for less ability to control the nature and social relations of the work by the worker became paradigmatic of this moment. It deeply alienated labour and increased disposable income. As such, it shifted a meaningful life away from work and towards

consumption. More than a century later, alienation is even more ingrained, even though conditions in workplaces have greatly improved. Enormous numbers of workers hate the sterility of their jobs and live for leisure. The re-socialization of work would counter this move, but it cannot 'organically' happen. Change has to arrive by the design of convivial work and the workplace.

The essence of convivial ways of life, communities and work is extremely simple: care for other human beings, friendship with substance and pleasure in the simple and vitally nourishing things that feed life (as the ancient Chinese knew[24]). Illich understood the liberatory force of conviviality and that the gains can outweigh the sacrifice – here, then, is what has to be developed and made a central plank of metrofitting.

---

[24] Jullien, *Vital Nourishment*, p. 14.

8

Post-sustainability

As a discourse and applied practice, sustainability is in general failing. There are two fundamental reasons why this is so. The first is that the concept has not been rigorously grounded in a thoroughgoing analysis of causality and thus what is actually unsustainable. The current understanding of this condition is dominantly biophysical, very reductive and centred on environmental and ecological impacts. For many practitioners, the unsustainable is treated as given and self-evident, this resulting in an immediate engagement with sustainability without any critical reflection. Consequentially, inquiry is arrested and action proceeds on a purely instrumental basis. Thereafter, it becomes just a matter of matching what are taken to be known problems with available, or developing, 'solutions', be they systems, technologies, designs, products or services delivered by establishing new industries, supporting economies and implementation policies.

Here, then, is a characterization of what has become the dominant domain of action for sustainable development, including addressing what are now familiar issues like: greenhouse gas emissions/renewable energy; polluting and environmentally damaging materials/industries/products/waste/waste management/recycling; deforestation/sustainable logging/plantations; clean water and its harvesting/conservation; urban sprawl/urban consolidation/ resilience, plus 'social sustainability' and more. The point is not that these actions are wrong and are not dealing with real problems but that they are inadequate in the face of the depth, scale and relational complexity of the fundamental causes of unsustainability.

These causal conditions cannot just be identified instrumentally, for they are far more structurally entrenched in the created essence of plural humanity and the world-within-the-world that, in difference, in large part it formed. So approached, unsustainability starts to look like a propensity of the conduct of our species that did not become a problem until it became amplified by our numbers and the gigantic technological utilization of planetary resources. What this means is that the ontological and the metaphysical constitute unsustainable modes of (our) being-in the-world have acted to prefigure and direct forms of instrumental and environmental action without having grasped the consequences or that we (in all our difference) are the causal core of the problem. Almost all the actions taken towards sustainability go to an engagement with symptoms that distract from an identification of, and engagement with, causes of the unsustainable grounded in 'us'.

At its most fundamental, the unrestrained anthropocentric essence of humanity has effectively meant that our species has unremittingly centred its own interests over its entire existence. This ontologically inscribed disposition has been central to everything we have collectively created *and* destroyed – recognizing the rate of destruction by indigenous peoples is very low, in contrast to the high levels by industrial societies. As a being without constraint we are the causal force of the unsustainable. Again it is apparent that everything associated with unsustainability slates back to us as an irrefutable fact. The more advanced our world transformative capability, the more of us there were, and the more rapid and large our negative impact on our earthly conditions of dependence became – thus the greater our unsustainability.

The metaphysical dimension of this disposition established world-making practices based upon flawed and perpetuated foundations of knowledge. The most obvious example here is 'capital logic' as it asserts the necessity (for capital) of unceasing economic growth as the basis of a global financial system – a 'logic' to which the reformism of sustainable development actually subscribes. Overriding this 'logic' is a fundamental pre-logical condition of exchange inscribed in the matter that is life itself (characterized earlier by reference to Bataille's notion of the 'general economy').

While none of this thinking is new knowledge, it has failed to arrive with a public, political or cultural profile and impact. This because it is couched in a conceptual language outside the means of expression of inscribed and available instrumental practice. Clearly, the ambition of metrofitting aims to address this problem in situated contexts that allow for a grounded extrapolation of localized implications of the unsustainable and the creation of a praxis to engage them. Such action implies solutions have to be made *in situ*, over time, and address fundamental causes grounded in human thought and action. It is likely that not all problems identified will be able to be solved – learning to adapt, and finding ways to live with those problems at present regarded as insurmountable has to become elemental to such a process.

So what has to be confronted? The most general and daunting answer is, as said, the challenge of ontological transformation of our being in the world. As totally anthropocentric entities, unless we ontologically change nothing fundamentally and directionally alters. Now even if an increased state of consciousness of 'the masses' could produce change, there are no available means to create this transformation on a sufficient scale for it to be able to redirect humanity away from its current fated path. But while astronomically hard, significant transformations can be contemplated by a massive exercise of ontological design. What this action recognizes is that our ontologies are a consequence of the agency of specificities that combines to constitute our mode of being in the world. Put more simply, we are designed by the world we bring into being, not least, by design. Thus intervention in this cycling can be contemplated by design itself transformed.

By implication, unsustainability equally requires recognition as being a psycho-cultural and epistemological problem, and one that biophysically and socio-culturally manifests itself in modes of action.

The ontological designing processes do not equate with idealized forms of design determinism of the past. Rather, they are lodged in complex relational factors that constitute the designing world in which our being is formed – as formed by language, inculcation, informal and formal education (from our infancy onward), our relation with the nature of the environments in which we live, work, learn and play. Plus the practices we learn and adopt that constitute our *habitus*, family, home, food, and the aesthetic domain we occupy, the diversity of relationships with each other. A great deal of which has just been outlined is complex, intellectually demanding and gathered within urban practices that fuse with ontological design and metrofitting processes.

Before going further, let us be quite clear: our anthropocentrism cannot be transcended, but once made present it enables responsibility for what we are to be taken. Clearly, this is no easy task. Neither is acting with the recognition of our inter-relation with other species, which is not its negation but an act of informed self-interest. Confronting such knowledge brings us back to ontological transformation, and to taking responsibility for what we are: this is not just a question of cognitive change but also an induction into a disposition – one arriving out of our placement in an altered mode of being-in-the-world. The instrumentalism of sustainability is incapable of comprehending and creating such change.

Rather than being placed in opposition to sustainability, a far more substantial and foundational strategy of change is needed in which ontological design and metrofitting are elemental – one grounded in the project and process of the Sustainment (already registered as a theoretically informed process understood as a post-Enlightenment project of a scale as great as or greater than the Enlightenment)[1]. The Sustainment is not posed in opposition to sustainability for it can co-opt much associated with it, but subordinated to a much larger frame of reference – one with a far more intellectual and political dynamic and transformative agency – that can be named as post-sustainability.[2]

---

[1] For a ful exposition of the Sustainment, see Fry, *Design Futuring*, pp. 197–208.

[2] Alain Findeli (2008), 'Sustainable Design: A Critique of the Current Tripolar Model', *The Design Journal*, Vol. 11, Issue 3, pp. 301–322.

To make what has been argued better situated historically, a brief critical critique of how sustainability was characterized in the World Commission on Environment and Development's Brundtland Commission Report ('Our Common Future') in 1987 will be presented.

Brundtland centred on the notion of 'sustainable development', and this essentially meant a reformist agenda directed at 'business as usual' in order to secure the continuation of economic development within the extant capitalist paradigm.[3] As such, and from the very start, sustainability lacked a basic understanding of the unsustainable at the level of fundamental (ex)change. Rather, it prompted a whole range of instrumental actions to reform the economic *status quo* from which many policy makers and practitioners constituted how sustainability could be attained instrumentally. At the same time, the concept rapidly entered widespread and popularist linguistic use, which further emasculated its descriptive agency. It was out of this setting that 'sustainability' was inducted into school and university education (including architecture and design). This action further reified and replicated a restricted understanding of essential change. Recognition that unsustainability is predicated upon the existing dominant form of the human ontology (anthropocentrism as lived, and thus is embedded in what we are and how we live) never arrived. So, by implication, what actually needed to change remained unthought and invisible.

As already argued, the ability to sustain humanity, and all it depends upon, cannot happen in conditions of global inequity. Again there was no real recognition of this by Brundtland. Likewise, the discourse did not acknowledge sustainability couldn't arrive in the company of endemic global conflict and the geopolitical and the political ideologies that underpin it. In staying within an Enlightenment division of knowledge, this discourse also removed itself from the very relationality upon which the praxis of the Sustainment stands. It aligned itself with those arguments that pragmatically reduced complexity to dislocated understanding (of exchange) based on Enlightenment divisions of knowledge. Whereas the very possibility of sustain-ability implicit in the Sustainment depends on advancing solutions to modes of adaptation, or ways to live with, able to fundamentally engage complex problems.

---

[3] The Brundtland Report was based on a number of very questionable assumptions. First, its anthropocentric bias meant that the interconnected interdependency of all biological life was not sufficiently acknowledged. Brundtland's idea of inter-generational equity needed to be subordinated to inter-species and linked to inter-cultural relations. Moreover, to appeal to the 'quality of life of future generations' failed to recognize the unevenness of the human condition. Second, and just as fundamental, the assumption that the future can be secured via economic growth needed to be challenged. This position has actually assisted the cultivation of a rhetoric of sustainable change and tokenistic actions. In large part, this approach was underpinned by an act of bad faith, able to be characterized as: 'unless capitalism was to be accommodated, any appeal to environmental protection would just not be taken seriously'.

Besides realizing that Sustainment demands an inversion (the *development of sustainment* rather the *sustainable development*), it exposes a lack of the reflective and critical knowledge of the unsustainable (needed to actually be understood to identify what has to be sustained). This condition of limitation, as indicated, cannot be separated from Enlightenment inherited, and still ruling, disciplinary divisions of knowledge that de-relationize problems from the contextual complexity in which they reside.

Once again climate change can be turned to as a discourse that exposes a dislocated understanding evident in the techno-scientific instrumental analysis that dominates. It is not that the way climate science is understood and discussed is wrong, or without use, but rather that it is totally insufficient in comprehending climate as 'effect' extending beyond system. One can consider, for instance, the climate's cultural agency and determinant relation to our species' *being in difference*, to demographics and associated migratory histories.

In summary, one can say that sustainability rests upon an epistemology and a worldview that is bonded to instrumentalism, and as such is part of the broken. In contrast, the Sustainment cannot acquire agency without being constituted out of a theory of knowledge that embraces the 'complexity of complexity' and the imperative of taking responsibility for (our) anthropocentrism.

The education of education

Bluntly, the academy needs to begin to learn how to think and act in ways able to more powerfully help secure a viable and enduring future for diverse humanity. Besides working to break down disciplinary barriers and move to trans-disciplinary and post-disciplinary modes of knowledge, there is a critical agenda that invites serious engagement, including:

1   Gaining the ability to sufficiently define and understand the problems of the unsustainable as they permeate every aspect of inner and worldly life of human beings together with gaining a more informed understanding of all that constitutes the 'world-within-the-world' that our species created over the millennia.

2   Countering the reduction of the relational complexity of the problem of the unsustainable to dominantly environmental issues.

3   Demonstrating the inappropriateness, widely held perception of and misplaced faith in the ability of instrumental action, especially in the form of a 'techno-fix', to resolve the unsustainability as it is reduced to damaged and completely broken natural and human-created systems.

4   Understanding that gaining knowledge of action claimed to advance sustainability as it actually often acts to 'sustain the unsustainable'.

5   Displacing the topic of sustainability within education at all levels (as an 'add-on' to the existing curriculum) and replacing it with the development of an understanding of unsustainability, the Sustainment (and the dialectic of Sustainment), adaptation and redirection, and relationality.

6   Recognizing that the humanities (remade as relational knowledge) are just as essential to the creation of sustain-ability as are the sciences, while grasping that for this to happen the humanities have to shed their historical attachment to humanism and existing inherited divisions of knowledge.

All of these actions have to be seen as being informed by gaining an understanding of the anthropocentric essence of the unsustainable and the advancement of the project of the Sustainment, which is vast and as yet still mostly an un-comprehended complexity. At the same time, and indivisibly, it requires an understanding of the nature, consequences and darker side of the Enlightenment (as the intellectual motor of modernity).[4]

Obviously, there are many implications from undertaking such an expansive and critical exercise. Three especially beg acknowledgement: first – the scale of the intellectual exercise needs to be embraced, recognizing it also requires unlearning, relearning and new learning under the guidance of a relational theory of knowledge; second – gaining reconfigured knowledge as it implies a total redirection of education at every level; and the third – acknowledging that no matter the urgency, such actions can only be realized as a mutually informing relational process of learning between each element over time.

The academy's attachment to the Enlightenment project has long gone, but the shell of its pedagogic structures lives on, including the divisions of knowledge it created still directive of a now dominantly vocational programme. The current and hegemonic neo-liberal academy now has no overarching project beyond being a service provider to deliver vocational capability to the economic *status quo*. Employability and income are the principal evaluative measurable norms of institutional success. Such an academy, even when engaged in innovation, is doing so in the context and spirit of market compliance – this in terms of the compliant subject (to capital logic) and its performative capabilities.

Conversely, the academy of the Sustainment would need to have an ethos that recognizes that learning what needs to be learnt is indivisible from

---

[4] On this critique, see Walter D. Mignolo (2011), *The Darker Side of Western Modernity: Global Futures, Decolonial Options*, Durham, NC: Duke University Press.

working with others collectively and in a spirit of goodwill, with honesty and respect as underpinned by an imperative of learning that takes responsibility for the inherent anthropocentrism of human beings. By implication, this also means thinking and acting in the medium of time and with urgency, while also recognizing the importance of informal education (a domain of knowledge the current institution mostly ignores). As a background to this massive and epoch-altering project, one has to acknowledge that complexity and challenges of the world at large are going to increase. In the face of such a scenario, the academy is on the line: it can find a way to a project that starts to futurally deal with this; or it can continue to serve the defuturing *status quo* and a deepening critical condition.

The future, the Sustainment, culture

The relation between climate and culture, as already intimated, is central to how we humans became what we are in difference in almost every respect. As such, climate is the starting point to comprehend the slow global distribution of and physical (but not genetic) changes of our species.

There are two theories: 'the multi-regional' and 'the out of Africa' (which is the scientifically dominant). This latter theory postulates that after spreading to various parts of Africa, *Homo sapiens* moved out of Northeast Africa into Asia Minor, the Levant and Arabia, this between 100,000 and 60,000 years ago, and thereafter to the East and West.[5] We were, however, not the first species to leave Africa – *Homo erectus* had done so a million and a half years before us. Movement was prompted by two related factors: climate and the availability of food. Migration patterns were complex, with nomadic territories being created, contested, established and abandoned. Movement within and beyond geographic regions was continuous. As the species moved very slowly over tens of thousands of years, biological adaptation to different climates and food sources occurred. So while we appear to be racially different (especially in skin colour and body size), these differences are just a product of adaptation to climatic conditions (in some instances to very extreme circumstances), food types and their availability. So no matter our seeming physical differences, genetically we are all almost identical.[6] If this view of movement and adaptation is brought to contemporary conditions, a number of problems become clear.

---

[5] Chris Stringer (2012), *The Origin of Our Species*, London: Allen Lane.
[6] Renée Hetherington and Robert G.B. Reid (2012), *The Climate Connection: Climate Change and Modern Human Evolution*, Cambridge: Cambridge University Press.

The first problem is time: while our biological ability to adapt remains the same, this process directly correlates with the speed of circumstantial change – adaptive change is very slow and so happens over a very large expanse of time, whereas the speed of the change of the climate can be and now is very fast. Second is an issue of settlement: the numbers of people in the world who are now nomadic in the traditional sense are minute. Thus the ability to move as the climate changes is far more difficult not only because human beings are now more sedentary and bonded to place but also because there are now so many of us. Moreover, populations are not free to move at will – national borders and migration laws make this increasingly clear. Yet the number of people being displaced is growing, and will increasingly do so. A new kind of involuntary nomadism is thus in the making within an unfolding crisis (destined to deepen).

The adaptive capability of our species now is, as said, no longer just bio-environmentally determined. Rather, techo-environments and ontological change employed to artificially deal with the necessity of adaptation are arriving – this based on two determinants: relational knowledge and advanced environmental technologies. Such knowledge can direct/redirect conditions of ontological formation intellectually, culturally and materially. As the conditions of being-in-the-world change, so do all beings. Technology obviously has, can and does contribute to this change – the most extreme, imminent and unpredictable example of this being geo-engineering.

Clearly, technologically sophisticated 'solutions' can be effective, but they can also be counter-productive (as with fossil fuel-powered air conditioning systems that improve the thermal comfort in specific environments at the cost of making the overall environment worse by adding to greenhouse gas emissions that in turn increase global warming). There are also dangers of increased levels of, and vulnerabilities coming from, technological dependence in areas like food, energy, water and waste.

In contrast, the scope of developing design directive knowledge and education focused on the advancement of understanding (rather than just knowledge centred on instrumental reason) can create ontologically designing environments that can change, for example, diet, ways of cooking, clothing habits, the working day and work patterns, the relation between indoor and outdoor life, cultural values associated with resource utilization like water, as well as non-fashion-based affirmative body images and far more modest space usage (on a domestic and urban scale). All of these types of change can contribute to the adaptation of modes of being, dwelling and habitats. They equally invite placing a lot of effort into the development of imagination able to prefigure new coping mechanisms and futural ways of life able to respond to the changing environmental, cultural, social and political circumstances. Again, all of these activities can be seen to be able to fuse with many modes and elements of metrofitting.

These remarks go to indicate that socio-cultural change is half the sky when dealing with climate change and unsustainability in general. Such change can contribute to countering the illusion that it is only science and technology that understand these problems and how to deal with them. It is actually essential to understand that the cultural sphere is critical in the creation of changes of perception, values, taste, lifestyle, desires and dreams, while recognizing the city as the key cultural catalyst for such redirective change.

The Sustainment and the future of cities

As now seen over several chapters, the creation of urban change cannot be divided from whom we are, where we live, how we dwell, the way 'we' think and the work we do. And moreover, for human and urban impacts to be significantly reduced the city has to be redirected. To do this in large, modern, well-constructed and operationally functional cities, is very hard indeed. For it to be done in often even larger, sometimes in old and frequently dysfunctional cities with large informal sectors is so difficult it can be viewed as almost impossible. Certainly, change cannot effectively arrive as an intervention from outside agents or via government policy alone, especially in dysfunctional cities where at best the rule of government is very limited. What this means is that change can only be created from the inside of such cities, this either by the creation of community demanding and enabling change or by independent action by communities. But how can such change happen?

Clearly, change on this scale cannot be imposed or created as a standard model. It has to arrive out of an organically constituted and situated collective leadership in a specific context that is formally and informally educated within a new relational paradigm of knowledge – one constituted out of a politics based on futural affirmative change rather than protest against the injustice of a defuturing past. But then how does this leadership get created? The generic answer is encountering the idea and form of a collective leadership via a designing event. This is a project in itself, and one that again can only arrive out of specific conditions of created possibilities and place likely made present by the recognition of coming crisis.

PART TWO

Contexts of Action

Having established the city as an object of familiar contemplation and then shifted to viewing it in contexts based on very different perceptions, problems and possibilities, metrofitting can now be approached in more detail, this to expose its potentiality as an important response to many of the futural challenges cities will face. Central to this task is an address to the disordering and reconfiguration of what is 'in place' or 'displaced' by the figure of the city.

To open Part Two, Chapter 9 overviews metrofitting, while Chapter 10 moves closer to design issues and then unpacks the importance of *habitus* to understanding metrofitting more strategically. Chapter 11 will explore questions of, and relations between, learning and unlearning. The notion of redesigning design will be the focus of Chapter 12. Chapter 13 will show the value of design fictions to advancing strategies of change. Putting a reframed understanding of space and time is the function of Chapter 14, and Chapter 15 will consider the remaking of modes of 'being in the city'. The final part of the book will support all of this material with two extremely different case studies, Cincinnati and Cairo – these to prompt projects that begin the process of grounding metrofitting in praxis.

9

Metrofitting:

Take two

As is now clear, the idea of metrofitting is not discrete, it could not be otherwise as it follows and exposes the plural paths that form cities. As already said, its intent is *the remaking of the city*, not as it was but *as it needs to be*. Previous chapters set out to show there can be no remaking that is fundamentally transformative without the city being understood as a relational complexity. Such understanding is not to hand, but as now should be becoming clear, metrofitting makes available conceptual approaches from where to begin to theorize redefined problems and relearn and redirect practices. Providing these capabilities is the key ambition of this work.

Let's start by asking what is an appropriate way to read the task of remaking a city? There are two suggested perspectives, the first being via time. In most cases, this view needs to be inter-generational and based on 'incremental learning in action'. Perspective two arrives out of (re)interpreting a few lines of Heidegger to fit within the remit of perspective one. Here is what he says:

> Abandonment of being is strongest at that place where it is most decidedly hidden. That happens where beings have – and had to – become most ordinary and familiar.[1]

Abandonment here means that we lose who and what we are in the taken-for-granted familiarity of the everydayness of our lives. As an entire literary history tells us, the city can often be the locus of a loss of being. Now what is layered onto this observation, especially via abandonment, is another kind of being and nothing, which means: understanding being and the deservered relation of 'not being together (as virtually being together)'. This is to say remaking cities

---

[1] Heidegger, *Contributions to Philosophy*, p. 77.

thus has to be as much about the remaking of direct human interaction in social space as it is about anything else.

Against this backdrop, metrofitting can be approached as focused on: 'the hard' (instrumentally biased) and 'the soft' (socio-culturally focused). The division is no more than a narrative device, the actuality of the two perspectives is far more graduated.

Framings

Although we all look at the city spatially from near or afar, it mostly remains unseen. Our spatial understanding of what we see is actually very limited, our temporal understanding of it even more so. While socio-culturally we traverse the city as our world, we are mostly oblivious to the others around us. They are the unknowns in the total materiality of a large city, which is ungraspable and mostly unseen. We simply get to know the fragments we want or need to know. Moreover, for the most part the synthetic metabolism of the city is completely out of sight (and hearing). Familiarity, of course, leaves much of the everyday as unseen.

As is now realized, conceptually and existentially the city is not one – the proper name of cities like New York, Mumbai, Lagos, Cairo, Jakarta, London and above all Tokyo is a misnomer. Nobody can actually know a city of 20 million people, or more, let alone one of 38 million (Tokyo). In reality, what has happened, as has now been recognized for a number of decades, is that urbanization has overtaken the city, it has subsumed it. In many cases, the city, as name, is an empty signifier be it with economic value. The boundaries bleed – the name does not correspond to this fluidity of place. Moreover, and increasingly, megacities become *de facto* city-states.

Architecture, urban design and planning are not adequately equipped to deal with the urban. The rise of the post-urban affirms this, as Stararchitects (practitioner proper name commodities) like Foster, Koolhass, Gehry and Hadid knew. Effectively, they created monumental markers exposing the defeat of the social function of architecture in a world in which soon almost ninety per cent of all homes being built will be informal (as is already the case in Africa). The extant city does not avail itself being of brought to aesthetic or fully managed order.[2] What late modern art architecture does is to create monuments marking the defeat of the social function of architecture. In a world heading towards eighty per cent of all homes built being informally (in the case of

---

[2] Remembering earlier remarks on Koolhaas and Lagos – for all his interest in the city, the nearest he got to addressing it by design was a proposed bus station with a roof market.

Africa it's ninety per cent), the social function of architects is surely to deal with the already built. This task is not a project of style but one of repair! Certainly, the age of exporting the European city as the design paradigm is dead. The largest cities in the world will belong to Asia and Africa, as will the coming disaster of the city (for example, nineteen of the most at-risk cities in the world exposed to sea level rises are in Asia).

. . .

The city is a ruin – some cities look like ruins, many do not – they are full of elegant buildings – but they are ruins of another kind. Disaster hides behind the façade. To talk of dealing with what already exists requires repairing/ adaptively remaking this ruin.

As already mentioned, remaking is not a return to the same. It is not a makeover. Rather, it is a foundational recreation (*palingenesia*): a rebirth from the ruins of the 'what was to become'. These ruins are not to be purely viewed via materiality of the city but are equally evident in the city's social, cultural, economic and political fabric. So while *palingenesis* does not exclude practical forms of repair, it does not necessarily do so to reinstate prior function.

Remaking is not a uniform instrument of action directed by the prefiguration of what should be or has been. It cannot be based on employing a standard template of the form deemed as a viable city. Even if such a template existed, it could not accommodate the scale and demands of many different cities. In contrast, remaking is an engagement from within which 'metrofitting' can be an active regenerative force. While its essence, *palingenesia*, does not exclude practical forms of repair, it does not necessarily, as already pointed out, return the repaired in order to reinstate prior functions. More than this, metrofitting also searches out what is broken in the normally unseen – which is to say the broken of what is taken to be normality and functional (the normality of the everyday and unconsidered destruction). As this it understands that functionality is not in itself an indicator of viable or desirable function: it can be good or bad, deliver or negate futures. Thus repair in this context is about redirection rather than performative correction, be it that 'the broken' to be redirected is a social, economic, political or cultural operative structure.

Metrofitting is predicated upon an ethos, which, as already argued, is put forward to be contextually understood as an order and spirit of conviviality in difference. In this respect, it does not overlook differential power but recognizes that the imperative of becoming futural allows the gathering of the unequal forces, resources and actors in a condition of exchange and mutual advantage wherein pain and sacrifice are implicit. The ethos of metrofitting enables the forging of those common interests upon which action against the 'defuturing unsustainable nature of normality' depends. The normality of 'now' does not define a condition of stability but the reverse. It is an undergirding turmoil created by continual destruction needed to maintain the *status quo* of economic growth, global development, technological progress and individuated hyper-consumptive advancement. The primary locus of this turmoil is obviously 'the city' as it currently accommodates the machinations of the entropic restrictive economy while also *enframing* the aspiration of 'the masses' – this as a conglomeration of commodity-centric desires spanning the richest to the poorest members of society. In this setting, 'aspiration' – and what produces it – has become another manifestation of the broken.

Of itself, metrofitting has no agency. For agency to become possible there have to be agents (people) and situated practices to give the concept a transformative potentiality, informed by a clear sense of what is broken together with deployable means of engagement. There is no assumption that metrofitting (or any other practice) can transform an entire city, but there is the view that well-conceived appropriative events can liberate 'seeds' that can give rise to processes leading to transformation in time (understood as: the medium and action with urgency). To this end, a language of metrofitting can be developed to evocatively characterize different methods and modes of engagement (practical, conceptual, cultural) that allows transformation to be imagined, spoken and constituted as specific projects. In so doing, it can liberate ideas, knowledge events and action enabling an unlearning and relearning. In this setting, failure is unavoidable, has to be embraced and understood as a step towards gaining resilience and attainment.

Over recent years, there have been a number of prefixes added to qualify the aspirational form of the city: the liveable city (an ambition that ignores the world's poorest and most unliveable cities); the sustainable city (a mostly narrow understanding of sustain-ability with a focus just on energy, water and waste); the smart city (a deceptive rhetoric of techno-centrism); the resilient city (again the focus is narrow and dominated by the infrastructure, and to some extent a population's ability to cope with/recover from disaster). Placed in this company, metrofitting implies not just action upon the plural nature of what constitutes a city but the enhancement of its fitness (so that *metrofitting* has no end but rather a relationally fit, connected and healthy *metro(polis)*).

Clearly, the health of all cities in every sense, and everywhere, can be improved. This is a general action that can enfold all other actions: the life of the body, the life of the city, environmental vitality. To attain such states of being requires 'vital nourishment' – a source from which 'to feed one's life' (as was indicated earlier, a common term in ancient Chinese thought[3]). To acquire a long life, and to eliminate those diseases that threaten life, requires continual

---

[3] Theorized by Zhuangzi (370–286 BCE) – see Jullien, *Vital Nourishment*, p. 9.

nourishment to sustain it. The city needs to be fit for life. Fitness here crosses from the organic to the functionally synthetic.

The language of the city is riven with organic metaphors in significant part due to those metaphors created by urban sociology a century plus ago. The view that underpins the notion of fitness now is one wherein the natural and the artificial have no clear line of demarcation. They interpenetrate each other, with the metabolic processes of the city being the most overt examples of this condition of uneven exchange. The redirection of the urban metabolism will be recalled as one of the key practices of metrofitting.

As registered, central to the destructiveness of the city is the propensity to consume/destroy ever more finite resources while accommodating an ever growing population generating constantly more waste. This situation is dangerous and potentially catastrophic. The enactment of de-consumption, and the rise in the significance of social technologies, as well as individuated cultural production, can lead towards less environmentally damaging and more equitable and materially modest ways of life. As has been presented, such action is a necessity rather than a choice. It can only be arrived at via a process of unmaking and remaking everyday practices (domestic and occupational). Such substantial transformative action is extremely urgent, yet it is not seen as such because 'crisis' is dominantly understood as event rather than process. Humanity, as well as being implicated in this process, is also its victims. Its privileged perpetrators insulate themselves against the arrival of this 'reality' via the purchase of waste-disposal services (by this and other naming).

The 'hard' edge: metrofitting and the instrumental perspective

The recognition of an absolute imperative to deal with the already created crisis means confronting the visible and invisible broken relational complexity of the urban (in particular, its post-natural metabolism, damaged material and socio-cultural fabric, psychotic-ontological space and defuturing fields of exchange). Not only does this require overcoming a whole range of professional perceptions and practices but also the very foundation upon which they stand (their *habitus*).

Architecture, landscape architecture, urban design, and planning have never recognized that the agency of design, in every respect, falls within the 'dialectic of Sustainment'. Consequently, the ability to understand what these practices destroy goes mostly un-comprehended by practitioners. So often, unwittingly, and so unknowingly, destruction is concealed by style. This situation is structural rather just being a result of individual failings. This is to say it is a product of an education of omission and a process of induction into professional practice that leave its fundamental dialectical foundations un-interrogated. Another huge overlooked omission is the imperative of acting in time (as previously qualified as: acting in the medium of time in the realization of things critical that require urgent action). Acting is space still rules. The way metrofitting approaches planning makes this perspective, and the insufficiency of the *status quo*, evident.

Here, then, are four really major planning challenges. They relate to events that are unlikely to arrive for a number of decades, which makes it 'easy' to overlook but disastrous to ignore:

1   *The relocation of a mass of internally displaced people (IDPs) as a result of changing environmental conditions.* It is already clear that millions of people are already being displaced (at the time of writing, the UN tells us that there are 57 million refugees worldwide). The displaced will number in the hundreds of millions in the coming decades. The point to be made is that the idea of moving and the planning of where and how to move masses of people should have already started by now. Such action begs to be viewed as trans-governmental, non-governmental and intergenerational.

2   *Climate change impacts linking to conflict.* This duo means that many cities will have to be abandoned – this is another trans-governmental, non-governmental and intergenerational action begging immediate research and planning.

3   *Moving some cities at risk.* Again this is a planning and logistics issue that information on past city-move projects can inform. What this history makes very clear is that it is another massively damaging process that spans decades (if it is done with any sensitivity). It likewise needs to start now.

4   *The creation of new cities in relation to displacement and massive numbers of people* (wherein any distinction between climate and conflict refugees will disappear). This is going to be another huge issue demanding urgent research and planning action. Who should build them, for how many people, and where is the money to build them going to come from? Who should answer these questions?

These challenges can be seen as counter to current planning trends and conditions of limitation. They recoil against a degeneration of planning into the micro-management of space and the built environment via codes, rules and regulation whereby design and 'master planning' is totally over-determined by compliance requirements. This action does not mean complete deregulation, but it does imply dramatically increasing the place of vision and dialogue within planning remade. The preoccupation with detail without recognition of the overall context has to end, and this can only happen by the recreation of what planning is and does. The second trend to counter is post-urbanism where the city is deemed to be beyond the reach of planning and is best left to the 'organic self-organization' of communities and interests. So 'informed', architects focus on signature buildings and let the city 'take care of itself'. In opposition to this negation another discourse that can accommodate the planned is needed – the discourse of spatial justice. A third and related trend to confront is working to negate the propensity to let the city take care of itself – this to the ultimate point whereby all urban infrastructure and services are allowed to become partial or totally dysfunctional. The oppositional action to these trends goes to the creation of a culture of material repair by local government, local business and community partner projects. Such action will not arrive unless the scales of the problems are made present and thereafter an open, broad and proliferating conversation is created.

As said, there can be no remaking of cities without a remaking of planning to become more socially relationally engaged, perceptive and dialogical and less bureaucratic, instrumental, developmentally orientated and gesturally consultative. Even as transformed, planning cannot be the sole driver of urban transformational processes. In this respect, it has to have a response/relation to the informal that supports the meeting of needs rather than imposing order. In particular, providing basic infrastructure to existing or emergent informal settlements is an obvious option.

These remarks beg to be seen within an existing expansive critique of planning, with its extensive literature that recognizes planning in the midst of a 'paradigm' crisis.[4] But equally within the context of metrofitting as a new framing and assemblage of practices that dislocates planning from its current service to 'urban functionalist reform' and economic development.

What is there to remake of planning? Many questions now follow: can it be brought within a more appropriate time-space model? In what structures (political and social) should controls and accountability be lodged? How can the Eurocentric epistemological basis of planning be undone? And then, how can the re-education process commence? These questions have go to the political agenda of metrofitting, including an acknowledgement of the deepening crises of rapid and informal urbanization, the momentum

---

[4] This critique shows planning's foundational principles, epistemology, culture and politics are all bankrupt (and responses to this situation, like 'new urbanism', are woefully inadequate). For an overview of this critique, see Stephen Graham and Simon Marvin (2012), *Splintering Urbanism*, London: Routledge, pp. 110–116.

of non-western population growth and the associated creation of megacities, as these concerns layer onto issues of climate change and other environmental impacts, urban conflict, and the fragmentation, breakdown and abandonment of cities. Finding the answers to these questions can only arrive via culturally and circumstantially located analysis, major changes in research and education (all of which transcend existing divisions and foundations of knowledge), plus the establishment of a higher and broader debate on the nature and fate of cities.

Certainly in the face of the scale of existing and coming challenges to the urban environment, the entire infrastructure of cities almost everywhere invites being (re)planned relationally via planning remade – this 'in time' and in a reconfiguration of economic and environmental priorities directed by the imperative of the Sustainment. This is especially so for new, futurally conceptualized cities and for those many old cities where the infrastructure is already breaking down. Responding to this problem implies a mix of new imaginaries, new knowledge, as well as repair and redirective action to introduce distributed and alternative infrastructure in areas like renewable energy, public transport, improved air and water quality, bio-waste management (for bio-mass energy and large-scale composting), and the generation of urban food production (this via 'continuously productive urban landscapes', CPULs)[5]. Such action can be combined with the recovery of good agricultural soil (which has been built over in so many cities – for which there is already an established body of knowledge and available technology). A comprehensive programme of retrofitting buildings and their adaptive reuse is another and very important action in many cities that can increase population density and utility without adding to their environmental footprint. This kind of action can also directly link to problems of homelessness.[6] While currently the exception, such action begs to be widely replicated in the future. Currently, however, many cities lack the political will, organizational means and the economic capacity to implement such innovations.

Forms of collaboration are increasingly deployed to advance community development, consultative and participatory design in cities where the social ecologies are broken. Such action has begun in places as diverse as the south side of Chicago, the 'no-go areas' of Johannesburg, and divided cities like Caracas and Karachi. In these contexts, the concept of the 'complete street' is arriving – a street locally designed to act as a catalyst for environmental and

---

[5] Andre Viljoen (ed.) (2005), *Continuous Productive Urban Landscapes*, London: Architectural Press.
[6] The most famous building reclaimed by the homeless is perhaps the Torre David building in Caracas. Many commentators have written about this building. They tell the story of how it was abandoned and then occupied by the homeless. See McGuirk, *Radical Cities*, pp. 175–186.

socio-cultural change. The challenge here is of course one of such action having sufficient scale to make a real difference.

The 'soft' edge: metrofitting, culture and perception

While we all live in a world at risk, the way risk is understood in and beyond the city is totally inadequate almost everywhere. For example, environmental risk is objectified by science, but thereafter is not relationally connected, and chronologically projected, to the general socio-cultural and economic risks a city faces. As a result, objectified problems are viewed as 'standing alone' and within a limited time frame. This imposes significant problems, in particular it creates the impression that the problem can be contained and met with a custom solution, either immediately or in the future. Such characterizations not only act to negate recognition of complexity but also fail to acknowledge that problems are now arriving for which there is no solution but to adapt. Climate change has already been mentioned as a clear example of this.[7]

In an age of globalizing consumerism, with populations disposed towards self-interest and socio-cultural conservatism, there is increasingly a dominant ontology of universalized self-interested individualism. The consequence of this, even among the educated classes, is 'akrasia' (understood as not acting upon what you know). So while large numbers of people understand that much in 'the world is at risk' – amplified by the unsustainable conditions created by human beings – they ignore this knowledge as evident in the way they act. At the same time, and by degree, people are increasingly unsettled by the state and defuturing events of the world, all of which fuels mass insecurity. Moreover, there is a widespread nihilist psychology that says, 'I have too much to lose to take risks, and anyway I have no agency to change anything.' Such a refusal heralds 'a fatalist mode of worldly habitation' that puts the very continuity of human life at risk, and remains dominantly directed towards securing the unsustainable *status quo*.

Metrofitting needs to be understood to be a counter action to such a sensibility – one that enables risks to be identified, examined and acted against as part of everyday working life. Such action has the potential to foster the socialization of the transformative measures that can enhance 'convivial work' and the building of 'communities of communication and cooperation' essential for the creation of adaptive change and sustainable working conditions.

---

[7] Deep-sea temperatures have already been increased and they take several hundred years to change.

The freedom of the modern world, authored and partly universalized by the Enlightenment, was predicated on 'freedom under the law'. Thus absolute freedom of 'nature raw in tooth and claw' – that is, freedom without restriction or protection – was sacrificed for a delimited freedom underpinned by the protection of the law. This relative freedom thereafter was contractually enshrined in civil society. A moment has now been reached when another sacrifice and condition of delimitation requires to be imposed – this because of the defuturing impetus of unsustainability. The Sustainment demands this sacrifice to securing the general conditions of human dependence (which extend to the conditions of biological and socio-cultural life at large). The argument for such change is vast and once waged will likely span many decades – but it has to be won. Not only will there be no future freedom without its victory but maybe not even a future for humanity itself.

By implication, the freedom to extend the unsustainable (by the destruction of environments of dependence, conflict and inequity – understood beyond the economic as a lack of social and spatial justice, services, utilities, food, education and meaningful and appropriately rewarded work) cannot and should not be condoned or tolerated. There is no viable path to the future predicated upon such violence.

Metrofitting, in the context of the urban, represents an enactment of the delimitation of freedom totally centred on the practice of the Sustainment. It therefore does not just mean taking action to secure the ability for urban life to continue to be. It does not presume one form of the city, state of mind or way of life, but it does assert that the current trajectory towards deepening structural conditions of unsustainability has to be halted. As indicated, this possibility cannot occur without sacrifice. There are actually only two scenarios: (1) the curtailment of unrestrained consumerism, excess and poverty, and the profligate use of resources and space, environmental destruction, and continued geopolitical conflict; or (2) allowing the ecological correction of a mass disaster, engendered by our action, to restore some kind of biophysical balance with or without the presence of a dramatically reduced number of human beings.

10

Metrofitting, thinking otherwise and a new foundation of change

The city is the most visible expression of our living in a 'world-within-the-world'. As such, it is totally a product of informal and formal design and artifice in time and space. Even most of the 'natural' elements of the city are managed and landscaped into their designated place. As we now recognize, the imposition of this world-within-the-world increasingly negates the nature of the biophysical world of our dependence. What is less recognized is that humanity is becoming increasingly unsustainable by design and that the sum of all the actions aiming to counter this (sustainability) are making little difference to this trajectory.

Metrofitting, it has been argued, has the agency to intervene in this equation with the potential to significantly help counter current anthropocentrically driven designed and designing modes of worldly negation. As such, it invites a cluster of critical perspectives being brought into view.

The discourse and celebration of the creative subject perverts the perception of human agency. The corrective (the dialectic of Sustainment) can bring the accompanying destructive consequences of this agency into view and in so doing reconfigure an assessment of its action – this to make visible how the home, the city and industrial production are equally sites of destruction.

Focusing, for instance, on the home (so often projected as a place of at least relative comfort, care and security) exposes it to be the locus of the creation of commodity grounded desires and the destination for a huge amount of industrial output to meet these created desires. So characterized, home is thus revealed as equally being a machine of destruction. To know this is not to devalue the positive socio-cultural significance of the home, but rather to bring it to presence as a required locus for a new imperative of responsibility. Effectively the city, as in part a sum of homes, is this observation writ large. But such an understanding also enables the city to be seen as a greatly expanded arena of transformative opportunity – one that metrofitting strives to name, develop and exploit. Yet this task is enormously complex: the city is ever changing, it produces increasing volumes of undirected waste and dominantly serves the economic *status quo*. Added to this, cities attract a continuous flow of people in this still ongoing age of rapid urbanization and displacement. All of this ensures the impetus driving destruction becomes increasingly excessive. Megacities and megaregions, so positioned as the planet's most 'advanced and dynamic' centres of production and consumption, show humanity being on the verge of a higher order of the unsustainable.

Could metrofitting have any redirective impact on large-scale industry? Insofar as it is deeply implicated in the city – as the city and the home are the locus of the demand for huge volumes of industrially made goods – the answer must be yes.

These opening remarks aim to make clear that humanity depends upon that which at the same time most threatens its continuity. In response to this situation, it is now appropriate to bring the nature of design and *habitus* into greater critical presence as they are both implicated in the ontological foundation of everyday urban life.[1] What this means is that in order for change to be possible, an attempt must be made to make present everything that needs to be changed. Revisiting design, and the work created by Pierre Bourdieu, will help in realizing this task.

On design

Design, as shown, is far more than it is presented to be by popular culture, education and professional practice. So acknowledged, there is an immediate need to make clear the distinction between a metaphysical (the sum of knowledge about designing and the designed) and an ontological (the nature of the agency of design in relation the being and beings) understanding of design. The essential things to understand are: that the designed world of human creation cannot be separated from the creation of the beings that inhabit that world; and that the act of prefiguration (design) is intrinsic to being human (we bring things into existence via giving intent to the form of an

---

[1] Martin Heidegger's notion of being-in-the-world situates *dasein*'s everydayness in 'being absorbed in the world'; see Heidegger, *Being and Time*, pp. 107–108. The concern with everyday life is variously engaged by sociology, cultural theory and philosophy. Michel de Certeau (1984) brought all of these perspectives and connected them to the city in *The Practice of Everyday Life*. A concern with everyday life and the city equally is present across almost all Henri Lefebvre's writing on cities.

idea). One can now reiterate: that the world we design in significant part designs us.[2]

Following what has just been said: metrofitting not only has the potential to change the city but equally the people who dwell therein, but not via the simplistic determinism that characterized the modern movement and its understanding of design, cause and effect. In contrast, an affirmative ontological understanding of design, as an underpinning of metrofitting, can be far more relationally engaged and dynamic in creating differentially situated dispositions to our being-in-the-world. One that is less destructive.

The city cannot be redirected to become other than it is without design itself being recreated to become more consciously ontologically attuned. Essentially, this means gaining and using knowledge of what has been designed and what it has brought into being. There is no assumption that complete identification is possible, but there is the recognition that gaining and applying such knowledge significantly increases the ability of design practitioners to take responsibility for what their work ends up creating. At the same time, a far more developed, and critically reflective, level of awareness by designers also needs to be fostered.

At the moment, design in its conceptual underdevelopment and bondage to the *status quo* remains dominantly understood instrumentally. Thus it is dominantly still part of the problem and still mostly serves the unsustainable. The discourses of architectural and design education, research and practice almost exclusively still operate within this paradigm. 'Sustainable design', as articulated to 'sustainable development', does not rupture this market connection.

To gain a kind of redirective capability, an appropriate level of awareness and ontological designing agency, not only does how and what to design need to change but also architects and designers need to transcend the limitations (and disarticulation) of the accepted divisions of knowledge that underpins their disciplines. They also need to shed the restricted vision of design held, projected and promoted by their professional organizations (especially in the context of service provision). The implication of these remarks for an architect, planner or designer who comprehends the necessity of the project of the Sustainment is that the very understanding of the essence of what design is and does has to undergo a radical change – this so that the relation between the prefigurative nature of things and human beings is fully grasped and thereafter acted upon.

---

[2] These remarks are actually the marker of a substantial history of inquiry presented in a trilogy: Tony Fry (2009), *Design Futuring*, Oxford: Berg, (2011), *Design as Politics*, Oxford: Berg; and (2012), *Becoming Human by Design*, London: Berg.

None of this can happen without strategic action able to direct the processes of transformation that metrofitting, as a situated practice, has the potential to commence. Such change for the majority of practitioners is unlikely to happen in the abstract. The ability to embark upon transformative action, starting with unmaking the foundations of existing design practices so they may be remade, requires new (and again informal and formal) modes of education and professional development. Central to doing this is an engagement with *habitus*. Unmaking and remaking are crucial to move transformative action from the conscious and specific to the general and (unconsciously) to that inscribed in practice.

Practice and the agency of the visible invisible

Practice, not least design practice, is underpinned by *habitus*. Pierre Bourdieu, in his *An Outline of a Theory of Practice* (first published in English in 1977), established a set of strong relational connections between *habitus*, structures and practices.[3] Although the concept is strongly associated with his work, it was not of his creation. Philosophically, the thinking on the concept has a long history passing from Aristotle to Hegel (as *ethos*) to Husserl (as *habitualität*) and in a variety of ways to Heidegger (as explicit in *dwelling* and inherent in *dasein*). Moreover, many social theorists commencing with Durkheim have evoked *habitus*.[4]

What Bourdieu made clear in his conceptualization was that *habitus* was an historically acquired foundational structure that framed perception, action and judgement enacted through, and gained during, an induction into a practice.[5] While part of the general reality of the everyday, *habitus* also has more specific meaning within particular 'fields' (contexts) of practice. So qualified, it is everything that is taken for granted in the passage of a practice from one (generation of) practitioners to another. Thus, what is acquired is an inhabitation of a practice enacted by habit, hence the relation to Heidegger's notion of dwelling.

In that *habitus* is manifest in everyday intuitive actions of the practitioner means that it can be viewed as the embodied common sense directive of the nature of habitual practices seen in a disposition displayed towards efficacious professional conduct. Such embodied knowledge Bourdieu tells us, echoing

---

[3] Pierre Bourdieu (1977), *An Outline of a Theory of Practice* (trans. Richard Nice), Cambridge: Cambridge University Press.

[4] See Karl Maton (2008), 'Habitus', in M. Grenfell (ed.), *Pierre Bourdieu: Key Concepts*, London: Acumen, pp. 49–65.

[5] Again see Bourdieu, *An Outline of a Theory of Practice*.

Heidegger, is not something that is simply learnt and consciously employed but is elemental to what you are.[6] *Habitus* is therefore a ground of professional identity as well as practice. To understand this is to realize that practices are constitutive of ontologies – we are what we do, are made by and make. So there is not 'a we' independent of practice, or 'a we' with an independent identity. The implication of what this means is profound, as in many contemporary societies large numbers of industrial and manual craft skills are disappearing with the rise and establishment of those socio-communicative digital technologies that are profoundly changing the ontology of (what) many of us (are).

The embodied knowledge of an established practice provides a sensed normative evaluative regime reflecting upon action to maintain induced learnt standards. *Habitus* is thus neither pure habit nor mechanistic repetition but something that is felt and informs action via received informal knowledge and a history of direct experience. It works to deliver things that work. Accumulatively this establishes what Bourdieu called the 'logic of practice'.[7] What the practitioner does within the 'logic of practice' is given, rather than consciously applied – this disposition to act is gained during the course of gaining a practice.

Bourdieu argued that practices are unable to be causally reduced to the material conditions out of which they appear to arrive. Rather, they come into being as a result of the structuring of the structure of *habitus*. This is to say that all that historically and circumstantially structures our disposition towards materially situated action, in relation to our perception of the potentiality of these material conditions, is already structured. In the context of our practices we all, *de facto*, 'arrive' in specific worldly circumstances biologically, culturally and socio-economically prefigured and disposed. This does not mean we are totally over-determined, but it does mean that our freedoms (given or acquired), in terms of our practices, are circumscribed by what an acquired *habitus* enables and disables. This acquisition can, of course, be strong (in the case of ontologies like those of a musician, farmer, architect, doctor, policewoman) or weak (in the case of casual workers and occupations with low skill levels).

Habitus, as the structuring of structures, is also implicated in the way social beings acquire their culture and values and exude them (this acquisition is what Bourdieu called 'cultural capital'), and thereafter how they appropriate their own cultural specificity from this process. In this respect, *habitus* functions in, and replicates, collective socio-cultural structures of exchange – language, material goods, symbolic forms and so on. In actuality, it means worldly occupation and actions, so understood, are not predicated upon a distinction between mind and matter, but result from inter-relational regulatory

---

[6] Pierre Bourdieu (1990), *The Logic of Practice* (trans. Richard Nice), Cambridge: Polity Press, p. 73.
[7] Ibid.

determinations as they structure, and are structured by, particular social conditions quite independent of seemingly overt rules.[8]

Effectively, a good deal of the actions of an educator of practice mimetically induct the learner into *habitus* by the transfer of unspoken rules and assumptions via 'showing the way things are done' – this in ways that the educators were themselves shown and learnt the particular actions, values and associated language of the practice. In this way, a 'common sense of the obvious' is established that negates the need for questioning and reflection. Thus the possibility of another way never arrives to *the way things are done*. Such action is foundational and establishes a starting point from which many other actions flow. Again *habitus* becomes habit as 'the only and the proper' forms of enacting the way things are done – if questioned: 'it is the right way things are done'. Certainly, this is evident when dealing with many physical practices, from using an axe or a chainsaw to dismembering an animal carcass, to the carving of the scroll at the neck of a violin or a myriad of other such skilled actions. All skilled actions are embodied *habitus* that become often inscribed in, and expressed by, muscle memory.

Obviously it is not simply a matter to overcome *habitus* (even if there were a reason to do so). However, there clearly can be, and is, a need to identify and bring it into presence so the particular practices (like architecture and design) can be questioned. The question though is how?

Well, while guiding principles can be created, they certainly cannot be done abstractly and with a formulaic methodology. On the basis of experience to date, change requires working with practitioners in the context of a specific project wherein actions and assumptions can be made phenomenally present, questioned, interrogated and reflected upon.[9] But such action goes nowhere unless there is a viable and appropriate counter-practice able to redirect or replace the condition of *habitus* rendered conscious. While the structuring of the structure of the practice can be changed, what is fixed is the relation between practice and *habitus* – there is no practice without it.

Much depends, of course, on the nature of the subject and the degree to which all that is taken-for-granted is embedded in their psyche, inscribed in their body and ontologically secured. Moreover, change does not necessarily produce an immediate and radical transformation of appearances or behaviour. Change takes time and is marked by gained evidence of considered consequences, the care and courage to create, manifest and defend difference – all in the recognition that such change has no end point. It is just process (redirected

---

[8] Bourdieu, *An Outline of a Theory of Practice*, p. 85.

[9] This experience is dominantly working with young designers on intercultural projects in unfamiliar settings understood to be learning environments.

and redirecting) in relation to practice, inscribed knowledge and exercised dispersed power.[10]

Bourdieu, technology and *habitus*

Bourdieu did not have a great deal to say about *habitus* and technology. What he did say was mostly about photography and television, and they were not the most insightful of his observations. Moreover, attempts to bring his thinking to technology have not been particularly illuminating, as they display little understanding of technology. In an article in *Cultural Studies* Jonathan Sterne writes that:

> . . . technologies are essentially subsets of *habitus* – they are organized forms of movement. In this way, technologies are theoretically unexceptional. They are very similar to other ways in which we organize social practice through the *habitus*.[11]

Such a statement shows little comprehension of the anthropological and metaphysical historicity of technology, especially in relation to its ontological designing significance, and the consequences of the complexity of technological transmutations.[12] Sterne shows even less understanding when he asserts that 'technologies' are 'socially shaped'. As such, both 'technology' and 'the social' are given an independent status. Ontological design tells us that this is simply not the case: the social/technology nexus is inter-relational.[13] Moreover, Sterne does not grasp that humans are technological beings, that technology has become metaphysical (knowledge), and that technologies cannot be understood by talking about specific technological things, for 'it' also exists as connected systems that constitute the technosphere. Technology thus intersects with, and appears in, particular individual and collective assemblages (like linked manufactured objects and utility services). An even weaker view of technology arrives when he says it '. . . may perform labour once done by a person, which is to say that people design and use technologies to enhance or promote

[10] Colin Gordon (ed.) (1980), *Michel Foucault, Power/Knowledge: Selected Interviews and Other Writings*, New York: Vintage.

[11] For example, Jonathan Sterne (2003), 'Bourdieu, Technique and Technology', *Cultural Studies*, Vol. 17, Nos. 3/4, p. 373.

[12] On the complexity of technology, the social and human evolution, see Bernard Stiegler (1998), *Technics and Time, 1: The Fault of Epimetheus* (trans. Richard Beardsworth and George Collins), Stanford, CA: Stanford University Press and (2009), *Technics and Time, 2: Disorientation* (trans. Stephen Barker), Stanford, CA: Stanford University Press; also Fry, *Becoming Human by Design*.

[13] Sterne, 'Bourdieu, Technique and Technology', p. 373.

certain activities and discourage others'.[14] The actuality is that people use and are used by technologies – there is no distinct division between the human and the technological. Technology is not merely a thing, and things do not remain discrete – by degree they have an animatory existence.

Times have changed in the technosphere. Beside the continued expansion and fusion between the mechanical and the electronic, the technological and the biological have also conjoined, as have communications, electronics, commodities and emotions (for many subjects, to be technologically disconnected is to be 'incomplete' and anxious – whereas to be connected is in fact to be enabled and complete(d)). The consequences of 'the hegemony of desevered relations' (connectedness) – where what appears to be close is mistaken for what is actually not near – is only just beginning to be understood (this especially in relation to much higher, and increasing, levels of depression among young people of both sexes – a condition especially now being associated with 'smartphone' use).[15]

The city is not outside this fluid reality: networks, data and the virtual are becoming as much a part of the functional operation of the city as its other infrastructural elements. Technology is deeply embedded in the lifeworld of humans. This has always been the case ever since the first hominoid picked up a stone and used it as a tool. But now the speed of this process is beyond comprehension and adaptive capacity. The illusion that humans were in control of technology has long gone – even popularist commentary on technology is starting to realize this. Like nature it has to learn to be lived with, and like nature it will bring delights and disasters, as well as a similar functional dependence.

Technology is constantly imposed in the name of freedom, protection and security. But in this setting we are viewed indivisibly, and as such, that to be protected and the danger to be guarded against.

Metrofitting, *habitus* and time

Metrofitting, as indicated, is a practice aiming to become praxis. This means it's an applied dimension underscored by a developed theoretical understanding of the afterlife of what has been, and what has to be understood and engaged in the present. It is beyond just an instrumental and functional comprehension of the problems to be confronted and engaged. For this change to occur,

---

[14] Ibid., p. 376.
[15] http://psychcentral.com/news/2012/06/17/heavy-cell-phone-use-linked-to-depression-sleep-problems-in-young-people/40262.html.

understanding has to be relational. The practices that metrofitting constitutes can only gain their full agency if existing unsustainable practices that constitute cities are confronted, contested and eventually displaced. Three implications of what has just been said now beg identification. The first is metrofitting is *de facto* a means and manifestation coming out of *habitus* being transformed. The second is this act of transformation is profoundly political without being attached to any particular institutionalized political ideology. Third, the transformation of *habitus* by the politics of metrofitting (remembered as a potential defuturing counter-force predicated upon a 'logic of the practice') requires being based on futuring and centred on 'acting in time' (again remembered as acting in the medium of time and with a sense of urgency).

For the possibility of the practice of metrofitting to arrive, in the way just outlined, there have to be available counter-practices for appropriation, plural structures of induction, and forms of learning, unmaking and making that disrupt and reconfigure extant thinking and the (il)logic of many practices that are directive of the urban and urban life. The next five chapters will be devoted to this exposition.

11

Unlearning and learning

The concern of this chapter is the making of the transition from a critical agenda to a process of change. It will do this by specifically examining the underpinning of existing practices of learning, the need for unlearning and an emergent foundation for a new learning.

Learning in the shadow of teaching

Mainstream Western education, with a few exceptions like Finland (where teaching is a high status profession), has failed to unlock the intellectual and creative potential of the majority of school students. It channels the young, predominantly at the behest of the policy of governments, towards serving the labour market, and as such it fosters a belief in a form of compliance that dominantly meets the needs of the national economy. Against this backdrop, universities have become mostly service providers to the economy as well as *de facto* acting as recruiting centres for government, the professions and the corporate sector.

Accompanying their functional narrowing, universities have become preoccupied with 'teaching and learning' increasingly via 'blended learning' (an euphemism for electronic technology in the classroom). These developments have been met with some criticism – one of the most celebrated sources being Sir Ken Robinson, a former professor of education from Warwick University in Britain.[1] Robinson's popularist semi-radical critique, which we will come to shortly, gained a high profile and a huge following on the Internet by using his voiceover to narrate a humorous animated cartoon ('blended learning') supporting his argument. What he put forward predominantly argued that current education methods destroy the inherent creativity of children. While this is not untrue, his sweeping claim fell completely in line with the misplaced view of many parents who live under the illusion that their child is being

---

[1] Robinson was knighted for his services to education.

unrecognized as exceptional, whereas in almost all cases their child was just a normal kid (exceptions exist but are the exception). Moreover, no recognition of the dialectical relation between creation and destruction was acknowledged.

Robinson's views are mild in comparison to those of actual radical critics of education from an earlier era, like those of Ivan Illich, who in *Deschooling Society* made very clear distinctions between teaching, learning and the regressive role of schools. While doing this Illich also put forward a powerful case showing that learning to function in the world dominantly occurred outside school.[2] Likewise, contrary to Robinson's focus on the individual, the famous Brazilian educator Paulo Freire identified the socio-political imperative of education in his most widely acclaimed book *Pedagogy of the Oppressed*. In particular, he exposed how adults having gained political agency thereafter acted as an enormous motivator to learn.[3]

Having so positioned the popularist critique of Robinson, let's now look at his arguments in a little more detail.[4] First, one can agree with him that few schools have the ability to create an environment that liberates the natural talents and creative abilities of children. Dominantly, 'schools do kill creativity' – as an educator who worked in art and design schools, I attest that this is true. Perhaps unfashionably one can argue that this situation has actually got progressively worse as more electronic media has arrived in the home and classroom. As earlier commentary made clear, image saturation exists to such an extent that it now colonizes and circumscribes imagination and establishes a strong propensity towards appropriative practice. In the misguided belief that creativity is teachable via formulaic techniques, and in recognition of diminished creativity among students, remedial classes have been introduced in many institutions. But more essentially, there is a huge problem of how creativity is comprehended and mobilized across the entire education debate. Again as remarked earlier, creativity is so often reduced to creative expression rather than being recognized as the exercise of imagination. Robinson, while acknowledging imagination is being diminished, sees it reductively as subordinate to 'the creative process'. His claim that the 'education system discourages creativity' folds back into a larger and structural reform agenda, rather than opening a path to conscious change that acknowledges it is stifled and circumscribed within extant divisions of knowledge and instrumentalized practices. As the philosophic debate of liberalism itself makes clear, the nature of a pluralistic liberal education system

---

[2] Ivan Illich (1971), *Deschooling Society*, London: Marion Boyers.
[3] Paulo Freire (2000 [1968]), *Pedagogy of the Oppressed* (trans. Myra Bergman Ramos), 30th Anniversary Edition, London: Bloomsbury Academic.
[4] The remarks on Robinson are drawn from his 2010 RSA video and Ken Robinson (2011), *Out of Our Minds: Learning to be Creative*, Chichester: Capstone.

essentially discourages and flattens all forms of fundamental difference[5] (an observation that repositions what Robinson has to say on conformity).

The second argument Robinson makes is a familiar one, and not without some truth. It is that school education is predicated upon the status given to academic ability and is orientated towards university entrance. However, the fact that university education has become a mass and vocationally orientated commodity in 'advanced economies', rather than an elite phenomenon, has radically changed this picture and weakened the argument. Another point Robinson makes that one can agree with is that schools fail to sufficiently recognize the plural character of intelligence. But his response to this that 'education should be personalised to every learning style' is not an appropriate one to the situation. For learning styles and methods are part of the problem, as are uniform teaching methods. Examples as different as the Finnish system and Freire's work in Brazil show that the key to effective education is the creation of a motivation to learn and the freedom to do so. Dominantly, method grounded teaching marks of a failure to do this. Progress here equates to the creation of conditions that focus on teaching methods delivering given curriculum content rather than on the creation of a culture of learning.

Again exposing only the partial flaws of liberalism, Robinson argues against subject hierarchies but defends disciplines. What he does not recognize (and what institutionalized education is light-years away from grasping) is that education is increasingly disarticulated from the operative complexity of the contemporary world – which (dys)functions as a relational complexity (which as we saw, Bourdieu recognized). Whereas Eurocentric education and at every level, but especially higher education, is structured on divisions of knowledge 'left over' from the Enlightenment. This epistemological framing worked to create the modern world, but it is now out of step with 'the reality' it assisted in bringing into being. This misfit framing lacks the ability to deal with the problems that were implicated in creating this world and are destined to continue to increase.

The same kind of half-way argument goes to Robinson's final and partial diatribe against conformity, which he sees as a problem of the standardization of curriculum and teaching assessment. Certainly this view is correct, but once more the problem he indicates is much deeper. Essentially, most school education dominantly creates (ontologically designs) an ontology of conformity whereby the path to success is assumed to be attained by finding out how to comply with the needs of the market. This is carried into university education

---

[5] A great deal of this debate centres on positions taken towards Thomas Hobbes, a claimed founder of liberalism, on civilization as an ideal and philosophy as politics. See, for example, Heinrich Meier (1995), *Carl Schmitt and Leo Strauss: The Hidden Dialogue* (trans. J. Harvey Lomax), Chicago, IL: University of Chicago Press.

where educators are constantly confronted in some form or another with students asking: 'what do I have to do to get the highest grades'. Here, then, is the true mark of the death of the creative spirit and the failure of education, private and public. What has been erased as one of the keys to learning is a willingness to embrace and reflect upon failure. What just does not arrive is an environment wherein it is safe to fail and where greater rewards of learning can (or should) come from glorious failure.

Finally, Robinson thinks he is making a case for a total and revolutionary transformation of education. He puts forward 'innovation' as one of the challenges this change would address. He is no revolutionary: revolutionaries don't get knighthoods! Innovation is not a value in itself – its value depends on what it is based on. Current use of the term is vacuous and generally folds back into the clichéd rhetoric of neo-liberal economics. The way Robinson discusses innovation is actually naïve, instrumental and mirrors how he views the time in which 'we' live as 'revolutionary' – which in any positive sense it is not. In so many ways, our time is defutured, dangerous and fragmented. He believes 'we' need to think differently about our abilities (whereas there is no universal 'we' and what is actually at stake is how 'a thinking' can arrive able to redirectively think different futures, and create them in a way that sustains us in our difference). Robinson recognizes there must be organizational change and a different education system. But his thinking is a long way from recognizing education in the larger context of change based on a project focused on securing human futures, one, as argued, underpinned by the imperative of the Sustainment.

What this brief critique of Robinson shows are the dangers of popularism. Certainly, there is some substance to his critique, but as indicated it also emplaces and re-enforces a good deal of fuzzy thinking and establishes a position of 'radical conservativism'.

The reactionary responses his argument have prompted don't even warrant a rebuttal: they turn on weak and essentialist positions resting on the defence of the existing teaching profession and an ultra-conservative view of education lacking a critical sense or recognition of the depth of the crisis of education's relation to the unsustainable.

The present ways in which education is discussed are lacklustre, and are at their worst when addressing performance measurement and technology in the classroom. This situation is partly a product of the intellectual sterility and instrumental tenor of the promotion and discussion of methods of teaching and learning. So much is missing from the discussion of education, such as for example: the disinterest and hatred of school across a whole swathe of ethnic and poor underclasses, and the recognition of teaching as epistemological violence when delivered by under-educated, uncritical and alienated teachers. Then there is the problem of the created narcissism of so many of the children of the demanding classes of privilege (producing children unaware of their privilege). In contrast, there is the love of, and hunger for, learning by significant numbers of student in underprivileged circumstances from and in underprivileged nations.[6] However, the most significant of all are two disjunctures of the educational institution begging recognition. The first is the schism between what is being taught and what needs to be learnt to be able to deal with a structurally unsustainable world. This problem grows by the day. The second, echoing Illich, is the disjuncture between the gaining importance of informal knowledge and the failure of formal education to comprehend its significance (as constitutive of *habitus*). This is what will now be considered.

Anthropocentrism: learning for unlearning

Education is grounded in the actuality of the dialectic of Sustainment and in the very moment of our becoming human. Remembering that: as a species we are born an animal but educated into becoming human (while biologically retaining our animality). But every one of us, under behavioural instruction and the ontological designing of the artefactual world of humanity, becomes ever more human during the passage out of infancy into childhood. We are all, across all cultures and by degree, the product of what has been destroyed and what has been created.

The gaining of a critique of human centredness (anthropocentrism) is the armature around which all education now needs to turn. It is only by this that the key to comprehension of what requires to be learnt and taken responsibility for can arrive. Without this knowledge it is not possible to establish the very ground upon which ethical choices and action need, and can, be made. Not only could such knowledge open education to a new vista of learning but it could also unlock the potentiality of unlearning – and in so doing provide the evaluative filter of extant knowledge. Unlearning is the corrective to the 'learning in error' that is at the core of the inter-generational continuity of the unsustainable.

At the most general, all humanity is required to learn how to live within the finite means of our planet, while also confronting the problems of our 'expanding global population, the growth of destruction resources and the propensity to conflict, all which are currently out of control (and increasingly becoming so). There are, of course, other factors in the meta-context of remaking cities. Again in our difference (climatic, cultural, economic and

---

[6] Speaking from experience: examples of classrooms that are no more than a hut with a dirt floor, a blackboard and a stick of chalk, with sixty or more children are not uncommon in so many poor nations.

geopolitical) there is a massive need to unlearn in order to relearn how to plan, design, make and appropriately dwell. However, and above all, there is the city as neglected, but rich and vital, a locus of learning.

In particular, the temporal qualities of spatial forces and practices of the city need to be far better understood. The configuration of urban space and its forms of use are directive of the speed of movement (walking, running, cycling, driving/being driven) and thus of time. Unlike the utopianism of 'new urbanism', in most urban space in most cities, time and movement do not flow but rather they are continually interrupted.[7] With this fracturing, striated space '. . . closes off a surface and "allocates" it according to determinate intervals'; but in smooth space one 'distributes oneself in an open space, according to the frequencies and in the course of one's crossings'.[8] The city thus can be seen as a space of territorialization/de-territorialization, appearance/ disappearance: such change in time is directive.[9] The point here, the relevance to metrofitting, is that there is a need to unlearn and relearn how one sees, constitutes and occupies space/spaces (of the city). One needs to view what seems static as movement in time (everything disappears in time) – the smooth returns – and the possibility of reoccupation (the arrival of the striated) is created. However, there is something else that can cut into these dynamics of time and space: fear. In cities of fear – cities of terror, violence and crime – public space ceases to exist, movement is restricted and territoriality is structured by the actuality or imminence of violence. Again the scope of what needs to be remade ever expands.

Human beings do not simply occupy space as an animal does, they create it, possess it, impose themselves upon it, increase their claim for it, mark it, transform it, and destroy it. There is no question that 'we' have assumed an absolute right to do so: the history of anthropocentrism is written in space, but it hides. A great deal of the city is hidden, as is knowledge of the city. Design is complicit in this concealment.

To be able to 'learn the city', it needs first to be opened up as a locus of unlearning: the illegibility of the seemingly legible, and the unfamiliarity of the familiar, both need to be exposed and then excavated. Things of the city are actually designed to appear to be not as what they actually are. The transitory frequency arrives with an illusion of permanence; likewise, so much of the fabric of the city claimed with lasting value is really expedient. The façade of

---

[7] In this contest whenever smooth (unbounded) space arrives, it is almost immediately claimed and '. . . translated, traversed into striated space: striated space is constantly being reversed and returned to smooth space'. Gilles Deleuze and Felix Guattari (1987), *A Thousand Plateaus: Capital and Schizophrenia* (trans. Brian Masumi). Minneapolis, MN: University of Minnesota Press, p. 474.
[8] Ibid., p. 481.
[9] Ibid., p. 480.

an office block does not merely conceal the functional structure of the building, for it also hides work, and the worker within the stratified order of an organization. Beautiful architecture may well mask an ugly organization. Lavish landscaping may well be a 'cover' for contaminated land. The spatial organization of an industrial complex may appear to be purely based on functional considerations, but could at the same time be organized to structure knowledge within a regime of power.

The language of how the city is presented to the world rarely matches the lived experience of place. Technological solutions are often short lived, traffic management systems being a clear example of this. The 'cleaning up' of a city with 'social problems' and its gentrification rather than solving problems so often simply put the displaced of the city out into its unseen margins where they can be (and frequently are) forgotten. Popular culture is ambiguously positioned in the play of all these relations: it conspires with illusions and exploits the concealed (in language, music and style).

Learning of the 'unnatural' nature of the metabolism of the city is an unlearning of it as operative system. The city teeters on, or falls into, dysfunction as its daily process of mass material and social destruction occurs – as is evident in its organic and intractable waste, sewage, pollutants and its social detritus (the dispossessed, the homeless, crime and the mentally ill). As this ungoverned machine of excess races on, the disease of consumption becomes ever more globally disseminated and destructive – so often concealed in the name of 'lifting people out of poverty'. How can over-production and globalizing hyper-consumption, as action that leads to a divesting of futures, be a route to the resolution of inequity? What is unthought, what cruel deception actually reveals, is the error, short-termism and pragmatic nature of globalization (which can break allegiances just as quickly it can make them).

In the polite quarters of modern wealthy cities, the endless struggle of concealment is enacted on a daily basis and life continues on sweetly. But on the streets of many cities of former empires, the squalor and stench of dysfunction is constant and is inescapably present.

At an even higher order of concealment, in one's learning of 'our' anthropocentric myopia, one unlearns the unity of the world of our existence and discovers the performative omnipotence of unsustainability as exercised by the de-worlding violence of the world-within-the-world of human creation. Effectively, due to the scale of our world-within-the-world making, our endeavours, combined with our numbers, have emplaced a situation of anthropocenic auto-destruction, with the city at the fore. Once recognized, this dangerous situation of implosion demands to be countered (hence actions like metrofitting). If ignored (which at the moment it mostly is), the prospect is apocalyptic. Extrapolating: the affirmative prospect requires a reduction in the scale of human planetary impacts by a reconfiguration of 'living well' within a condition of substantial constraint; the negative prospect is whatsoever can start anew from whatever remains after the apocalypse.

To authentically learn (that is to be ontologically newly in-formed), one has to unlearn that there is no intrinsic relation between teaching and knowing. Learning is now 'learning to understand' what needs to be understood for humanity to become futural. It is extremely clear that humanity has no future unless this lesson is learnt. It is also very evident that little progress on this count is currently being made. A vast amount of knowledge exists about *how* to continue to extend and elaborate the world-within-the-world constantly being made and occupied. For the comprehensive case for *why* the process of the auto-destruction of (our) time needs to cease, and then the question of *how* to redirect human energies towards establishing the project of the Sustainment (which can but extend our finitudinal moment) now needs to commence (it has needed to do so for many decades). Knowledge itself cannot produce this change. It can only come from an understanding that recoils against that myopia inherent in anthropocentrism and the nihilism of 'our being now'. Without this leadership of the understanding, fundamental ontological transformative action cannot arrive.

Let us again make clear: learning only happens if those who wish to learn unlearn the(ir) already learnt (*habitus*). And what learning in the face of unlearnt structural unsustainability demands is discovery, via a situated disclosure of crisis, how they/we become futurally other than (individually and collectively) they/we are.

In a broken world (seen and concealed), understanding depends upon an exposure of breakdown, breaking points and breakouts. The broken is already here, but is frequently unseen or seen mostly under conditions of misrecognition. Metrofitting placed in this context is learning what enables the remaking of cities to be situationally learnt (contra to externally implemented knowledge, methods and techniques). It does not presume to be the sole project of learning, for as we are about to see, other relational kindred areas of action are already forming.

Breaking out of striated space and the borderlands

Gaining recognition of a new way to understand the hybrid constructs in those 'in between' spaces of difference afforded by border thinking will be shown to have the ability to deliver new learning able to comprehend what response-ability can be created in the afterlife of modernity. Essentially, what is being evoked here is thinking that re-enforces metrofitting (as an ontological design agent) in the remaking of how the city is understood and engaged in contexts of decoloniality and inequity.

Border thinking exists and arrived out of that cultural space between the epistemological afterlife of modernity lodged in the Eurocentrically configured world at large together with being on the inside of the darker side of that afterlife. Here is the space of a decolonizing subject trying to think with and against the past and ongoing imposed knowledge, but also with the recognition of the presence and importance of the trace of indigenous knowledge. As put by Madina Tlostanova and Walter Mignolo: 'border thinking means a specific epistemic response from the exteriority of Western modernity, a response from the outside created from the perspective of the inside.'[10] There are still many subjects historically 'enframed' by colonialism who live without any sense of belonging to the afterlife of their past. Learning in this context requires unlearning what was learnt as a consequence of an education under the tutelage of the colonial matrix. Only then does relearning become possible.

Such action does not happen in an ethereal space but often in a city equally marked by its visible traces of a colonial history. Ontologically, for both the subject and the city, a borderland forms – a space of detached betweenness never totally delinked from what was imposed and lost, but not belonging to it either. This ontology and place are not simply of one scale – it can be of a minor or major dimension. From the perspective of metrofitting, this issue raises the possibility of a particular way to think 'spaces of betweenness' (not to be confused with left-over urban between spaces). Just as the unlearning associated with border thinking should not be seen as a chosen position, but rather one recognized as ontological condition borne out of alienation from what has been learnt. It follows that borderlands are a product of alienation underscored by the violence of imposed thought.

For the colonized subject, violence stems from the imposition of reason as negation, and for the city (as was seen with the example of Delhi) as an ordering of structure and space from elsewhere. Border thinking and borderland design give this recoil from violence somewhere affirmatively to go.

Lest there be any confusion, this thinking is not grounded in the past for, as needs to realized, the colonial matrix retains a corrosive and ongoing Eurocentrically grounded capability enacted by epistemological colonialism and technology. From points of reception of the colonized, the West now imports (in the form of expertise and products) the mirror of what it once exported – mimesis hereby can be read in the afterlife of colonization. Two observations follow: first, just as metaphysics became elemental to technology

---

[10] Madina V. Tlostanova and Walter D. Mignolo (2012), *Learning to Unlearn: Decolonial Reflections from Eurasia and the Americas*, Columbus, OH: Ohio State University Press, p. 6.

(now overtly expressed as 'artificial intelligence'), second, so too has colonialism (as historically Eurocentrically authored knowledge). Both become delivered via design, systems and globalizing products. Hegemonic capitalism has managed to commodify every dimension of everyday life everywhere. At the same time, there are fissures, betweenness, contradictions and critically alienated subjects, as well as those nihilist and violent returns of the repressed that manage to combine a fundamentalist ideology/theology with advanced technologies.

Contrary to Western belief and rhetoric, the humanist spirit of 'civilizing humanity' became an endless process of physical, economic, cultural, emotional, sexual and epistemological violence. The scale and damage to the very being of anthropos by European global colonization is beyond measure, and the view that it is over, is of the past, is miscast. Rather, it returns universalized in new forms.

Between the extremes of violent imposition and violent recoil, borderlands form. In this context, border thinking is not a matter of choice any more than confronting the unsustainable is (an action it is in fact indivisible from). It is a matter of survival, and survival is more than a matter of biological continuity. It is the survival of the fullness of (our) being, and thus the totality of what we are and can become. But to survive there is a price to pay. For, as a thread running from ancient philosophy to the present tells us: 'unless one is willing to sacrifice one's life in order to be, one does not have a life able to be recognised as such'.

It is not hard for the halfway-informed people of the present everywhere to recognize that the challenges humanity faces demand action. The hardest part is to come to terms with that nihilism that prevents taking action (expressed as 'I am just one person, what can I do?'). It starts with the action of and on the self within a change community. A life lived in the avoidance of pain can never be futural. To find oneself in the borderland is a discovery of being in a place where there is no choice but to act in pain – it is a place opening into metrofitting as action.

12

Metrofitting and the de-signing of design

Architecture, planning and urban design lack the intellectual means to remake the city. The constraints of their disciplines, the pragmatics of service provision, the perceptual limitations of functionalism, the aesthetic preoccupations with style and the form of their practices, all combine to obscure what needs to be engaged and how to do so. Moreover, one cannot any longer simply evoke 'the city' as if it were a transparent and visible form with clearly grounded meaning. The plurality of its form, the complexity of its systems and the diversity of its economies and cultures have overwhelmed the signifying capability of the city as sign, object and place. In this general and global moment, the uncertainty of what cities actually now are meets the uncertainty of what they might become. Metrofitting cannot but be this mix.

. . .

Metrofitting cannot happen without design (as it spans, and goes beyond, all of its disciplines); this means, as indicated, it cannot be enabled with design as it is. Design has been placed among all that which has to be unlearnt and relearnt, but reiterating, this most importantly without its being reduced to mere instrumentalism. Adding to what has already been said on design, four foundational pathways of action will be now introduced and brought together to assist in its unmaking and remaking: ontological design, design in time, elimination design and design intelligence. These actions are not exclusive.[1] But they and others referenced[2] are posed as affirmative responses to a substantial critique of existing defuturing approaches to design in its current

[1] See Fry, *Design Futuring*, for a larger range of examples.
[2] Ibid.

implication in the form and future of cities.[3] It is with these qualifications that the four examples of how to remake cities by design are put forward.

Ontological design

Ontological design has a strong theoretical underpinning and a history.[4] It arrived out of and stands upon a philosophical understanding of ontology brought to the performative quality of things. Within the totality of all that is (the ontic), all the beings (animate and inanimate) that constitute it have a particular (ontological) mode of being. The study of this mode of the being of beings and the relation between beings and things, together with its historical and futural agency, is at the core of the understanding that underpins ontological design.

The world in being is not stasis, for worlds are ontologically active: worlds world – they bring their futures into being. Martin Heidegger named this process as 'worlding'. As beings among beings, 'we' are not external observers of this process but are both recipients of, and active agents within, it. This 'worlding' process of multivalent causes and effects has no *telos*, no evolutionary trajectory. Yet the nature of those things that over the eons our species' progenitors, and then we as *Homo sapiens*, brought into being can be understood by Heidegger's notion of 'equipmentality'. Along with the ontological designing of all such things, which is the sum of the agency of all the physical, tactile and mental abilities exercised, they enabled our species to accumulate huge worldly transformative consequences. Here, then, is an unbroken passage from the most rudimentary of stone tools to the equipmental super-abundant and ultra-complexity of the technologically hegemonic present: computers, nuclear power stations, smartphones, laser-guided bombs and robotics, space travel, biotechnology, deep-sea dredgers, dental drills, 3D printers, road rollers, automated space laboratories and so on in almost incalculable quantities. All of this techno-world is overlaid with the knowledge that enabled such an accumulation of things, and the minds that brought them into being, to be created.

There is an inescapable need to remind ourselves that what resulted from all of these human attainments established a condition of profound ambiguity – an extraordinary 'world-within-the-world' in which the city is but one manifestation. Yet, as has been seen, at the same time this created world, as

---

[3] Defuturing directly links to the dialectic of Sustainment – first outlined in Tony Fry (1999), *A New Design Philosophy: An Introduction to Defuturing*, Sydney, NSW: UNSW Press.

[4] See Anne-Marie Willis (2006), 'Ontological Designing – Laying the Ground', *Design Philosophy Papers: Collection Three*, Ravensbourne: Team D/E/S Publications.

it now has arrived in its most developed from, is revealed as placing the very conditions of the biophysical world upon which we, and all other sentient beings, most fundamentally depend upon, at risk. Thus as is becoming ever more apparent, in making our world without cognizance of the consequences of our actions we are effectively defuturing ourselves. We are making our/the world gradually inhospitable to ourselves and other species. Here, then, is our equipmental nemesis.

Being in *our world* and being in and of *the world* now exist in a compromised condition (for us). To know this brings the knowers to a recognition of the place of design in its conflicting agency over humanity's futuring and defuturing modes of being-in-the-world. This agency centres on the prefigured abilities (the ontological designing) of 'things' as they design the performative conditions under which designed things are used and the capabilities that users then acquire.

So positioned, there are four features of our world that advance an understanding of the nature of ontological design:

1   The essence of any *thing* brought into being by design is that it will go on designing (no matter if it is a building, chair, automobile, atomic clock, video game, toaster or an air-traffic control system), which of course means that the operative efficacy of the designing ('*thinging*') of all designed things is their ongoing consequences.

2   These consequences can be negative or positive – and in this context, design ethics, as such, becomes futurally decisive.

3   Causally, such consequences (ranging from the microscopic to the global) always impact upon the environments of our being and so upon our biophysical, mental or psycho-social being in the environments in which we inhabit.

4   The ongoing designing of the essence of ontological design means that 'the designed' is always an active agent in time.

There is also one additional and crucial caveat to make: the objective of exploring what design designs is not that all consequences can be foreseen and dealt with. However, the resultant knowledge significantly increases an ability to take responsibility for what design brings into being.

Design in time: a developed reiteration

Not only does design, as understood as the ontologically designed and designing, dynamically exist in the medium of time, but now in its global totality it is acting to negate (defuture) the time of our being (at least if our collective worldly actions continue to be as they are now).

Somehow the most obvious of empirical facts of the auto-destructive nature of our planetary life seem to have escaped the notice of the world's political and economic leadership. Whatever has come to their notice has seemingly been put to one side so they can address pressing shorter-term issues. Even if known, the simple fact is that collectively our species is a finite being on a finite planet, and our planetary existence is dependent upon how we act. The inescapable fact is that if those things we depend upon as a species are increasingly destroyed, then existence will be shortened, but if we sustain these things our duration will be much longer. While short-term imperatives and pragmatic political agendas seem to rule the day, there is clearly a deeper problem. It centres on a crisis of (a lack of) imagination. Put simply, how to get from the unsustainable present to a future condition of being that can be sustained cannot currently be contemplated – it is certainly beyond tokenistic and shallow acts of sustainability that fold back in sustaining the *status quo*. Design, as designing in time, is an absolutely critical futural factor in breaking out of this lacuna.

When making reference to 'design in time' earlier, it was pointed out that it also meant acting with urgency in recognition of global problems that are already present and are all going to get worse as they relationally enfold each other. These are the types of problems already noted: climate change, resource stress, rapid urbanization, inequity, increasing population pressures, rapid technological change, and asymmetrical conflict. But over and above these situations, as was mentioned earlier, biologists are now indicating that humanity is at the beginning of the sixth global extinction event.[5]

Since 1500, more than 320 terrestrial vertebrates have become extinct. Populations of the remaining species show a 25 percent average decline in abundance. The situation is similarly dire for invertebrate animal life. And while previous extinctions have been driven by natural planetary transformations or catastrophic asteroid strikes, the current die-off can be associated to human activity.[6]

Here we remind ourselves that 'everything has its own time' and time should not be confused with the measurement of time. There is no single and overriding definition of time. So said, what both Aristotle and Einstein have

---

[5] Kolbert, *The Sixth Extinction*; see also Bjorn Carey (2014), 'Stanford Biologist Warns of Early Stages of Earth's 6th Mass Extinction', *Stanford News*, 24 July [http://news.stanford.edu/news/2014/july/sixth-mass-extinction-072414.html].
[6] Ibid.

told us is very relevant to our concerns here: 'Time is that in which events occur', as such it is change.

These remarks also return us to acknowledge again our species' being-in-time, with the city as the dominant environmental designing event of our being. In ontologically designing terms, recognizing cities are designed, the future of our species is becoming indivisible from the future of cities.

The city's past is in significant part always prefigurative of its future. However, in the present era, it is not just that design action stands before the critical moment of 'now' but the very condition of criticality of being now is destined to get more critical. Yet an enormous motor force – that of the short termism of 'business-as-usual' together with the human propensity towards 'chronophobia' (the fear of time coupled with the illusion of permanence) – by disposition rather than by conspiracy, acts to conceal this situation.

Identifying a problem is one thing, finding an appropriate and an ethically viable means to intervene to engage it is clearly another.

Elimination by design[7]

Sustainable design has been preoccupied with designing things – sustainable products, technologies, buildings and systems. Far less attention has been given to the retrofitting of existing products and buildings. This activity still represents only a very small market segment, with environmental low impact/high social function retrofits representing an even smaller part of this small market. Meanwhile, the impact of new 'green buildings' on urban unsustainability is negligible. The global reality is that the rate of growth of problems totally marginalizes 'solutions' in areas like waste, energy, building construction, urban population pressure and food security. Metrofitting as idea, practice and ethos, in 'hard' and 'soft' forms, can be inserted into this context, not as a ready-made solution but as an opening into transformative processes and practices, albeit that they are still nascent.

It is also clear that in a 'world of unchecked consumerism', designing and manufacturing 'environmentally improved' versions of existing products or buildings is not going to get anywhere near delivering the conditions for the Sustainment. The sheer number and momentum of unsustainable mass-market products overwhelms impact reductive gains made. Moreover, their performance is relative – none are completely sustain-able. 'Eco, green,

---

[7] The concept was first outlined by Tony Fry (2003) in 'Elimination By Design', *Design Philosophy Papers*, Vol. 1, Issue 4, pp. 145–147.

sustainable' commodities – such things now simply add to 'consumer choice', and in the main, just for the privileged.

Against the backdrop of extant and counter commodification, the design of the nothing of 'elimination design' is now to be considered.

The fundamental proposition of elimination design is very simple – there are huge numbers of unsustainable things that need to be eliminated in order to increase the possibility of humanity acquiring a greater ability to sustain itself. An argument already exists that asserts that products can be replaced by services. But this is only partly true, and services themselves are not without impacts. It is certainly not easy to get people to give up their attachment to things or to the convenience of having them to hand. More essentially, there are things that cannot be replaced by services, and equally there are both products and services that just should not exist because they are dangerous and/or damage the environments of our dependence and thus defuture.

While elimination by design is an enormous challenge, it has an entry point that is graspable and which invites engagement, critical inquiry and development. Elimination design in this context is about the recognition that there are many obvious and concealed things that beg elimination. One can easily list obvious 'dirty high greenhouse gas emitting' industries, stockpiles of nuclear weapons, a vast range of environmental pollutants of air, land and water, carcinogenic and high volatile organic compound construction materials, many health harming processed foods, products that sustain unsustainable practices (like those that are made from timber coming from the world's dwindling old growth and rain forests). But far more problematic are those perhaps less obvious, like excessive leisure technologies that have no relation to actual needs – each of us would have their own favoured list of things like: jet skis, leaf blowers, children's mini trail motorbikes, quad bikes, a whole range of shoddy home exercise equipment, fad kitchen equipment, and short-life plastic garden furniture. Then there is gratuitous travel, reject shop plastic trash (with its accelerated journey to landfill), disposable products like razors, cameras, eating utensils and cheap plastic coat hangers. There is also the huge amount of trash goods and food on supermarket shelves (from high salt, high sugar, high animal fat health harming processed food products to a great array of disposables and bottom of the market household goods). Such lists endlessly run on!

Identification is one thing, effective elimination action is another, especially as the instrumental and political means to take such action would meet massive resistance and, if imposed, would be seen as being a totalitarian measure. But notwithstanding, imposed elimination, at the scale required to reduce the level of impact able to deliver the kind of adjustment is needed. It would mean curtailing individual choice and 'freedom to consume'. Yet such elimination is essential, as sooner or later will be recognized – so how can it happen?

The answer is not easy, and requires leadership and a transformation of everyday practices rather than in most cases alternative products. Such action mostly centres on a reconfiguration of values and what constitutes a quality of life and the creation of the ontological design means to materialize it. This is a challenging design task with almost no material output. To deliver such change by government and voluntary action would be a collective task of enormous proportions. It would require a huge amount of support, research, imagination and applied communication skills – yet it can be seen to be in the realm of the possible. Thus 'elimination design' can be viewed as both an occupation and a praxis.

Design intelligence[8]

The difference between ontological design and design intelligence (use of the term is being distanced from its usage in artificial intelligence and interactive design) is that the former is directive of actions of the subject, while the latter is something inherent within mind. However, both combine as an intrinsic quality of human being (this as prefiguration is directive of the form of what action intends to bring into being).

Design intelligence was once implicit in *habitus* as the underpinning of craft practices, well before design became constituted as a specifically named division of practice and discourse. This was especially evident in the ancient world of the East where the creation of a craft object was understood to have an efficacy and propensity well beyond its discernible function. Likewise, in the West inchoate forms of this intelligence were evident in the practices of designer-makers from the rise of the first machine age in the eighteenth century. What these examples, as two among many, make clear is that craft workers displayed an ability to identify and resolve design problems with very refined tacit knowledge (which is to say with knowledge carried by *habitus* rather than that which was formally acquired and named). Sadly, such proto-design intelligence has faded along with the many craft skills in which it was lodged.[9]

Framed by this history, one observes a lack by designers and design educators, across the entire range of contemporary design practices, to be able to identify the fundamental importance of 'design intelligence'. This lack

---

[8] Tony Fry (2005), 'On Design Intelligence', *Design Philosophy Papers*, Vol. 3, Issue 2, pp. 131–143.
[9] This loss underscores much of what Richard Sennett has to say in *The Craftsman*.

has hindered its development and then communication of its significance to the arts and science communities. This failure, notwithstanding attempts over time, was to bring such knowledge to the notice of both these fields of human endeavour.[10]

Within the context of metrofitting, design intelligence can be defined in, and situated as, a comprehension of design's ontological designing essence and possible consequences from a perspective grounded in an awareness of anthropocentrism. Thus it is predominantly seen as being about understanding what the designed designs in time and place from a position where the ethical implications of an enacted dialectic of Sustainment are grasped.

It is only by having the understanding of this intelligence that the designer/manager/client can get near knowing what they are really doing (and so be in a position to take ethical and socio-environmental responsibility of whatever they bring into being). To understand this does not displace instrumental design, but it does undercut it as a design rationale. Equally, it follows that without design intelligence the ability to recognize the ontological designing consequences of contemporary technologies is very low. Put in the context of remade design education, design intelligence would be elemental to the formation of (a) new *habitus*.

In the defuturing circumstances of structural unsustainability, the oft-heard argument is that the designer simply does not have the power to control what happens to what they bring into being, because they are simply providing a service to a client. This is an indefensible position. It mirrors the economic expediency of the restrictive economy at large and erases any claim to ethical authority. There is no future (for 'us') unless the unsustainable present is sacrificed on the altar of the future. If follows that design intelligence needs to become futurally prefigurative through the process of remaking design practices that are not subordinate to the direction of clients. What this means is the creation of a convergence between design intelligence and design leadership.

Convergence

All the applied practices of metrofitting in combination with the political projects of remaking imagination, unlearning, relearning and new learning converge to constitute that politico-space designated as a borderland – to constitute a situated pro-praxis of a neo-humanities. To do this implies moving

---

[10] See, for example, David Pye (1974), *The Nature and Aesthetics of Design*, London: Barrie & Jenkins; Peter Dormer (1990), *The Meaning of Modern Design*, London: Thames & Hudson; and Sennett, *The Craftsman*.

away from the corpus and divided structures of knowledge provided by the extant academy and towards the acquisition of new understanding and knowledge gained from located projects within a worldly situated setting of praxis. To argue for this change is not to suggest that existing knowledge no longer has a value. Rather, what is of value has to be the result of a selective and critical evaluation and thereafter 'rescued' from its current misplacement. Knowledge, it should be understood, is not outside the efficacy of the dialectic of Sustainment. It is also to argue that in the conditions in which professional practice, architecture and design education and science and the humanities currently find themselves are exposed as being ethically unsupportable. Essentially, this means showing how in many instances they uphold the structural unsustainability of the anthropocentric world of the *status quo*. Gaining and acting upon this knowledge is crucial in the creation of a *habitus* with a praxis wherein there is a convergence between design intelligence and design leadership. Not only does doing this imply a huge project of unlearning, relearning and new learning but also a major exercise of applied post-disciplinary research – all leading to the formation of a new (post) designer (as it is) ontology.

The formation of a politico-space designated as a 'borderland' is significant here (as the space between how things are and how they need to be). It is a space of creative alienation wherein a drive to create a condition of transformation can be nurtured and realized. Metrofitting can be seen as an example of such a space. More than this, and working in the betweenness of the borderland, it is also a space in which the creation of a non-idealized 'convivial culture' can be formed.

Technological unthinking

It is already apparent from diverse sources of research that mobile devices and computer games continue to have an increasing cultural, physical and psycho-social impact upon young people in particular (diminished interpersonal skills, reduced attention spans, obesity and depression are some of the more evident examples of this situation, but there are also far more complex consequences being wrought, including cognitive transformations and the industrialization of memory[11]). Anecdotally, is it not unsettling to be on a bus, in a doctor's waiting room, in an airport lounge or the like with everyone's face glued to their smartphone?

---

[11] See, for example, the account of these changes given by Stiegler, *Technics and Time, 2*.

Here one needs to understand the political configuration of design as an ambiguous figure of power and freedom. Without the power to design in the context of everyday life freedom is delimited, and while the ability to design is an expression of freedom, it can also be used to negate it. This is exactly what happens once a condition of technological dependence has been created (in contradistinction to the promise that whatever the technology on offer, it will bring freedom). The more one sees conformity and compliance, via the embodied instrumentalism of the metaphysical essence of so much of contemporary digital technology, the more one can conclude that freedom to think for oneself is being curtailed negatively.[12] To reiterate, this loss exists at the most fundamental of levels for prefiguration (design at its most basic), which is a feature of humanness. Thus design by technology is ontologically present in an inverted form. In the way it is directing numerous human actions of making, organization and communication, technology has turned from being a formative agent of our becoming to an agent of negation, and at its most extreme may well be 'willing us' towards extinction in the name of a saving power (be it called development, progress or sustainability). In the nihilistic state of helplessness that is increasingly intrinsic to contemporary humanity, salvational power is posited with technology (as an act of faith). As the now naturalized (as the natural artificial) technology, like nature itself, is both wondrous and terrifying.

Design intelligence and conviviality, as a counter ontological designing, can be posed against an absolute, totality negative and fatalistic view of the arrival of technologically delivered oblivion. In a defuturing world, it is only possible to get to the future (with a future for us in our difference) by design. Clearly, such a statement asserts that design remade is of absolutely huge importance to our continued being. Metrofitting expresses this in a very basic way – humanity has to deal with what it has already created. As argued, it does this in the context of cities.

The already designed so often acts reflectively as the prefigurative foundation of designing – the object that is brought to mind is seen as it might be rather than as it currently is. In this respect, design intelligence is a part of intelligence in general, as manifest not only in the prefigurative act but also in the hermeneutic nature of the way of seeing things 'as they might be' – which is to say that things are seen in relation to things which are absent, and as they exist in a field of historically constituted interpretations. Seeing so understood folds into a larger 'reading of the world' whereby an interpretative relation to the designed environment around us (including the semiosphere) is

---

[12] Here one can note that ontologically designed, 'menu options design the restriction of choice and create an illusion of control'.

ontologically directive of our actions. Driving, shopping, dressing, playing tennis, singing and so on are all contextually directed actions based on our knowing of *how to act* in the specific context that we immediately recognize. So again it's affirmed that while we prefigure we are equally prefigured.

Thus in the final analysis, the de-signing of design for the remaking of design, the designing that emanates from the borderland of design, is to create by imagination revitalized, a new foundation of the prefigurative – this of those material and immaterial prefigurative objects that ontologically act as the foundation for an other designing that futures. So said, humanity cannot save itself. Moreover, as has been made clear, design as it is cannot provide a solution to this defuturing situation. There is no solution to hand. But transformative processes can be created that have the potential to change the ontological condition of being out of which our becoming otherwise can be constituted. There is no assured future and all that can be offered and claimed is a process of engagement with the complexity of the defuturing forces of the unsustainable that now dominate the conditions of human existence, including cities.

13

Metrofitting and urban design fictions

Designing trades on fictions: the idea always prefigures the created. Likewise, the idea always has a historicity (an unnarrativized history) that draws on the past (the imaginary of, for instance, an object that draws on others that already exist). Equally, the design idea of what could be also feeds off metaphorical projections – being as free as a bird, travelling through the water like a fish, having the strength of an ox, moving with the speed of the wind. Language is never other than image, and naming is the first act of design.

Fictions, as they are understood in a more conventional literary sense, can and do provide a ground of learning. Critical fictional writing – writing that brings a conceptualized future into confrontation with the conditions of limitation and potential of the present can and does fold into a design process. From the perspective of metrofitting, the aim is now to explore such possibilities.

. . .

While reactive to identified threats, metrofitting requires thinking and projecting with a longer view of the city. For this to be possible, one needs to embrace design fictions grounded in well-researched and clearly communicated determinants and conditions of limitation. A number of narrative tropes already exist able to help realize this objective. Some have already received prior comment (like: the Chinese notion of 'vital nourishment' as an affirmation of convergent means to sustain being). But many other observations can prompt forms of fictional elaboration. For example, the destruction of the illusion of permanence brought to the city, the recognition of the home as a locus of material destruction, and the city as implicated in the end of the distinction between the public and the private as it arrives in the epoch of surveillance and fear. These proto-narratives will be revisited and others developed.

Prospects and possibilities

The expectation is that by 2050 two-thirds of the world's population will live in cities, with this trend continuing onward. How will food production support this population in conditions of increased global warming? Likewise, how will the relation between the city/city-state and the nation-state change (as it certainly will)? What will be the impact of the abandonment of some of the world's major cities? And then, how will significant geopolitical changes and conflicts affect cities? These are a few of the huge questions to be faced.

The point about fictions is not that they are going to disclose the future. They do not provide all-revealing crystal-ball images. Rather, they can and do provide objects of discussion, correction and strategic evaluation. More specifically, fictions can help identify the needs and opportunities for redirective urban action via the visualization of possible urban futures. And while data on existing trends can provide a limited and available way to do this, to think prospects beyond these trends requires more liberated imaginaries. In this setting, metrofitting does not simply ask why and how the city needs to change but what will change look like? How can the city be given 'fitness in time', and how can such change be comprehended and engaged? These questions are all prefigured by another one: what does the city need to be fit for?

Against utopias/dystopias

Uninhabitable and destroyed environments – disasters will arrive in myriad new forms. Clearly, they are going to increase, but not everything is going to get worse. However, 'we' are certain to face a very uneven future.

Humanity now lives beyond the possibility of utopia, and for a great many people the future will be dystopic. However, what many of the privileged will experience will not become a continuation of the conditions they currently enjoy. Large numbers will fall out of privilege. There will be loss and resistance produced once it becomes widely recognized that humanity does not have a future with increased equity – not on the basis of an ideologically expressed imperative. Redistributive justice is the only way to deal with a vast population and finite resources, as well as lessen the prospect of related major global conflict. But this will only happen if such change is seen to be materially in the general interest in the face of a confrontation with felt crisis. In this situation, so contextualized in critical circumstances – ways of life will be unmade and remade. Equally, adaptive change will become a major concern for almost everyone everywhere. 'Deconsumption' (living with less), the democratization of cultural production, and the social reclamation of technology are likely to become future pragmatic imperatives if the global population continues to increase while renewable resources diminish. In these circumstances, a new economic paradigm is not optional but essential and unavoidable. Without fundamental economic change, spatial and socio-economic justice, and the overcoming of a geopolitical propensity towards conflict, humanity will not survive in any recognizable form. The longer the confrontation with the fundamental economic problems of structural sustainability is deferred in critical circumstances, the more serious the defuturing consequences.

Against the backdrop of such prospects, nothing is solid, nothing is certain except the bankruptcy of the economic *status quo* and the politics that supports it. The facticity of the human condition is that there is no viable choice but to act upon a fiction, one generated out of substantial evidence. What such action recognizes is that to wait until one has all the facts is to be doomed. Moreover, to restate, there is very little correspondence between the materiality of our existence and what is perceived to be real. Thus fiction is not an alien frame of reference but an under-recognized norm lodged in all our respective cultures. Plato knew this, as evidenced in his understanding of mediated reality expressed by his allegory of the 'Simile of the Cave' (in *The Republic*). Over the millennia, many other thinkers – of both the East and West – have reiterated the 'truth' of Plato's observation.

Seeing cities, design and fiction

The idea of the city blinds us. The image on 'the screen', projected by the idea 'of the city', is no more than a memory of the fragments that acquire symbolic form and structure. Such fragments become deployed to represent an un-representable whole: the city as a complete image. For the most part, the banality, functionality and hyper-real dislocation of the city – even when seen – goes unnoticed. And beyond this, the city increasingly becomes swallowed up and overtaken by the spatial colonization of the urban conurbation. When viewing the city, does it occur to us that what we are looking at will be displaced, replaced or abandoned? The disjuncture between seeing and the seen demands attention, no matter whom-so-ever we are, not least because the city ever oscillates between what we want to see and what there is to see.

A part of what hides in the way the city is viewed is what actually designed and designs it. So much of what brought it into being to form materializations in space that is rendered and animated in everyday life is not evident in the read meanings of the plan, architecture, streetscapes, open spaces and topography of the city. The marks of political ideology expressed in the social, economic and cultural configuration of urban space, its colour, form, condition and location require to be learnt via a hermeneutics of disclosure. Likewise, at a greater extreme (especially in cities of fear of civil unrest and conflict) there is an increasing trend towards the bio-political management of bodies by the physical management of space, surveillance and policing – all instruments of direction that need bringing to presence. Religion, and religious divides have from almost the very beginning of cities played a significant part in their design. This trend is increasing and moving rather than declining. Finally, the power' of logistics is acknowledged as a designing force – this enfolds everything from the movement of people, goods, materials, power and information: this is all elemental to a bio-political quantified and inscribed urban system.

For 'us', so much of the presence of the city is mute, unseen and unreachable. It does not hide from us; unknowingly, we hide from it (we don't think about things we don't want to know). Design fictions cannot create the power to read the city in contra-ways. They can be given representable narrative and animatory forms, however: pleasure, poverty, cultural diversity, history, expressed craft skills and so on. Fictions do give voice to the city!

In sum, how the city is seen and how its design is comprehended and realized cannot be divorced from the way it is imagined, projected, read and spoken. Fiction is not divided from fact: it ever remains present awaiting exposure. Designing and design fictions are equally implicated in each other. Both invite being brought out of their complicit relation into, as will be seen, a frame of critical inquiry and development. Fictions having a capability of exposing how the city functions, as a designing event, cannot simply be regarded as abstractions.

The ontologically designing essence of the city and the urban environment thus constitutes the everyday life of the changing urban fabric and its ontologies. What this means is a determination of specific forms of 'being-in-the-world' materially, functionally and psychologically. In part, this is evident in particular urbocentric subject positions that manifest a certain 'giving over to the city' that produces conditions of independence and dependence. Of course, the form of such 'giving over' changes significantly within the conditions of varied classes and ethnic groups of the city and the disposition of their individual, gendered and cultural geography. No matter the city, its meaning is never totally unified, yet as we are seeing this difference is never fully reflected in how the city is projected, for this is always mediated by the power that commands the systems of its projection. As a result, all recognition of place is misplaced.

The existential condition of living towards a seemingly uncertain future fraught with dangers is of a scale unique to the present age. Unlike any other time in history, a composite, globally constructed, media-authored 'world picture' arrives as ideologically inflected everywhere. The constant flow of mediated images of and from 'the world' shapes modes of cognition that inflect how the future is perceived. But increasingly this overload of imagery establishes a deepening psychology of unsettlement directive of a condition of nihilism: a sense of helplessness in the face of problems that appear before us. Again the seen turns to the unseen. So ambiguously, according to the individual's state of mind, the city, and the individual's domestic place within it, are framed by the world picture, and so often become a locus of recoil. Consequently, and in general, the home is not only so viewed, while equally being treated as a place of haven in an uncaring world. More than this, it also often becomes a locus of fiction, and thus a place of pretence.

The city, being and time

Ever since its arrival, the city has been a meta-designing force of humanity, as seen in the ways it has functioned as an economic armature, as a place of learning and creative expression and of worship. But conversely, it also seems to have degenerated into a location of oppression and destruction. Yet the city is moving beyond the reach of the contemporary imagination. Certainly, there can be no certainty that the city, as it is, will remain the dominant human habitat. As they get larger, as the risks of environmental disasters, conflicts and pandemics increase, urban populations will become more vulnerable. One catastrophic event striking just one megacity already has the ability to wipe out many millions of people.

Distributed and mobile populations are not in the same danger. The point here is not that this prospect is being posed as a creative, desired or utopian possibility but rather it is a registering that events external to the city will increasingly direct its future form. Now that humanity is living on the edge of a new extinction event, neither our future nor our ways of life are assured. Currently, fictions do not disclose the future lived forms of this fact. While it might be imagined that change will be incremental, with examples like sea level rises as projected over centuries, this may not continue to be the case. Certainly, ecological and climatic systems can reach a tipping point when order breaks down and a condition of system disorder arrives at great speed. In this context, the demand upon design fictions is to imagine the unimaginable, and in so doing take current cultures beyond their limits of vision. The objective of such action is clearly counter to assumptions of the future as either being determined by a single and unstoppable trajectory of technological advancement or the arrival of an apocalyptic ending. What a whole range of indicators around issues of already rehearsed events (like climate change, food security, geopolitical change and conflict, population pressures, resource pressures) all suggest is that human futures will become more plural, diverse and fragmented. Perhaps if this change arrives at its extreme, the very integrity of the species will be challenged. Such a prospect brings to the fore one of the fundamental and unavoidable lessons of biology as learnt from Darwin: if a species cannot adapt, it will not survive.

Design fiction and the imperatives

As should now be clear, design fictions needs to be distinguished from pure fantasy and be grounded in real imperatives as articulated, like responding to climate change, which itself is an interesting example of just how thin the line dividing fact and fiction is (and of information redundancy: rate of climate change is so rapid that whatever one says or writes, as based on available research, will always be out of date).

A plethora of climate change scenarios now exist. The Australian Commonwealth Science and Industry Research Organization (CSIRO) and Bureau of Meteorology told the Australian peoples nation's landmass will warm faster than anywhere else in the world. This could produce as increase of 5°C by 2090 (even with major cuts to greenhouses gases (GHGs), it would rise to just under 3°C).[1] It is already acknowledged that 2°C would create severe problems for the nation. Against this backdrop, the pledge of late 2015 in Paris by all the world's nations to reduce their GHG emissions so that warming would not exceed 2°C is a political fiction: the chance of all these nations complying with their pledges is remote, moreover there could be any number of events and new research findings in coming decades that dramatically change the picture. Already five Pacific Islands have been lost.[2] Yet there is nonetheless an imperative to respond to scenarios as designing contexts.

Kevin Hennessy, a principal research scientist at CSIRO, said that hospitals, transport infrastructure, construction codes, and fire planning should all already start to prepare for these changes.[3] But Hennessy's view is partial. What really are the actual social and cultural adaptive challenges that are required? What really has to be confronted (such as the fact that already high-risk fire areas would become just too dangerous to live in, or that some parts of the nation with more heat and less water would simply have to be abandoned)? In this setting, design fictions provide: a contained means to

---

[1] Oliver Milman (2015), 'Climate Change Will Hit Australia Harder than the Rest of the World, Study Says', *The Guardian*, 27 January [http://www.theguardian.com/environment/2015/jan/26/climate-change-will-hit-australia-harder-than-rest-of-world-study-shows].
[2] Reported by Reuters to the world's press on 10 May 2016.
[3] Ibid.

think the unthinkable so what has to be thought can be enabled; and a means for 'the people' to understand the kind of issues and change they will have to confront in not too many coming generations.

Measured by an individual human lifetime such events may appear to arrive slowly, whereas in evolutionary and geological time they arrive very quickly indeed. Even so, such events have a considerable ability to unsettle: and unsettlement, as indicated, is not an external factor – it's part of the problem and has causal consequences. The fears that unsettle are amplified by the media, which means that unsettlement becomes an enflamed condition of uneven and variable intensity of mind. Yet it is felt, but rarely named or talked about, thus it goes unaddressed and becomes just another contributing factor of nihilism.

Frames of fictions

An opening into four design fictions will be briefly outlined below to give a little more substance to the idea. In some way, they all embrace an ontological understanding of care (which means care as a performative quality of an object, system or process), and the recreation (recoding, remaking, rewriting) of something that already exists.

These fictions will go to the notion of the creation of the city as a structure of care.[4] It does this by undertaking a fictional description of the metabolic reconfiguration of the city that transforms urban functions. Now of course this is a large task that can only be suggestively illustrated: here with four examples able to direct the writing of fictions.

The first example is the creation of an illustrated narrative based on clusters of 'crisis avoidance workscapes' able to create situated demonstration projects showing how a city needs and can adapt to significantly improve its ability to cope with the coming climate, while also making clear what kind of local research is needed to be able to undertake such action, by whom and how. The whole point of the fiction is not to claim the creation of a 'solution' but to make dealing with coming problems present and to counter abstract notions (which have been one of the major problems of the climate change debate). The form of this fiction would be the construction of a 'theatre of crisis on the street' with the content being the theatrical set not the play!

Foodscapes provide example two. The demand for food security means that cities have to become far more horticulturally productive. To do this, the

---

[4] See Martin Heidegger (1988 [1927]), on the care structure in *Being and Time* (trans. John Macquarrie and Edward Robinson), Oxford: Blackwell, Part One, VI, pp. 225–274.

relation between the rural, peri-urban and the urban has to be broken down, with a significant percentage of urban open space being potentially reclaimed and dedicated to food production – gardens could be interconnected, public land resumed, businesses established and workforces trained. Doing so would increase local food production and the food industry. Based on a grid laid over, say, a 'Google' map of a city, food-growing areas could be designated. Thereafter, this map would be able to provide a community with the content of negotiation and consultation with public and private landowners. Such an exercise would not be just about land-use reconfiguration for food production but also be a key resource for education on issues of future food security, adaptive change and community development. Such an exercise could, for example, be narrated, videoed and uploaded to YouTube.

Example three goes to the concept of 'passage' – the city recognized not just as a place of settlement but also as a site of transit, transition and temporary dwelling. Again while this is already the case, this dimension of the life of cities will substantially increase in scale and as a problem, as the numbers of internally displaced people within many nations grow due to climate change and conflict. So what would a transit-organized element of a city look like (either as strip, segment or distributed structure), and then how could it be made to work geographically, socially and economically? The delivery of this fiction could be via a fictional documentary based on a range of interviews with constructed characters: a senior police officer, a social worker, several displaced people plus a range of vox pop street recordings.

The last example considers how the viability of a city requires the development of its social ecologies – this is to say, that the ability of a city to be/become resilient is indivisible from it having functioning communities that can act organizationally before and after a disaster. In a broken world, such developmental action does not happen of itself – it has to be created: the cultural ecologies that constitute and structure power within communities have to be remade. A fiction that makes this very clear would aim to make an important contribution to such a process.

This fiction to be based on a reporter writing a series of articles for an online newspaper following the fate of a farming community of 800 people on the edge of a delta coastal city who have to come to terms with the prospect of salinization of their land as sea levels rise, eventually making it unsuitable for farming. The focus of the story being centred on three of the most affected families and how they managed to join together to face and deal with the problems the situation created – by the planning and creation of an alternative economy based on growing tomatoes hydroponically with the help of community-provided labour, skills, knowledge and loans.

Fictions, writing and remaking

Let's be clear about the position presented: the city is a fiction. This does not mean it does not exist but rather that it is not what it is thought to be as an object and imaginary. Pointing this out is not new.[5]

There is fiction within science and there is science fiction[6] – obviously they are not the same thing, but in both cases science lends authority to fiction. In design and architecture, the same is not true (as the 'science/design fusion' produced by science fiction writer Bruce Stirling evidences[7]). Whereas literacy fiction, drawing its authority from 'creative' practice, so often simply uses the city as a backdrop (as, for example, with Paul Auster's *The New York Trilogy*, 1985) or as a dramatic stage (as employed by Carlos Ruis Zafón in *The Shadow of the Wind*, 2005)[8]. In contrast, when a design fiction arrives (like, for instance, with Buckminster Fuller's ideas for an imaginary city), cultural questions evaporate and the technological character of the project situates it as an object of scientific evaluation. The attempt to counter this propensity by casting experimental design within the realm of neo-avant-garde art practice aesthetically does not solve the problem of cultural paucity, it just smothers critical content.

The discourse of design fictions is still in the making and likewise the way the future is now being thought and brought to presence is changing. This is clear in a number of recent texts, for example:

> . . . a shift in science fictional representations in text and film, a temporal relocation in which scenarios imagine not the future but our own present as apocalyptic. Whereas the classical literary device of science fiction derives its estrangement effect from the way it utilizes future scenarios as an indirect commentary upon the present, these texts 'represent the apocalypse as already happening, unnoticed or unrecognized, within the contemporary'.[9]

---

[5] It was, for example, the basis of discussion at 'Public Space: A Philosophical Idea of the City', a conference led by Josep Ramoneda at Yale University in 2003.

[6] The science/fiction relation is made very clear by Isabelle Stengers: 'In the perspective I am constructing, it is the obviousness of this power of fiction that constitutes not only the "terrain of invention" for modern science, but also *the means by which it will stabilize itself so as to better detach itself from it.*' Isabelle Stengers (2000), *The Invention of Modern Science* (trans. Daniel. W. Smith), Minneapolis, MN: University of Minnesota Press, p. 79.

[7] Bruce Stirling (2005), *Shaping Things*, Cambridge, MA: MIT Press.

[8] Paul Auster (1985), *The New York Trilogy*, London: Faber & Faber; Carlos Ruis Zafón (2005), *The Shadow of the Wind*, London: Penguin.

[9] Cunningham, D. and A. Warwick (2013), 'Unnoticed Apocalypse: The Science Fiction Politics of Urban Crisis', *City*, Vol. 17, No. 4, p. 434 cited by Nasser Abourahme (2014), 'Ruinous City, Ruinous Time', *City*, Vol. 18, Nos. 4/5, pp. 577–582.

Yet against this picture of the 'present as ruined time', the future can be seen as already tainted (for what the past has already thrown into it means it also is in part ruined).[10] So contextualized, design can nonetheless provide rich stories able to tell a city's defuturing history and its futural projection – both demanding critical interrogation. These stories of course should not, and cannot, be either ungrounded dystopic nightmares or utopian dreams. Rather, what they offer are realistic ways to think how to engage situated, existing and coming challenges of the age. Here specific issues already commented upon, like social ecology, resilience and conviviality, invite becoming employed as a basis for storytelling within an elaboration of city futures. Such stories have the potential to provide a fertile terrain of fictional expositions able to rework the very basis of what a city is as a 'signscape', or as a pedagogic domain in which new modes of earthly habitation can be researched, explored and learnt.[11]

Certainly, the leap that design fictions make can go beyond seeing cities as they are: as dysfunctional wastelands, historical tourist attractors, pleasure playgrounds, industrial centres, financial hubs, hives of poverty, squalor and crime, or movie-land techno-futuristic fantasy lands. Such thinking can obviously go to existing cities and their transformation or to the new. Metrofitting's aim is to be prefiguratively developed in, and part of, the response to this situation in fiction and in fact.

---

[10] David Scott (2014), *Omens of Adversity: Tragedy, Time, Memory, Justice*, Durham, NC: Duke University Press, p. 12.
[11] Fry, *City Futures in the Age of a Changing Climate*.

14

Space, time, dwelling and movement

Climate change will alter how cities are viewed in the coming decades. Some that are currently desirable to live in will not remain, so public space may radically change, extreme weather could make damage to building stock a frequent occurrence, and adaptive action to deal with, for example, storms, rising sea levels and heat will become very visible. Abandoned coastal villages, towns and cities will become commonplace along those coastlines of the world at risk from sea level rises (an impact projected to eventually displace between 200 and 700 million people according to varied sources), which will have huge economic, social and psychological consequences for entire populations. Any sense that people have that cities are things of permanence will go.

It follows that such circumstances will force an enormous number of people to become more mobile, less settled and increasingly nomadic, meaning many cities will have to deal with very large transitory populations: a situation the beginning of which is already very evident. Thus the idea and reality of totally or partially moving existing cities (materially, socio-culturally and economically), and the creation of cities specifically designed to move, will eventually become widely accepted. Many of those other forces of transformation that have been explored over previous chapters, such as unchecked urbanization, rapid technological change, conflict and food security, will contribute to the changing perceptions of the character, form and fate of cities.

As is about to be elaborated, and at the most profound level, situations are starting to unfold, being seen and experienced that will modify ways that human beings negotiate space and time. To support this claim, four indicators of change will be registered.

The re-marking of space and ways it is understood

We humans make a space for ourselves by the selection and designation of symbolic boundary markers, the drawing of lines in law and on the land, the building of fences or walls and so on, all of which position ourselves in striated space. Yet we originally came from, and moved out of, smooth space: plains, grasslands, deserts, hillsides, mountain regions, forests, marshes and coastlines. As stated by Gilles Deleuze and Félix Guattari, the action of passing into and staying in spaces of containment within cities changed us ontologically, and continues to do so.[1] The breaking of the limit of the striated is an act towards spatial freedom, a freedom to move beyond the political actions of constraint coming from the imposition of law that brings (nomos) order to space.[2] In its formation within the striated containment of our becoming, the act of the occupation of space (prefigured by an act of interpretation that deems it available to be occupied) ruptures our 'being in the environment' from its/our animality. As such, it was an ur-moment – a moment prior to our moment of becoming, out of which we arrived (and into which 'we' can, and sometimes do, fall back). This is a long forgotten moment about which Martin Heidegger could say that 'there is no space without human beings' for the 'animal does not experience space'.[3] Rather, for the animal space is simply whatever constitutes its environment. The key point underlying these observations is that we humans do not occupy space naturally and that space is not a fixed empirical fact but a plural and variable social construction. More specifically, our making and placement of things in a place actually constitutes the making of space by things[4] – there cannot be space without an object in 'it' (be it a park bench or a planet). By implication, there is no such thing as empty space.

Reconfigured notions of 'the event' of space and the city

As is now evident, space does not arrive of itself. It requires an idea and act of production by a subject whereby it is perceived to be via an interpretative

---

[1] Deleuze and Guattari, A Thousand Plateaus, pp. 474–500.
[2] This relation is outlined in detail by Claudio Minca (2011) in his chapter 'The Question of Spatial Ontology', in Stephen Legg (ed.), Spatiality, Sovereignty and Carl Schmitt, London: Routledge, p. 169.
[3] Zollikon Seminar 19/16. Of course, there is no binary relation between us and animals for while we become human we biologically remain animal.
[4] Heidegger, 'Building, Dwelling, Thinking', in Poetry, Language, Thought; see also Andrew J. Mitchell (2010), Heidegger Among the Sculptors, Stanford, CA: Stanford University Press.

encounter with a located object/objectified condition that makes space itself present. This making present means space exists by virtue of the events out of which it arrives, thus it only exists by virtue of being in the company of time (hence 'time-space'). While time and space are not the same they are interdependent – they have 'nothing in common as a unity', rather what they share is 'what brings them to one'.[5] All questions concerning space and time remain unanswerable, and even un-askable, as long as space and time are not grasped within 'time-space'.[6]

Nothing remains the same, so everything changes. Our world-space is thus grounded in proximity to the near and the far as experiential and perceptual.[7] World-space should not be confused with global space, which is purely a political construction. All of these characterizations of space need to be differentiated from notions of it being measured and quantified.

Now in common with all concepts, there is no philosophical meta-discourse able to be appealed to in order to provide a resolution of theoretical difference. Neither can there be anything other than an anthropocentric view. What, however, can be acknowledged is that there are experiential differences in the encounter of space that carry epistemologies with them that ensure theoretical contestation within and beyond the Eurocentric. Obviously, what has been said here is positioned by these remarks.

Addressing Western philosophy, Yoko Arisaka argues that there are four dominant theories of space – the absolutist (where it has an independent existence and within which all things are contained), the relational (whereby space is not independent of things), the Kantian (deeming it *a priori* and subjective), and the Heideggerian (who after Kant acknowledges 'the human character of space as a condition of experience' but rejects it 'as an *a priori* feature of mind' in favour of seeing it as directly connected to 'our practical involvement in the world').[8] Our spatial modes of 'being-in-the-world' are equiprimordial – we are always among and in relation to things but, as has been recognized, things also exist in relation to us. Ontologically, in our actions in the company of objects, we design and make them as specific things in place – thus we make, and are in part made by, assemblages of things in space.

What has just been outlined, as linked to time of our being, brings with it three modifications: our being in the city, space itself and 'the world' (as the situated locus of our being). What this means, as we shall see, is that these three views of conditions of being are layers of the same.

---

[5] Heidegger, *Contributions to Philosophy*, p. 268.
[6] Ibid., p. 270.
[7] Ibid., p. 451.
[8] Yoko Arisaka (1995), 'On Heidegger's Theory of Space: A Critique of Dreyfus', *Inquiry*, Vol. 38, No. 4, pp. 455–456.

Being in the city

Where is it that one *actually* is?

We urban dwellers live among the visible and invisible, the interwoven imaginary and the real. Buried pipes and electronic infrastructures all go unseen, as does a great deal of inequity, suffering, pleasure, labour, exploitation and pain (unseeing here being a consequence of what is hidden from view and what is deliberately ignored). And then there is the waste, excess and uncaring concealed by beautiful façades. We may live in a neighbourhood that watches or is watched; our locus may be fixed in place or mobile. We perhaps believe we belong to where we are, or we may long to be somewhere else. We can view our city with pride, interest or regard it with contempt. Whatever and however we see it, we do so with a spatial imagination now dominantly born of the city yet corrupted by the world of which it and we are a part.

Beyond the visible urban fabric, beyond place and location, are the systems that interlace the city and globally connect it. Here we find those communication networks of finance and commerce, surveillance, crime, sociality, information and entertainment. Along with them is another complexity of: transport systems, goods and services, corporations, mobile labour, migration. Life in such an environment results in our being simultaneously in the here and elsewhere. As such, we exist as desevered, whereby the near, close and far all no longer exist in anything like a legible geometry or geography. Now, to be in the city (however understood) is to be emplaced and displaced as the hyper-real and connected constitute it as, as said, the here and the elsewhere

Being in space and the space of being

The implication of what has been outlined is that contemporary urban subjects exist in a fracture-zone – which is to say that they are disseminated across dislocated spaces rather than simply being in a collective space. Thus wherever they are, they are also somewhere else: they are disconnected even when connected. This is again to say that the smartphone, tablet, computer via Internet connectedness all combine to produce a geography of deseverence. Identity has now become a menu item selected according to which space the subject posits its self within. So while Heidegger tells us that only human beings have space and that all other beings only have environments, what 'we' now have (by degree according to our global circumstances) is the experience of multivalent space that is temporally co-existent.[9]

---

[9] Martin Heidegger, 'Building, Dwelling, Thinking', in *Poetry, Language, Thought*.

What is also becoming increasingly evident is that the technological ontological transformation of our 'being in space' remains poorly understood, while at the same time it is moving into a higher register of complexity as artificial intelligence (AI) becomes more pervasive and uncritically embraced. For example, already in the wealthier cities space is becoming organized into managed zones (via automated systems of flows of traffic, soon to be extended by driverless vehicles, robotic delivery services and even embodied tracking communication[10]) wherein the technological construction of space will dis-place the social construction of space, with the result that the subject in space becomes objectified as that to be tracked, positioned or moved.[11] Such 'innovation' layers onto the city of fully automated factories, warehouses, driverless vehicles, and virtual holographic on-line educational institutions powered by learning machines. What is already being constituted is post-human space in which the distance between human biology, technology, idea, fiction and fact ever diminishes.

Interestingly, the dangers of this urban technosphere link to the dangers now being recognized of globally high-profile technology, as advocated by the astrophysicist Stephen Hawking and by representatives of the digital technology industry such as Microsoft's Bill Gates.[12] They are voicing the now growing fear that AI poses an increasing threat to human agency. Their concerns transpose to the immaterialized of the city as a depopulated socio-cultural and economic/political structure.

When climate change makes the external environment increasingly unpleasant, as it will, technology will become ever more pervasive. The privileged are likely to withdraw further into the technosphere, whereas vast numbers of the under-privileged will be abandoned to their environmental fate. If such a scenario is realized, and the chances that it will are very high, it will again have an enormous impact on the psychology of our species, together with convergent forces of change produced by climate change that create new and deeper divisions between peoples.

---

[10] Tracker chips are already being implanted in dogs worldwide and in small numbers of mostly wealthy people in countries where hostage taking is commonplace.

[11] The ambition expressed by AI extremism, voiced by supporters of 'singularity', is that it becomes a regime of total control. Singularity supporters, at the most fanatical end, assert that the human brain can and will eventually be downloaded and the body dispensed with. However, between the state of the art of AI now and crazy AI futurism is a developmental impetus, supported by corporations like Intel, Google and Apple, that is giving the advance of the technology its head ('because they can') without having any idea of possible impacts. The best known promoter of singularity is Google's chief engineer Ray Kurzweil [http://www.kurzweilai.net/]; see also the Singularity University [https://su.org/] (Kurzweil being one of its founders).

[12] See, for example, http://www.huffingtonpost.com/james-barrat/hawking-gates-artificial-intelligence_b_7008706.html.

Being-in-the-world now

Futurally, our very being-in-the-world is at stake as a result of what we humans do, have become and are becoming. Restating, effectively by dint of our numbers and actions, the world of our dependence is being put at risk. We humans forget, or have never been aware, that our familiar world environmentally arrived out of one of the many climatic and geological traumatic events our planet has undergone – most of which are beyond the reach of our imagination and representational capability. That condition we take to be normality is but a passing moment of relative tranquility between past and future trauma. Against this background, the implications of our actions *en masse* have made our conditions of existence far more fragile. One thing is certain: no matter what we do or don't do, planet Earth will endure in some form long after our species has disappeared. The mode of our being-in-the-world is now a de-naturalized condition of active anthropocentric construction, and as has been made very clear, our world-making has turned to unmaking – this as a result of a past and unwitting creation of 'structural unsustainability' in combination with a contemporary myopia towards this defuturing situation.

The making of the world of human fabrication was obviously taken well beyond material appropriation and artifice – it became cultural as well as material. At the most basic, this is evident in the language, classification and bringing to presence of 'what ontically is' (as knowledge, image, meaning and posited values). Remembering, taking such world-making action, in its many varied forms, equally made us (individually and collectively): our feelings, psyches, traditions, ways of life, practices of exchange and so on. It follows that being-in-the-world was also, and still is, the making of our own fate in the company of other animate and inanimate beings. Yet our ability as a species to actually see the consequences of what we are doing remains extremely limited.

It is crucial to recognize that our being-in-the-world is equally a being in difference. We are not one. The very notion of 'the one' (the human) was an imposition of modernity over many indigenous designations of species being. Eurocentrically inculcated humans are predominantly disconnected from the natural environment (in large part by cities), whereas many indigenous cultures see themselves as organically connected rather than as individuated. It follows that 'their' being-in-the-world and 'being in space' is not the same as 'ours'. And as the comment on modernity suggests, colonialism made major efforts to destroy the difference of 'others', whereas one of the objectives of the Sustainment is to work towards creating, and learning from, 'commonality in difference'. No matter who we are, what we believe or our world view, we all need to be sustained – as such, it becomes the ground, a place between, a borderland, upon which to build mutual respect, reciprocal learning, and conditions of exchange that address inequity.

To be present is 'to be' in space and time. To take action, as with metrofitting, is to be involved in and potentially transformative of each of these mediums of our existence. It follows that if our disposition towards space changes, so equally does our being in time: this to be addressed from the remaining vantage points.

Matter in time

Matter marks time as expressed in signs of change, which design and architecture romantically celebrate as patina, the distressed and the ruin, but equally such marks also sanction the erasure of matter and time via destruction and demolition (often to make way for contemporary signature architectural structures)[13].

While there are structures that are unsafe, unusable and beyond repair, and thus cannot be saved, the ethos of metrofitting, at its most basic material level, is that if a structure can be economically repaired it should be (this notion of economic being understood in the context here as a clear end-use rather than as an abstract claim). Even if the structure is beyond repair, the recovery of materials for reuse has to be seen as an action in time, and therefore an act of communication against the erasure of the past in an age of accelerated change (which itself equates to an increase in the speed of the destruction of time). The use of reused materials may or may not be driven by an aesthetic, but its primary function (beyond the structural) needs to be seen as resistance against forgetting fundamental material value(s).

Currently, arguments for keeping the old are too restrictive and aesthetically taste-given – heritage, historic interest and conservation being cases in point. What gets overlooked is the utility and significance of memory as an articulated time-space attachment. This in turn links to conjuncturally situated architecture – an architecture of place that denotes locus. By implication, the erasure of memory in this context is the erasure of the specificity of space (place). This in turn folds back into the old being removed to make space for a placeless hyper-reality of the same.

While no structure can claim to be absolutely permanent, almost all of those now built have a market designated design life (say 50–80 years) that *de facto* means they are temporary. In contrast, many buildings built as temporary (like those in refugee camps) are now destined to become semi-permanent (which history suggests looks like 50 years).

---

[13] As the slogan of the Deen Brothers, an infamous Brisbane demolition company, put it: 'all we leave are the memories'.

Unquestionably, what is not being grasped and employed by architects is the imperative of building in time – that is, in the medium of time for the time in which we live, which in turn means *building in the recognition of the time of earthly dwelling* (a recognition that totally revalorizes materials and their use). More prosaically, how the 'design life' of structures is now often thought and approached is completely discredited by developer economics, as it is based on building turnover and redevelopment. Such development is effectively a crime of capital against the future.

Time, city and world

There is no reducible and singular definition of time. What so far has been dominantly employed in this text is a phenomenological understanding: time as event and change. Classical time was divided between *Cronos* (a formal, eternal and universal understanding of time) and *Kairos* (realized and fulfilled time). The nature of time that we take as the familiar and the everyday was understood by Heidegger to be the existential condition into which we have all 'fallen'[14] – we share this along with the notion of time as measure. He also observed, following Aristotle, that 'things have their own time', which is but another way of saying all things exist in a condition of differential change. In all but its abstracted and measured characterizations, time is discontinuous. We know this existentially: events of the same duration are experienced as being of variable length of time according to the state of mind of the subject and the interruptions and distractions of the moment.

Seeing things in time, not least cities, is to view objects in a passage of events that at best we can only in part discern. What we do know is that those structures that constitute the material fabric of the city came into being at a particular moment and that they all travel to a moment of eventual destruction assured by change. Overlaid on this mode of seeing is the imposition of political time whereby the nature and objective of change is imposed. In the city, nothing is left to its own time. All human interventions are within time-space. What such interventions do is to create an historical rupture that breaks historical continuity. This produces a spacing and disjuncture in how being-in-the-world, at any particular moment, is experienced. As a result, what is taken for granted goes unseen, and so is not available for critical engagement.[15] As can be learnt from Walter Benjamin, whenever one views the past (or projects one's mind into the future) a political position of sight becomes adopted in the present.

---

[14] Martin Heidegger (1992 [1979]), *History of the Concept of Time* (trans. Theodore Kisiel), Bloomington, IN: Indiana University Press, p. 320.
[15] See Lindross, *Now-Time/Image-Space*, p. 18.

These considerations of time are in no way incidental to our concern with design and metrofitting – which is centrally about making change to make time (as qualified). Action for the Sustainment is action in the medium of time-space. Making time here denotes a consciously understood human action in the medium of time and in the spatial specificity of place. This in the recognition that design, architecture and planning have fundamentally failed to pay sufficient attention to time because of the power of market forces, and a lack of acknowledgement that whatsoever is brought into being exists in time-space. These defuturing practices continue on in time and as such have designing, environmental and socio-cultural consequences that are mostly overlooked, and thus are not taken responsibility for and therefore cannot be futural.

The time of process is 'the always now (*jeztzeit*)' – this is to acknowledge that neither the past nor the future can be occupied. 'Now' is thus always that border-time of the eternal in-betweenness dividing the historical from nothingness – yet the past is constantly being draw into the present with the result that 'now' becomes re-animated. Events do not just end: structures may be completed but they are not finished. Notwithstanding how we view the city, it exists and functions in the now. It operates in a regime of time-space that designing and regulatory practices do not sufficiently recognize, make present or take cognizance of. A part of the agenda of metrofitting has to be to address this problem within the wider context of seeing the city. For action on the city to be directed towards sustaining, the city has to be seen differently – this via a seeing intrinsic to metrofitting.

As Henri Lefebvre pointed out, modernity aimed 'to make time . . . vanish from social space' and reduce it to that 'recorded solely on measuring instruments'.[16] The intent was to neutralize time and strip it of its difference. Yet cities, like trees, flowers and people have their own time. Metrofitting placed in this context is action that recovers 'the time of difference' and its existential comprehension through the experience of 'being-in-the-world'. Such time is not amenable to being controlled by any order or understanding of chronological time.

---

[16] Henri Lefebvre (1991 [1974]), *The Production of Space* (transd Donald Nicholson-Smith), Oxford: Blackwell, p. 95.

15

Metrofitting and being
in the city

*Behold, Damascus is taken away from being a city, and it shall be
a ruinous heap.*

ISAIAH 17.1 (KING JAMES BIBLE)

Metrofitting is a diverse and necessarily enduring project of urban transformation that acknowledges the negative environmental impacts of unchecked urbanization and urban dysfunction, and the associated economic and psycho-social problems, all of which make a very significant contribution to global unsustainability.

Like the city itself, metrofitting represents a broad range of instrumental, economic, socio-cultural and political activities that cannot be reduced to a single form or practice. By implication, metrofitting action is not just the responsibility of the state, or of non-government organizations, the private sector and individuals, for it spans the entire gamut of the structures of the formation and conduct of contemporary urban life. This action has no specific aesthetic, nor is it something to be created by any specialist industry, profession or practice. Equally, it is no mere pragmatic viewable as a bricolage of base forms of human survival.

Rather, metrofitting invites being *thought* as a field of action directed towards new modes of earthly collective habitation informed in ways that recognize a critical assembly of material practices, imperatives, understandings and responsibilities that draw on the analytic, conceptual, political, economic and organizational domains of knowledge. This intellectual agenda is a key element in its praxis. While all this activity can start from a very modest beginning, it is essential that it is understood as an accumulative and continuous process grounded in building teams, new knowledge, capability and efficacy over time. As a major contribution to advance the Sustainment, metrofitting has no end point (for the propensity towards the unsustainable is unceasing). In this respect, metrofitting begs to be seen as an integral feature of being futural. As such, it is not a matter of choice.

Analytically, the specific risks, challenges and potentials of any particular urban environment, across every aspect of its life and function, need to be: (i) studied comprehensively, (ii) thoroughly understood and (iii) well documented. All other actions stand on the adequacy of these three activities – including instigating a new political order better able to deal with the relational complexity of overcoming a dysfunctional urban metabolism. Obviously, the intellectual capacity to undertake this action is not likely to be readily at hand. It has to be created. Without this level of knowledge, transformative action will be rendered impossible because what requires to be transformed has not been adequately grasped. It thereafter follows that once metrofitting begins, it does so on the basis of the situated knowledge, a rigorous conceptual framework and the organizational leadership capability essential to bridge it to the project of the Sustainment. Doing this means going well beyond existing ways of dealing with the unsustainable urban fabric and the modalities of life of existing cities, including addressing the inequity of cities – most evident in the informal sector and the social dysfunction and distress these conditions create.

As has been argued at length, establishing a convivial culture able to adopt, lead and deliver metrofitting in action is crucial: among this in the first instance is the establishment of an extremely well informed cadre working to develop metrofitting – as outlined as idea, theory, practices and thus praxis. Without this change culture, the generalization of action to wider communities is just not possible. The development of this culture requires being supported and informed by well distributed arguments that clearly critique the madness of unconstrained material accumulation, environmental and social destruction, inequity and the proliferation of global asymmetrical conflict.

Here it is worth reiterating a point made when introducing this book:

Notwithstanding the urgency of the situation, gaining a comprehensive understanding of metrofitting, and then instigating a significant level of action globally are going to take time (several decades). We need to make it extremely clear that our ambition is to assist in the development of this understanding and informed action.

Being in the City

How might metrofitting alter being in the city? Naturally, any answer to this question has to realize that such conditions of being are enormously varied. Having said this, there are two general trends and a few observations to register. While these trends present massive challenges, they nonetheless invite consideration as positive scenarios.

Trend one goes to a fundamental reconfiguration of the way of life of the privileged (defined as a way of life that goes well beyond having adequate food, shelter and a liveable wage), as it fuels destruction by excess. Downsizing excess to create a condition of lived spatial and material modesty has to become a normative basis of social and spatial justice. This vital and extremely tough metrofitting task indicates the enormous scale of the challenge of reconfiguring the indivisible relation between design, economic and social action. Central to this action is countering the loss of 'standards of living' of the privileged by improvements in the quality of their life (as previously discussed in the context of enhanced modes of cultural production, but additionally by enhanced modes of sociality/conviviality). Such action – which clearly can take multiple forms – requires being seen as essential and directed to advance the global equity upon which the Sustainment depends. As such, it has to be structurally socio-economically inscribed, and thereby removed from the realm of 'consumer choice'.

Trend two goes to the counter context of the first: an engagement with the conditions of the poor. Their conditions require to be up-scaled to a condition of material modesty, to counter the destructive force of poverty in which they live (with its lack of ability to renew). For the poor, culturally productive practices need to be recovered and revitalized as well as newly created.

Both trends would obviously take on hugely different forms in different contexts, but even so each would lead to widespread changes in everyday public life wherein being in the city would be a far more active process of constant remaking. Such politically challenging action cannot arrive by yet more vacuous gesturalism based on goal setting, guidelines and development targets. Rather, it needs to centre on actually undertaking specific projects of material, socio-cultural, environmental and economic change that are demonstrably shown to be major employment generative and transformative modes of being. This is to indicate that metrofitting is not something to be done for the urban population but something that has to be done with and by them. Public life here begs to be understood as equally as much a project of social reconstruction as it is one of material transformation. Within this project, the marginalized and non-Western cultures have a great deal to contribute, and this requires recognition.

Even from these brief remarks, 'being in the city' can be discerned as potentially becoming very different in the future from what it is now. But this prospect can go two ways: towards the enormous task of transformation implicit in the ways outlined; or towards dysfunction and dystopic breakdown leading to a non-retrievable and disastrous condition of suffering, including a collapse of many of the functional aspects of everyday life (this trend already is evident in those cities suffering massive inequality and infrastructure systems failure).

The politics of change indicated to deal with these situations will not be voluntarist or arrive via currently extant democratic process. Rather, it will arrive under 'a state of emergency' that imposes limits and conditions of opportunity. This notion of imposition has a nasty history that spans dictatorship, and the excesses of fascism plus the more recent suspension of the rule of law by executive powers centring on an abandonment of compliance with *habeas corpus* (the requirement of bringing 'the body' of an accused before a court or judge). 'Rendition' and detention without trial at Guantánamo Bay by the US government are recent examples of such action.[1] What doing this rests upon is a suspension of the judicial order by the executive, as Giorgio Agamben has pointed out.[2]

While such a state of emergency, deemed 'a state of exception' (as classically defined by Carl Schmitt as whomsoever has absolute power is sovereign and the sovereign is 'he who decides on the state of exception'),[3] has been enacted now by numerous regimes, it cannot be assigned to the past. It still remains a critical issue of concern in relation to the present and future of state power. The context of such concern is that under the seeming rule of democracy, 'freedoms' are being eroded in the name of its protection. As we saw in an earlier chapter, this is already slowly happening in late modern society with surveillance, in overt and covert forms, becoming a structural feature of everyday life for everyone under the threat (and guise) of terrorism.

In contrast, a 'state of emergency' is now being evoked in the conditions of a major disaster (psycho-social, economic and environmental) – such a situation would arrive with a loss of certain freedoms and the enactment of material restrictions is almost always met with resigned acceptance and mild resistance. To counter this, a massive campaign to communicate the imperative to which to respond would be essential. A global disaster has already arrived: our lives and the conditions of dependence (life as we know it) are in grave danger. From the measure of a human life, the disaster is slow but from a geological-biophysical perspective it is rapid. The imperative of the Sustainment has to be directive of what freedoms are lost and given. To deny this is to feed crisis by a wilful refusal of recognition and to aggravate that 'crisis of crisis' that currently denotes the human condition. Clearly, the key

---

[1] On 13 November 2001, the president of the United States 'authorized the "indefinite detention" and trial by military commissions (not to be confused with the military tribunals provided for by the law of war)'. Cited by Giorgio Agamben (2005), *State of Exception* (trans. Kevin Attell), Chicago, IL: University of Chicago Press, p. 3.

[2] Ibid., p. 33.

[3] Ibid., p. 1.

issue is how to ensure a state of emergency arrives with an adherence to social justice. Democratic nations at war have shown this to be possible.

Notwithstanding the unfolding of events in coming decades, what is now unavoidable is that humanity is travelling towards hugely complex political and legal problems that no government or transnational organization currently appears to be facing, at least publically. At its most basic, the indicated actual and emergent state of the world environmentally and geopolitically seems to be beyond the capacity of contemporary political paradigms to deal with. Neither nations nor transnational organizations have the means (and maybe the insight) to establish a ground of commonality. One of the reasons for this is that governments across the entire political spectrum, from China to the United States, depend on maintaining a trajectory of consumer-led economic growth. Certainly, it is also extremely doubtful, at least in democratic nations, that electorates are going to vote for a reduced standard of living or the equally needed redistribution of wealth that now transcends any ideological project, yet taking such action now would be purely pragmatic. Thus the future – our species' future – is being sacrificed for the present.

As made clear earlier: an ever-growing profligate human population on a planet of finite resources is a condition of impossibility. To act as if this were not the case is a path to an assured disaster. Draconian immigration controls, as they are eroding the freedom of movement for many people globally, coupled with the growing numbers of refugees and internally displaced people in the world sets the scene of this impending drama. Increasingly, 'freedom' is becoming reduced to 'the freedom to consume', but under global conditions where a crisis of consumption is certain. If a freedom to life is to be secured, then it is this freedom that more than any other needs to be curtailed.

Recasting the two scenarios already briefly rehearsed, there are two options. The first is a needed realignment of human conduct to start to bring it into line with the imperative of the Sustainment. The second is simply to do nothing and let the unsustainable defuturing forces of the *status quo* run their course. In both cases, the end point (which obviously will be of the same moment) is the same: crisis. In the first scenario, the crisis is acknowledged and met by effective political management directing transformative action. In the second scenario, crisis is ignored (or sought to be concealed by tokenistic measures) with apocalyptic consequences beyond any form of political control. That the scale of the challenge presented by the proposed actions seems overwhelming is not an argument for not rising to it.

The absolute objective of metrofitting is to contribute to averting scenario two while being part of those activities working towards the realization of scenario one. But, as indicated, this cannot happen unless very substantial political change occurs. Reference to the need for a new political imaginary has been one key change factor – as acknowledged in an earlier chapter. But as indicated, this correspondingly heightens the problem of overcoming the politics of the *status quo*. Now obviously resolving this problem has to be incorporated into the very challenge of creating a new political imagination itself. New concepts of political theory, action and agency are thus integral to this task. Certainly, elaborating this task is well beyond the capability of this text, although it has in part commenced elsewhere.[4] Linking the imperative of a new political imagination to the implications of a non-voluntarist politics of change, enacted under a recast 'state of exception', can make the problems of framing imposed limits clearer. Saying this brings us into direct confrontation with the issue of dictatorship, as a contemporary global political reality and as a complex historically constituted phenomenon.

Dictatorship has and does take on various forms: there is the sovereign king or queen who inherits or claims full dictatorial power; the sole dictator heading the single state political party; or a state where all parties but the ruling party are emasculated. Sovereign dictatorship is the exercise of absolute and unlimited power no matter whomsoever exercises that power (by implication 'the people' are completely powerless), whereas the assumption of dictatorial power during a condition of crisis – a state of exception – is a commissary dictatorship. Carl Schmitt provides a good summary of what this dictatorship actually is:

Dictatorship is the exercise of state power freed from any legal restrictions, for the purpose of resolving abnormal situations – in particular situations of war and rebellion. Hence two decisive elements for the concept of dictatorship are on the one hand the idea of a normal situation that the dictatorship restores or establishes, and on the other the idea that, in the event of an abnormal situation, certain legal barriers are suspended in favour of resolving the situation through dictatorship.[5]

'Democratic' states are not untouched by the problem of dictatorship – they have the seed of it within them – this as 'constitutional dictatorship' where in a 'time of crisis' democratic rule is modified or suspended as 'a state of exception' until 'normality' is restored. This is clearly an opening into the needed condition of limitation indicated, but it is not sufficient unless the 'exception' is understood in time and any notion of return to a condition of normality is removed. In truth, it is likely that the emergency is now the normal (continuing critical) human condition for the imaginable future. Thus all

---

[4] Fry, *Design as Politics*.
[5] Carl Schmitt (2014), *Dictatorship* (trans. Michael Hoelzl and Graham Wood), Oxford: Polity Press, p. xxiii.

freedoms would be subordinate to the dictatorship of Sustainment and in need, therefore, of being clearly thought out and articulated within its theoretical/intellectual remit of the problematic of control. These matters again cast us back into complexity, one that Carl Schmitt partly illuminates by pointing out the plural character of dictatorship.[6]

Constitutional dictatorship has become an applied principle of constitutional governments and comes with the obvious danger of slippage from a temporary act to a permanent condition.[7]

The debate of most interest to our concern with metrofitting and the Sustainment centres on the relation of two things: the notion of the dictatorship of an imperative; and the question of acting in response to a specific basis of 'need' (to be).

As stated, the imperative of the Sustainment is absolute, for without securing the conditions upon which we humans depend, we have nothing. To appropriately further position the significance of this statement requires to put it alongside the rule of law. Freedom in modern democratic societies is conditional and delimited – it is a relative condition under the law. The limits of the law create a relative freedom – absolute freedom, evoking the famed words of Thomas Hobbes, is 'nature raw in tooth and claw'. A point has now been reached when freedom needs to be recalibrated and circumscribed by the establishment of conditions of delimitation to emplace 'freedom under the rule of law of the Sustainment'. Hereafter, the question is how, not why.

This imperative was first provocatively expressed as the 'dictatorship of Sustainment' in my *Design as Politics*.[8] The fundamental proposition is that unless humanity (as we know it) gives way to its rule we, as a species, will not survive. The Sustainment, it should be re-emphasized, is not merely the sustainment of our biophysical environment but a project that intellectually and culturally aligns us with all that acts to sustain us. As such, it understands that our future is threated by inequity and conflict as well as its indivisibility from the damage we humans do to the world around us.

The concept of necessity does not exist independently from an anthropocentric designation, and need itself cannot be reduced to an essentialism, for cultural norms of sacrifice can override its materiality.[9] There is no intrinsic need for humanity to survive. Yet a designated primary need to do so can be posited as *the* political imperative of humanity.

---

[6] Ibid.
[7] Agamben, *State of Exception*, pp. 8–9.
[8] Fry, *Design as Politics*, p. 211.
[9] Agamben, *State of Exception*, pp. 30–31; and Tony Fry (1994), 'Against an Essentialist Theory of Need', in *Remakings: Ecology, Design, Philosophy*, Sydney, NSW: UNSW Press.

Framing 'the state of exception' as able to be justified and resolved by necessity, as so argued fundamentally, rests upon turning human self-interest on its head. The issue now becomes not one justifying the Sustainment imposed as a crass enforced 'state of exception' but rather how and in what form it arrives as a way of delivering material modesty and equity together with a much greater degree of peace, and conviviality, as well as spatial and social justice. To recognize this turns us full circle to confront the formation of a politics able to answer these questions.

Part of the answer may well turn on a reconfiguration of 'the common good' beyond its past moral determinants. The Sustainment is 'a need' absolutely everyone needs in order to continue to be: it is 'a need in common'. It effectively transcends an evaluation of it as good or bad, for the Sustainment names the foundational condition upon which human welfare depends.[10] To understand this is to realize the extent to which the law currently fails to secure what is most vital to 'our' wellbeing. It fails to protect 'us' against those unsustainable forces that defuture – forces that are structurally part of the economy, property relations and institutions that the law upholds. At the same time, it allows 'a state of exception' to be normalized that erodes away freedoms in the name of national security, while at the same time ignoring the hegemonic 'existential state of exception' in which the oppressed and dispossessed underclasses of the world live without the protection of the law (while frequently being the victims of unjust laws).[11]

The whole contemporary discourse of national security has created a crisis of authority. Moreover, as Agamben has identified, there is now confusion surrounding the distinction between authority and dictatorship – a problem first addressed by Schmitt in 1931 and then by Hannah Arendt in 1961 (unknowingly echoing Schmitt).[12] This view was that the experience of authority (as, for example, acquired capability ontologically grounded) had vanished. As a result, authority became understood as authoritarianism, hence linked to dictatorship.

The failure of the law (both national and international) to protect that which is most fundamental – a liveable life, and life itself (a determinate of the Sustainment) was grounded in its attachment and service to the unsustainable *status quo*, thereby making it unable to protect the world's most vulnerable people and resources from conflict, exploitation and environmental destruction. Consequently, in one direction the law has lost much of its authority and gravitas, while in the other it has gravitated towards authoritarianism. The

---

[10] These remarks recast those of Adolph Nissen addressed by Agamben, *State of Exception*, pp. 45–46.

[11] See Agamben, *State of Exception*, p. 57, on the Benjamin-Schmitt dossier.

[12] Ibid., pp. 74–75.

incongruity of the free nations of the world is that the very means they claim to employ to protect freedom transpire so often to be either hollow or the actual instruments by which it is taken away.

The loss of freedom produced by the unsustainable is a restriction of life, a diminishment of liberty (by the national security state and 'the state of exception' as a normalized form of dictatorship) and a dialectical counter force: the freedom of consumption. The mantra of the Chinese state today asserts that accepting a loss of political freedom is offset by what is gained through the freedom to consume. Effectively, this mantra is now a global dictum – sometimes agreed in silence, at others in indirect language, and frequently as direct expression. Against all of this, what metrofitting offers is action to reclaim the freedom to act for the self while equally doing so with an understanding of, and towards, a redefined common good.

PART THREE

Introduction to the Case Studies

From the very opening of this work, the scale of metrofitting was presented as an enormous undertaking. Now many chapters later, the task no doubt looks ever larger and one that extends over a substantial period of time (enfolded within the Sustainment it can actually be taken to be a structural and unending process in the life and operation of a city). The two case studies that follow will show very different approaches and starting points to the metrofitting project. The contrast is deliberate. The first city is Cincinnati, in the state of Ohio, USA. It is a well-established city that does not appear to have any immediately evident major problems. Study two is of New Cairo, a desert city in Egypt around thirty kilometres due east of the centre of Cairo. It has discernible major problems that bring the very question of what a city is into question. Obviously, these case studies illuminate issues that are common to other cities in similar circumstances.

16

Cincinnati case study

FIGURE 1 *Downtown frames.*

How is it possible to find a starting point to commence metrofitting? The answer is that there are many and that they are all circumstantially determined. For many cities in economically advanced nations with repairable problems of 'the broken', risk analysis is one way to start. This is what will now be shown.

FIGURE 2 *Movement of goods by road, rail and the Ohio River.*

Introducing Cincinnati

Cincinnati largely owes its existence to its position on the Ohio River – initially, it was a crossing point of the river and consequently became a centre of trade. Its growth was modest until stimulated by a mass influx of German migrants in the 1830s. By the early twentieth century, it had grown to become a commercially viable, mid-sized American city and the home of several large corporations. But like many 'old economy' cities, by the end of the twentieth century and beginning of the twenty-first its population began to shrink as the US economy faltered and began to restructure. Fortunately, many corporations stayed in the city and a slow process of recovery was begun.

While the city has experienced flooding, it has had no major environmental disasters. However, in common with a lot of other US cities, it does have a problem with inequity. Poverty is especially evident within Afro-American and poor white communities. This situation erupted in 2001, when there was a significant 'race riot' in Cincinnati. Things have not improved, although they have been made less visible.

Why Cincinnati?

Notwithstanding its social problems, Cincinnati shows itself to be unexceptional. It is a city with a mostly sound building stock, cultural resources, a modestly improving economy and is located in a region that is not, at least in the short term, likely to be exposed to extreme climate change impacts. Nevertheless, it still faces risks, including those of tornadoes, as do many other similar cities in the region. The city would very significantly improve its ability to deal with its current and future risks if metrofitting was embraced. To highlight this, a Cincinnati metrofitting risk-mapping workshop was held in early February 2014 at the University of Cincinnati's Niehoff Community Design Urban Studio.

The workshop was based on two assumptions. First, like almost every city, Cincinnati is not sufficiently prepared for the environmental and social challenges that will arrive in future decades. Clearly, not all of these challenges can be recognized, but many can. History, local environmental data, social and economic studies, regional, national and global trends, and available regional climate change data, all make this very clear. Assumption two is, again like most cities, Cincinnati is not prepared for future challenges predominantly because the threats have not been significantly researched, considered and documented as a composite picture of risk. The workshop provided an opportunity to review these assumptions and initiate a process of risk evaluation.

Framed by the agenda of metrofitting, the entire 'hard and soft' risk assessment process has the ability to make an important contribution to civic education, public education and community awareness, as well as to identifying a more instrumental range of concerns. As such, it enables a city to better prepare for disasters and thereby commence building social resilience, while at the same time contributing to the identification of needed practical adaptive actions.

Around forty people attended the workshop, including architects, planners, city council and state government representatives, environmentalists, academics, and postgraduate students, as well as members of community organizations. While the risk-mapping workshop assisted in developing preventative and post-disaster planning, it equally established a sound starting point for building group understandings of the contextual complexity of critical and prospective crisis situations. It also exposed what knowledge needs to be developed and communicated to all at risk as well as to those who are responsible for risk reduction and disaster response. In so doing, risk mapping actually creates triggers for making decisions about what and when specific critical metrofitting tasks need to be undertaken. Instrumentally, it can also specifically identify and confront problems that have to be resolved to reduce negative impacts upon human populations, be they bio-physical, material (with particular reference to food and shelter) or socio-cultural (in the context of poverty and inter-racial tensions).

The existence of a 'Green Cincinnati Plan' helped set the context for the workshop.[1] However, what the plan lacked, and what risk mapping provided, was a clearer sense and wider picture of present and future threats environmentally, socially and to a lesser extent economically.

So positioned, the risk-mapping exercise was a geographic mapping exercise (whereby risks are visually marked) that enabled:

- a picture to be constructed of the relational complexity of risk factors to be grasped and engaged so as to inform communities, and direct policy and planning by local government, the corporate and the commercial sector, and NGOs; and

- a programme of research and works to be identified and equipped to start to deal with that which threatens.

The time frame for the creation of a resolved risk map is of the order of one year (although subject to the size of the city, and the problems it faces, it could be more or less).

Understanding local contextual complexity

Clearly, before the mapping process can start, the local contextual complexity needs to be identified and documented. Typically, this includes assembling publicly available information about the city, its geology, state of its building stock, demographics, social and economic history, historical climate data and so on. This material needs to be read from the perspective of anything that has, or could have, determinate consequences for the future of the city and its population. Added to this activity is the need to address and critique the sufficiency of existing risk identification, management, information materials and approaches (like the disaster plans of utility services and local hospitals). All existing local maps also need to be gathered as a workshop resource (planning, zoning, vegetation, flooding, housing density, infrastructure, etc.).

---

[1] This plan was produced by the City of Cincinnati in 2013. It reflected on 'greening' accomplishments in the prior five years. It looked at changes being prompted by the 'sustainability agenda' and then addressed the process and implementation processes that need to be adopted. Thereafter, the vast bulk of the document reviewed the familiar technical areas of sustainability: energy, waste, land management and use, food and water. The document ended with material on climate change and adaptation, an implementation plan and recommendations.

The starting point for a risk-mapping event is (and for Cincinnati was) a briefing on the workshop to identify its ambition, tasks to be undertaken, methods to be employed, its defined outputs and a realistic timeline. Specifically, the complex nature of risk also requires unpacking, including potential consequences triggered by a cataclysmic event (like the breakdown of public services, fire, floods, an outbreak of crime and civil unrest, extreme water or air pollution, major chemical spills and the spread of disease from contaminated water and food). The city also requires to be understood as social ecology (culture, the social power structure and the viability of community) – what this means is having a picture of the diverse social fabric of the city, the relations of power between groups, and levels of risk of social dysfunction and conflict (with the most socially disadvantaged always being most at risk and unstable).

The primary aim of a risk workshop is not to try to take on the huge task that the event reveals needs to be done. Rather, it is to build an informed cadre to produce and present material able to influence the local power structures, especially the city council and at-risk communities, and thereafter to adopt and develop processes of detailed research, planning and change with community participation.

Pragmatically, a predesigned documentation template (plus dossier and map notes) was created for the workshop showing how information gathered could be recorded in a common format and deployed in the production of material to communicate to the media. Finally, the workshop was divided into four groups, which after some modification, were as follows:

- *environmental* group with a brief to review existing disaster plans and supplement available information, identify existing documented environmental risks, and undertake such activities as an audit of the critical building stock and the state of infrastructure of the city;

- *economic* group with a brief to review and supplement available information, and develop an analysis of the local economy from available information;

- *socio-cultural* group with a brief to review and supplement available information; draw up a plan to map the social ecology of the metro area, and review historic and current social problem 'hot-spots';

- *design, documentation, communication and map-making* group with a brief to gather documented output from the other groups, keep those groups informed of the work of others, develop a schematic map for information uploading and disseminate data when available.

As indicated, the two-day workshop was no more than a means to expose and communicate the risk-mapping process to the organizations represented at it, all being mostly registered in a series of risk maps. What is essential to understand is that these maps do not present the attendees with solutions. Rather, what they do is to graphically illustrate tasks to be done with map-based detail and to be corrected as more information is gathered and knowledge gained. So, for example, a flood evacuation route might be marked on the map, which will be required to be reviewed and then corrected by the city's traffic engineers and emergency services, and thereafter materialized as, for example, signs fabricated and comprehensively placed on the designated roads. Such action requires to be seen not merely as informative, and an expression of civic responsibility, but also as an element of public education that among other things raises awareness that climate change adaptive action is underway.

The workshop

Besides introducing the context and content of the workshop, the opening session confronted the need for 'thinking otherwise' on how risk was understood and going to be approached.

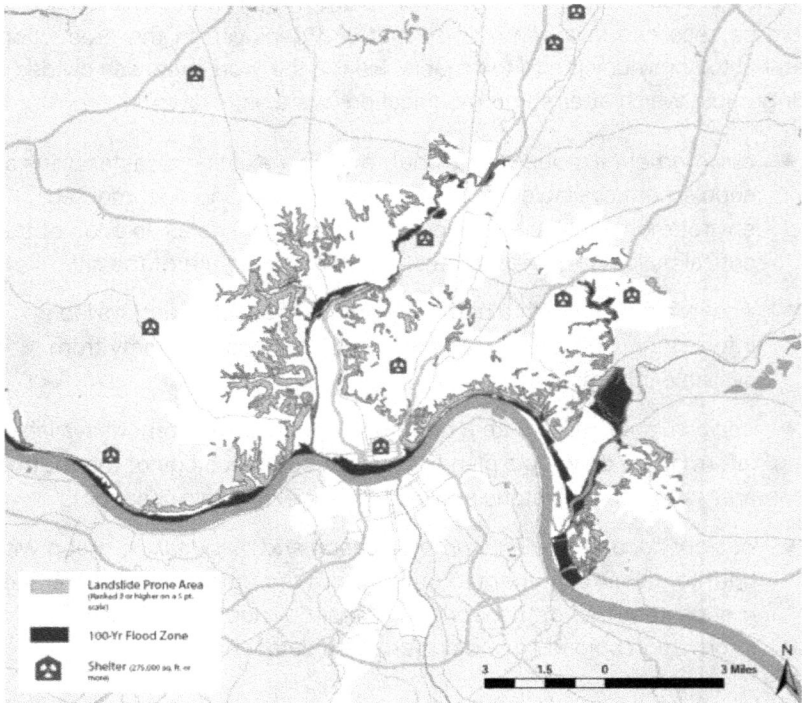

FIGURE 3 *Landslides and flood.*

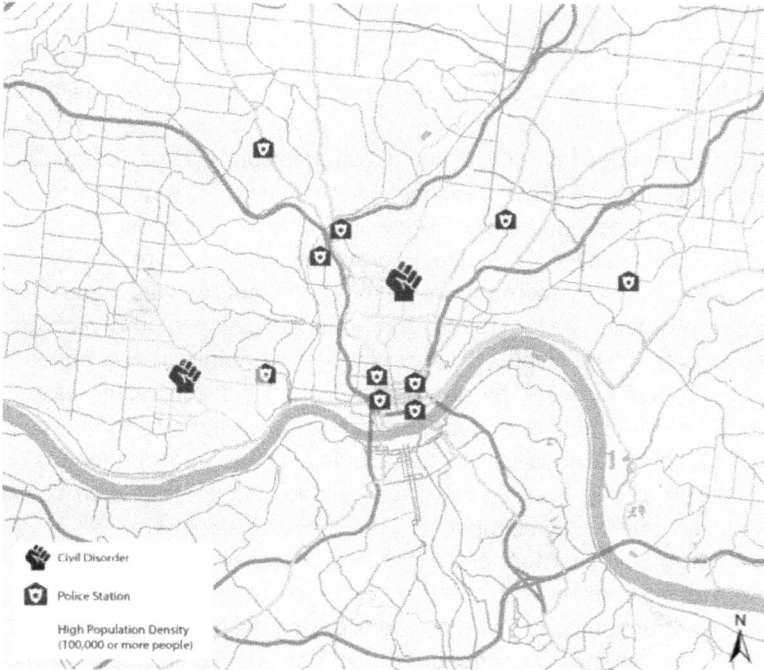

FIGURE 4 *Civil disorder.*

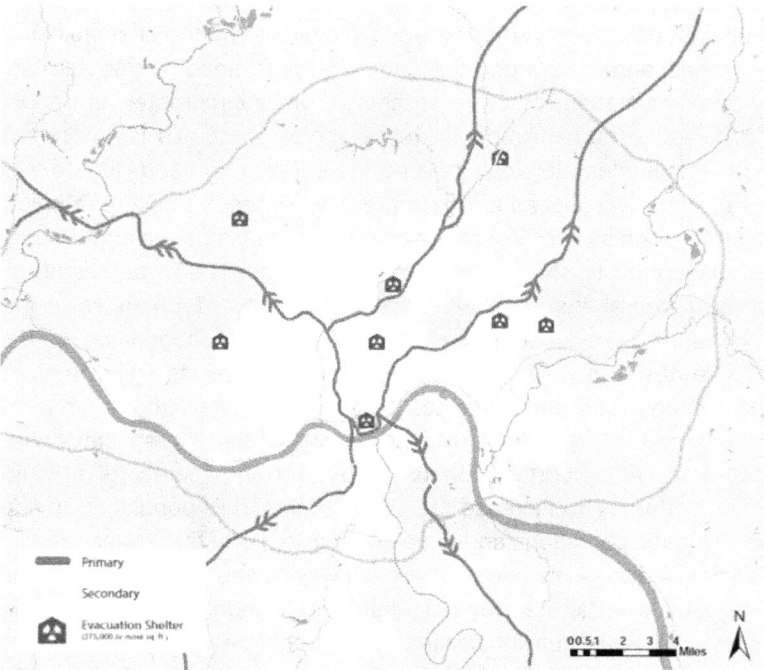

FIGURE 5 *Evacuation routes.*

'Thinking otherwise' essentially named the need, as well as a way, to interrogate the familiar by making it unfamiliar. To clarify this point, what actions were needed for a city to 'become sustainable' (the kind of instrumental actions outlined in the Green Cincinnati Plan – actions like reduced greenhouse gas emissions, the adoption of renewable energy, the reduction of waste, better land use policy and practice, improved management of fresh water and so on) were shown to be important but not sufficient. As was made clear, this because they failed to go to the fundamental cause of the problem: the anthropocentric disposition of human actions. Notwithstanding appearances of normality, we humans, by degree and globally, are in many ways out of control. This disposition is evident both collectively (in the form of the world's economy) and individually (in the acquisitiveness that underpins hyper-consumption and in the extent of global inequity together with social and spatial injustice). There is simply no correlation between what we all need to live in reasonable comfort and what we materially want and acquire. In contrast to the deployment of the intelligence that has made the world of human construction possible, our world-making, as this book makes clear, is not only becoming out of control but the human population displays almost no sense of the consequences of their/our actions in time. Put simply: we bring things into existence frequently with very little sense of what they will cause socio-culturally and environmentally.

There can be no substantial advance in overcoming the unsustainable until our anthropocentrically directed actions are constrained by transformation of our worldly habitation, by our own choice, or by circumstantial impositions that will reduce human impacts. To recognize all of this is to dramatically expand what is meant by 'risk' beyond the environment and climate.

Metrofitting was placed in this context as a means of situated unlearning and learning, and as such it was deployed as a means not an end. Specifically, it was elaborated to show how understanding needed to be based upon: a relational comprehensive view of the complexity of urban socio-material interconnectedness (ecology beyond ecology); and recognition of the key imperative of dealing with what already materially exists (in contrast to just adding systems and structures to those already established). None of this was presented in opposition to the proposals of the 'Green Cincinnati Plan' but rather as an important means to extend and realize its ambition by providing pathways to increase the ability of the city's population to adapt to coming climatic conditions and in doing so gain a greater resilience.

As acknowledged, historically there is always a need to review documented local disaster events, the way risks have been understood and managed in the past, and what current hazards have been identified. However, rather than just working with such generalized perspectives, more fine-grained characterizations of place, risks and exposed populations are required. Many other tasks also invited consideration and grounding in more specific and detailed practices. Likewise, rather than just undertaking a 'desk study' to generate a disaster management plan that objectifies risk and risk-levels from available data, the practice of risk assessment can and should be supported by fieldwork research, which should be made a publicly visible activity. Gathering information via consultative processes, the physical examination of structures, and photo documentation of identified dangers (and exhibiting them), besides having analytical value again become a means to communicate and educate the public on the fact that risks exist, are not always immediately obvious and need to be known if they are to be dealt with.

Additionally, there is a pressing need to recognize that humanity is now in a rapidly changing situation environmentally in which risk is continually increasing (albeit unevenly). Unfortunately, not only is there insufficient recognition of this fact but also information can be (and sometimes is) publicly withheld or repressed.[2]

One obvious way to make the changing picture of risk evident is to undertake and publish a local risk audit – of built fabric, infrastructure vulnerability, the exposure and coping capacity of essential services, as well as the location of vulnerable communities. Such an audit needs to ask, for example: how well can the existing built fabric deal with the expectation of the increasing severity of extreme weather notionally projected over this century and beyond? Are there unsound built structures that should be removed? What buildings are in need of structural repair to make them storm-safe, and which buildings offer safe shelter in extreme weather events? Does 'public liability' insurance beg rethinking? And then, under what conditions does infrastructure currently deemed safe become unsafe? Has contingency planning factored in rising risk levels? Are there effective, operative and tested inter-utility and services communication and command systems available? Then, returning to the issue of communities: what are the specific risks to which vulnerable communities are exposed, and how could such risks be reduced? And last, in this non-definitive listing, what and where are the pressure points that indicate where the breakdown of social order might occur?

Self-evidently, making risks visible and understood cannot be divided from the ability to deal with them. This applies to preventative and post-disaster action. The scale of coming disasters will be well beyond the economic and material resources of many local and national states (in many poorer nations this point has already been surpassed). This makes 'community' a crucial

---

[2] For example, in 2014 a local coastal council in Queensland, Australia, was prohibited from making reference to rising sea levels as it might affect property values.

factor of resilience, and 'community development' a key preventative action. To simply reduce resilience to instrumental means and action (a current trend) is to demonstrate a fundamental lack of understanding of what the nature of resilience in coming circumstances will require.

Against the background of these observations, and prior to group work, in order to help develop group understandings a range of risk reduction actions were reviewed that centred on making risks more visible via processes of continuous communication, education, discussion and practical material action in the city. This included thinking about hazard reductions based on historical data (like flooding, storm damage and heat wave data), community participation in planning risk audits, as well as providing a basis for more interesting and developed city signage strategies (with community input). Signage, for example, addresses routes of evacuation, the visual marking of shelters (be they existing structures or specially built ones), evacuation centres, the location of emergency equipment and disaster prevention works, and so on. Again, to restate, making risk visible by such means not only becomes part of a process of public awareness and education, but is also an expression by the local state of enacted and normalized civic responsibility towards tangible forms of preparedness. So often disaster management plans are created yet remain on computer servers, on office shelves or in filing cabinets, whereas their adequacy requires public scrutiny, exposure and forms of available and tangible presence. Likewise, understanding disaster 'risk and response' begs curriculum development related to cities at all levels of education and professional development (especially in those services responsible for responding to disasters). On this basis, such educational activity requires continual updating and the embracing of action directed at fundamental cultural, environmental and climatic change. Such action also links more widely to educational and social reform, in the context of social and civic responsibility in conditions of now assured change. Adaptive action is as much a question of mind as it is one of matter.

It was made clear to the workshop groups that beyond the visualization of risk, what risk maps also importantly enable is the identification of needed strategic and organizational actions informed by the complex relational picture of risk. Again, as such, they also provide a learning experience. Finally, they provide an effective communication tool to employ in winning community, political and economic support for risk reduction action as well highlighting the associated importance of metrofitting.

The workshop groups were formed by matching the considerable and particular expertise of each of the event's participants with the specific task focus of the group – design, planning, history, policy, environment and local knowledge were all well covered. There was, however, one important area – economics – that was engaged with but professionally under-represented. The groups worked independently, but with everyone contributing to a dialogue of information and knowledge sharing. As indicated, while the scale of the task was beyond the capability of a two-day event, it succeeded in planting the idea and providing the potential and motivation for metrofitting and risk mapping to be incorporated into individual professional practice.

Most significantly, one of the participants, the Director of the City of Cincinnati Office of Environmental Quality, took the event extremely seriously, and employed a postgraduate student to assist in the development of the approach within council policy. In September 2014, the Director and I gave a presentation of the context, concept and the application of risk mapping to a council committee – with a specific focus on local and regional existing and prospective climate conditions. At the same time, we made clear that risks are always globally connected and do not respect local containment. One clear illustration of this was that while Cincinnati was well over 1,000 kilometres from New Orleans, Cincinnati nonetheless received over 2,000 people displaced by Hurricane Katrina in 2005.

Final focus of the event: what is resilience?

The issue of resilience was presented and discussed at the workshop. It was outlined as the capacity of urban infrastructure, and its management, to withstand trauma, function under stress, and rapidly recover – this especially from climate change-related, high-impact extreme weather events. Consideration of the structural integrity of the built environment to withstand and recover from such impacts was also included. The workshop also acknowledged the huge importance of communities' socio-cultural and psycho-social capability to confront the prospect of a broad range of disasters, as well as deal with them when they happen. Central to this capability is the viability of local communities to retain their integrity under extreme circumstances.

Community is a misused term. So often it is reduced to a loose grouping of people living in a particular area, or the gathering of ethnic or religious groups. However, historically the true character of community was based on the sacred in tribal and religious societies. Underpinning this was belief. Belief, of course, can be secular, positive or negative (as with nationalism and reactionary political ideologies) and be developed and thereafter fostered.

So framed, a key to resilience in the age of a changing climate and resultant unsettlement (environmentally, economically, culturally, psychologically) is a belief in something that has the ability to constitute 'commonality in difference'. The concept of the Sustainment was put forward at the workshop as a way to meet this need. In naming and materializing the concept, as an ongoing process than can support human life, and which all life depends upon, the potential foundation of a secular belief based on the Sustainment was registered and taken seriously (including it being seen as an important prefigurative means to build community). What makes such action so important is that as environmental conditions become more critical, and as the impacts of climate change become far more severe and more widespread (as will be remembered), the ability of the state to adequately respond will increasingly diminish. This will mean that whatever the situation, in very many cases, the only available resource will be action by the impacted community itself, and perhaps other communities that are in a position to offer assistance.

On reflection: what was learnt at the workshop?

It was immediately clear that a good deal of information and knowledge already existed within the groups and more generally in the city. But there was, and is, a problem of stasis: in the main the knowledge is arrested in history, is not being sufficiently used and is locked into documentation systems. Disaster management plans are a good example here. So often, once created, they await a disaster rather than being made visible as a directive instrument in preventative and preparative planning and action. Likewise, with perhaps a few exceptions, they do not become the basis of public education and media content.

Certainly, risk identification and response need to be a public process, and directly connected to education and communication strategies that enable local populations to grasp coming dangers and prepare for them. Explicitly, this means that the nature of risks and responses to them are made comprehensively publicly visible in schools, homes, businesses and on the street. At the same time, this activity needs to be directly linked to metrofitting at the level of the repair of the local social and material fabric of the city. Again such action should not be viewed simply pragmatically, for it also has the ability to provide a great deal of positive socio-cultural change and informal education.

Against this backdrop, the workshop recognized the time to take action is now, not least because it takes a long time to inform and transform the perceptions, values and conduct of local populations. Likewise, spreading public works over time makes the financial burden more manageable. It was also recognized that for progress to be made, a 'community of interest' with political agency has to be created – this cannot be divided from the development of community and the formation of a sensibility that recognizes negative environmental conditions are already arriving and will progressively get worse.

It was also clear to all that change is not going to come via a grand vision and vast public programme, but rather will grow out of a proliferation of modest actions that gain momentum.

Appendix

Here is some of the content of the workshop that was spoken to and addressed by the groups. In addition to this information were a collection of articles and an example disaster management plan that were circulated and displayed. Each group was given a series of themed question sheets to review.

Documents Review Sheet

- What disaster planning and management documents exist in the city and are available to review, including those by the local council, energy providers, water providers, medical services, emergency services and corporations?

- Additionally, what other such documents exist of similar types of climatic regions and do any include mapping?

- What contemporary 'critical demographic' social data on the 'state of the city' have been published or are available?

- What contemporary environmental data have been published (web and reports) and are regional climatic data available?

- Have local climate projections been created?

- What economic data are available to review – economic climate of the city, income distribution, poverty levels, expenditure on disaster management planning, and risk awareness and management education/training and resources (current and predictive)?

- More?

Historical Questions Sheet

- Historically, what disasters has Cincinnati suffered?

- What impacts did they have and do empirical data on them exist?

- What was the public response to these events?

- Do localized historical climate data exist?

- What disaster planning and management exists in the city now?

- What historical and geographic factors might be related to these disasters and their impacts (building in flood-prone areas, bad housing, a lack of or poor quality of emergency services, etc.)?

- Is there any relevant historical 'critical demographic' data that should be sought (especially in terms of 'at-risk communities')?

- What urban improvements have been made as a result of past disasters?

- More?

Information Issues Documentation Sheet

The output of the workshop needs to be:

- visual: a map with information and relational connections made – this requires designing

- an outline of critical issues in a supporting document.

Groups need to:

- agree a common documentation and visualization format within groups

- work on overlays to the visualization format

- create a reporting template.

There are three communication strategic and content questions/issues to address:

- Who to report/present the workshop output material to and in what form

- What content to report to the media, and to what media outlets

- How and what to communicate to those people from whom support is sought.

Risk Sheet Questions

- What are the actual and potential extreme weather events that could impact Cincinnati now and in the future: extreme storms, tornadoes, landslides, hail storms, floods, extreme cold, extreme heat, more?

- Demographically, who are the most 'at risk' and where?

- What is the risk of a pandemic in the US arriving in Cincinnati?

- What is the likelihood of civil unrest in the city and what might cause it?

- Does the city have any specific industrial/chemical hazards?

- Does the city have any known terror targets?

- Is 'peak-oil' still a risk, and if so what would its impact be?

Additional risk questions:

- Is an influx of IDPs possible and from where?

- What is the level of knowledge and training on disasters in emergency and medical services (and of what type) in the city?

- Where are the actual or prospective evacuation centres in Cincinnati?

- What emergency food, water and energy supplies/facilities exist and where?

Social Ecology Questions (also issues to be discussed and clarified)*

To deal with risk, it is essential to:

- generate adaptive social change

- develop the coping capacity and resilience of all communities

- engage and strengthen the social ecology of the city.

In this context, how should 'the environmental, political and social state of Cincinnati' be understood? Thus:

---

* Where social ecology is understood as: the social and cultural relations of power, symbolic forms of exchange and function, and the viability of community.

- What is the formal and informal power structure and how can it be mapped, and how can the following be added to this map?

- What is the social fabric of the city and how does it symbolically express itself across all classes and ethnicities?

- At a meta-level: who interacts with whom (the functions and nature of exchange politically, economically and socially, specifically in relation to direct and indirect information pathways)?

- What are the socio-cultural divisions and tensions of the city (the obvious and the not-so-obvious)?

- What is the social formation of faith communities, sports and the arts in the city?

- Which social ecologies in the city work well and which do not?

17

New Cairo case study

FIGURE 6 *Day workers' breakfast.*

As a case study, it would be totally inadequate to present New Cairo (a desert 'city', the centre of which is twenty-five kilometres outside Cairo) as the name of an agglomeration of places, spaces, structures, social-formations, cultures and economies that in sum represent it as a whole. Whatever the elements there are, they simply cannot be meaningfully gathered under the name. This is not to say its disparate forms and numerous problems are completely un-located – they do speak of themselves but indiscernibly they also are utterances of many other places. New Cairo is a sprawling location of dislocated fragments.

So said, the aim of the case study is to start to explore ways to describe the kind of field of complexity that metrofitting needs to examine in such a place if it is to begin to create an agenda of repair and redirective action of that which the designation 'city' strives to mask. In itself, this task is substantial and is clearly a major research project in its own right. To recognize this imperative is to acknowledge that there is no way the scale and problems of metrofitting a 'place' like New Cairo can begin to be contemplated without attempting to establish a clear conceptual grasp of what has to be addressed. Certainly, without the knowledge delivered by a whole raft of research there would be absolutely no chance of creating anything like the beginning of an effective metrofitting programme. It is against this backdrop that the case study will aim to expose the magnitude of the problems, the character and the enormous scale that the project of metrofitting New Cairo would present. Even if commenced in a well-organized, adequately resourced and energetic manner, it would take many decades.

FIGURE 7 *One of many illegal shops.*

FIGURE 8 *Motorbike taxi.*

FIGURE 9 *The rare 'real deal' taxi.*

FIGURE 10 *The image meets reality.*

FIGURE 11 *'Good' public housing 1.*

FIGURE 12 *'Good' public housing 2.*

FIGURE 13 *El Rehab Gated Community new shopping.*

FIGURE 14 *Business estate development.*

FIGURE 15 *Machine and driver for hire.*

FIGURE 16 *Desert housing.*

FIGURE 17 *Hyde Park Gate.*

FIGURE 18 *Hyde Park – the site develops.*

FIGURE 19 *Hyde Park – the image.*

FIGURE 20 *Hyde Park – the reality.*

FIGURE 21 *Hyde Park – the scale.*

FIGURE 22 *Selling the idea.*

FIGURE 23 *Madinaty entry gate.*

FIGURE 24 *Madinaty 'the biggest'.*

FIGURE 25 *Waiting for water (from the Nile).*

New Cairo in context

New Cairo exits by virtue of problems coming from the population pressures of Cairo. Major among these problems has been the failure of the city, especially its old sections, to cope with the volume of people and traffic. The city actually 'functions' in a condition of dysfunction: a situation that has huge economic and social impacts upon it. Added to this, as we shall see, are clusters of political, economic and increasingly environmental problems directly linked to climate change and national security.

In 1985, Egypt had a population of 50 million. By 2015, it was 85 million and by 2035 it is expected to be 110 million (thus having doubled in 50 years). This population is concentrated in the Nile Valley, which occupies only five per cent of the landmass of the nation. What remains is mostly desert. Almost a quarter of Egypt's population lives in Cairo, or travels to work there.

The poor and broken infrastructure of the city buckles under the weight of this number of people (around 20 million, plus 3 million more who arrive each day to work, or to look for it[1]). Cities like New Cairo were conceived and then built in the desert to accommodate people and industries relocated to reduce pressures on central Cairo. It was also done to open up central Cairo for new commercial development. Yet alongside 'official' projects of resettlement, another counter-trend was taking place. From the 1970s onward, the informal settlement of Cairo started to rapidly increase. As a result, by 2009, 63.6 per cent of the city's population lived in informal housing.[2] Government's ability to plan and control the city increasingly became diminished.

Forces of change

Climate change is going to have a very significant impact on everyday life in Egypt, its economy and future. There are areas of the 270-km Mediterranean coastline that are 1 m or less above sea level and which are already significantly impacted by sea level rises. In fact, the IPCC has classified the Nile Delta as within the top three most exposed regions in the world. Besides salinity created by sea level rises, there are major land erosion problems.[3] Alexandria, the nation's second city, is only 7 m above sea level, its lower districts (in whole or part) are likely to be inundated and thereafter cut off from the

---

[1] In a city with a large informal community, official figures are always below the true number.
[2] David Sims (2012), *Understanding Cairo: The Logic of a City Out of Control*, Cairo: The American University Press, p.96.
[3] Jack Shenker (2009), 'Nile Delta: "We are Going Underwater. The Sea will Conquer Our Lands"', *The Guardian*, 21 August [https://www.theguardian.com/environment/2009/aug/21/climate-change-nile-flooding-farming].

mainland. While the seriousness of this situation has been reported, recent research has indicted a far more critical situation is emerging.[4] The Delta region enfolds 16,000 m[2] of farmland that produces 60 per cent of Egypt's food. A sea level rise of 1 m would reduce this region's food output by 20 per cent – this at the same time that the nation's population is growing rapidly. The longer-term view, one coming from research in progress in the West Antarctic, suggests the situation is going to get very much worse.[5] As John Vidal, on reporting current environmental events in Egypt has made graphically clear:

> . . . the Mediterranean Sea is remorselessly battering the Egyptian coastline. Salt is leaching into the rich soils and invading drinking water wells, 1,000 year old homes are being eroded from below and hundreds of square miles of land have been inundated by rising water in just a few generations. Sea levels are inexorably rising and storms are becoming more intense.[6]

Sea level rises are expected to displace several millions of people from the Delta as the agricultural system starts to increasingly fail. No matter where families resettle, many of the displaced young men will seek work in Cairo, this influx adding to the pressures on the city. This situation in turn creates another problem. The water supply and irrigation demands of these cities will increase stress on the already overused supply from the Nile. This water crisis is not a crisis of the future: it has already started.[7]

While climate change impacts are certain to have increasingly serious consequences for Egypt, they will equally impact on the geopolitics of the region. Effectively, the nation is already being governed as a 'national security state' under a regime acting under 'a state of exception' that centralizes executive power. The greater the pressures on the domestic population, the more the threat from external forces increases, the more terrorist attacks there are within the nation, the more the militarization of the city, and the greater the negative economic consequences, including upon tourism.[8]

---

[4] On 13 May 2014, Suzanne Goldenberg reported for *The Guardian* that the 'Western Antarctic ice collapse has already begun, scientists warn'. The two separate studies confirmed that the loss of this ice sheet was inevitable and this, over coming centuries, will cause up to an additional 4 m rise in sea level.

[5] Ibid.

[6] John Vidal (2011), 'Drier, Hotter: Can Egypt Escape its Climate Future?', *The Guardian*, 18 November [https://www.theguardian.com/environment/blog/2011/nov/18/egypt-climate-change].

[7] Isabel Esterman (2014), 'Water Shortage Shrivels Dreams of Good Life in New Cairo', 4 September [http://www.madamasr.com/en/2014/09/04/feature/society/water-shortage-shrivels-dreams-of-the-good-life-in-new-cairo/].

[8] For example, conflict in the Sinai is continuous with no means to resolve it imminently and Egypt's tourist industry is already on its knees: in the first quarter of 2016, tourism fell by 66 per cent [http://egyptianstreets.com/2016/04/26/egypts-tourism-earnings-fall-by-66-in-first-quarter-of-2016/].

Introducing New Cairo

Built on a huge plateau over 200 m above sea level, New Cairo is obviously well protected from sea level rises (in contrast to Cairo, which is only 23 m above, but with some areas of the city adjacent to the Nile less than 4 m above sea level).

New Cairo is one of the eight desert towns created under the Egyptian government's New Towns Programme commenced in 1977.[9] The actual physical formation of New Cairo started in the 1980s by the amalgamation of three dormitory suburbs.[10] Officially established as a new town in 1989, it had three specified modes of development: public housing, privately developed compounds and individual plots.[11] This information gives the impression of a coherence that is in reality totally lacking. Notwithstanding the existence of some public housing, the provision for people with 'limited income' (translate as 'the poor') is tokenistic when measured against need.[12] The original target population for the city was 2 million but it has got nowhere near this number.[13] The actual projection for 2027 has been put at 3½ million, which would require the existing population to be increased by a factor of 20.[14] Unless a vast number of jobs are created, and housing becomes more affordable (which is certainly not the current trend), New Cairo's population growth will continue to remain weak for the foreseeable future.

A huge number of houses are incomplete, partly finished, or finished but unoccupied. Many are illegally occupied.[15] The mode of development was based on land allocation rather than any kind of comprehensive planning programme. It assured that there would be sprawl and structural fragmentation from the start. The management of New Cairo is under the auspices of the New Urban Communities Association (NUCA) – a semi-autonomous organization run by ex-generals which operates without transparency and which has sold, and continues to sell, vacant land for huge profits. It also has a history of allocating parcels of land to 'friends of the regime'.[16]

To understand the scale and complexity of metrofitting New Cairo, one has to comprehend the enormous geographic scale of what has been created. New Cairo now exceeds the original plan of 264 km² (which equals half that of

---

[9] Sims, *Understanding Cairo*, p. 171.
[10] Ibid., p. 78.
[11] Ibid., pp. 177–179.
[12] Ibid., p. 286.
[13] Ibid., p. 80.
[14] Ibid., p. 199.
[15] Ibid., p. 79.
[16] Ibid., p. 189.

greater Cairo but with only something like one-thousandth of its population). Ambiguously, Madinaty (a development of 45 km²) has been added to the area but it only appears on some maps. Actual boundaries and location names mean little when viewing a vast panorama of this urban (con)fusion.

Of place

The rhetoric of New Cairo itself invites confusion. Within the town there are cities that are not cities, and the name 'town' itself does not denote a town – issues of translation and the dislocation of the representational function of language fold into this confusion. However, what is actually clear when viewing New Cairo is that operationally it is a designated area of regional development that touches on other such regions. By implication, both the name of the place and the mapping of borders are arbitrary. Numerous areas bleed into each other, and lines in the desert that appear on maps are meaningless on the ground. One cannot grasp what this form of development is without understanding that it is predicated upon a particular perception of space – one based on an incursion into the seemingly unlimited smooth space of the desert that allows for the creation of undisciplined striated space. A road is used to draw a line. It authorizes, for example, a progressively expanding area of dense or low-rise housing development to occur within compounds via its delineation. What this action facilitates is urban sprawl on a vast scale – compounds proliferate and get ever larger. They have populations of the size of cities but without the transport and economic infrastructures of the city, its commercial amenities (shops and offices) or its social fabric. There are two very obvious results that flow from such 'planning': an extremely large dependency on cars and delivery services; and social atomization (which means in many cases social withdrawal into a domestic 'bubble' that effectively excludes the world at large).

There are two contradictory factors underpinning the dramatic growth in compound living. First is their deployed significance as places able to codify and communicate a conspicuous expression of wealth and status. The most expensive of them offers a 'life style of fantasy' created by a themed architectural style and landscaping that presents a simulacrum of almost anywhere in the developed world. The second attraction links fear with exclusion. Fear of the actual amplifies the dangers of everyday life in Egypt and exclusion from its dirt, disorder and a shunned underclass of old Cairo.

The life of privilege in ordered and clean space of a compound, with its less polluted air and irrigated greenery, clearly improves the environmental quality of life, but it equally allows the privileged to ignore the squalor on the other side of the wall, abandon the underclass to its fate, and so tolerate the intolerable.

In a country with a seemingly incoherent and outdated modernist approach to its 'development' (including an obsession with grandiose architectural statements), much large-scale development centres on the wish to attract foreign investment. The government seeks such investment and establishes policies to support it, this because it generates income from land sales and taxes. Such base economic pragmatism is indivisible from a governmental failure to comprehend, plan and create cities that are of an appropriate size, scale and sustaining capability. Moreover, there is a clear political failure to recognize the merit of making a far more viable food bowl for the nation, while also establishing urban development that is far more compact and economically, socially and culturally functional.

Notwithstanding the arrival of the rhetoric and some of the technology of 'sustainability', the environmental stress and impacts of infrastructure are continually being moved ever further into the desert – doing this seems to continue to go unrecognized. Clearly, if development in the desert does take place, it should be contained within very clear and sustainable conditions of limitation. The arrival of the proposed new capital city of Egypt is a major expression of exactly the opposite perspective. Looking at the 'vision' of this city it reads like a shopping list of excess to advance the creation of a global example of the unsustainable. While aiming to become the ultimate example of the nation's projection of the 'conspicuous display of wealth', as a global communication it will be a semiotic, social and environmental disaster in the making. The president and his minsters naturally think otherwise. They cling to a late nineteenth- to mid-twentieth-century idea that somehow a big, new and sparkling capital city will bring the world to recognize Egypt as a modern advanced nation.

If the city is to be created in the form in which it is proposed, and with a projected population of 5 million plus, it would be the largest custom-built capital city ever constructed. In reality, the government would do well if it even reached 2 million. As a desert development it is totally environmentally inappropriate and as such it could well set a new standard for the unsustainable – for instance, the impact of the infrastructure of such a city would be massive, not least in terms of the demand for irrigation. One asks: does anywhere need a park twice the size of New York's Central Park, or a theme park four times the size of Disneyland? Does any city anywhere need 663 hospitals and clinics or 1,250 mosques and churches?[17] Does anyone who has any experience at

[17] Patrick Kingsley (2015), 'A New New Cairo: Egypt Plans £30bn Purpose-built Capital in Desert', *The Guardian*, 16 March [https://www.theguardian.com/cities/2015/mar/16/new-cairo-egypt-plans-capital-city-desert].

all of building construction in Egypt for one moment believe government claims that the city could be built in five to seven years? And likewise, does anyone believe the housing in this city would be affordable for those millions of poor Egyptians who need decent homes?

And then what of the fate and fact of those thirty desert towns/cities that in almost every case are not in any real sense cities, massively under-populated, partly functional and the product of poor planning? Surely problems that these urban areas display require urgent address, this before another maniacal urban development problem is commenced? This situation is very evident in New Cairo and the adjoining area of Madinity.

While the scale of the bad political and planning judgement of the new city is incredulous, one can partly agree with the objective of moving government and its departments out of downtown Cairo. If this happened and was done well, not only would this action make a contribution to taking pressure off the city but it would also enable its much needed 'repair and restoration', not least to the ancient areas, to take place. However, getting people with strong family ties to move to a city in the desert is no easy task. Meanwhile, there is a contra expectation: that within a few decades Cairo's population is going to reach 40 million.[18] On the basis of current practice, managing this growth in population seems beyond contemplation. However, one thing is certain: it will generate a huge increase in the creation of informal settlements.

As for a new capital city, conceptually (but not politically under the current regime) there are alternatives: metrofitting New Cairo would be one option to explore. Another would be a small number of modest relocation cities in the Nile Valley with populations of say 250,000 to 400,000 people – these to drive the regeneration and development the nation's agricultural sector and to accommodate displaced people from the Delta.

Traffic without enforced law, transport and the people

The rules of the road in Cairo are *de facto* created by the collective practices of drivers rather than by the law and its enforcement. Traffic police are effectively non-existent. Traffic lights exist but are mostly ignored, except at a few mystical intersections where somehow a consensus has been agreed that they serve a useful purpose. Some of the traffic lights have cameras, but nobody takes any notice of them, and even if they worked they would be

---

[18] See M. Osman http://www.thecairoreview.com/tahrir-forum/rapid-population-growth-imperils-egypt/.

unable to record the volume of offences. Technology was destined to be worthless from the start, this because there is no system to deliver fines as the majority of the population live in informal housing without addresses. Even those with formal addresses do not receive mail on a regular basis, as the postal service is so operationally and financially poor. Almost all vehicles carry the marks of close encounters with other vehicles – the only assured way to keep a new car pristine is to be a compound dweller and only drive within it. What this driving environment has produced is a language of the car horn. It is essential to know: it is key. Perhaps surprisingly, although driving conditions are very bad, drivers are not aggressive. To drive in Cairo it is essential to have a really good spatial sense of your own vehicle, and its distance from others. Vehicles travel at speed extremely close to each other, and in traffic jams at slow speed often just a few centimetres apart. Minor dings, as said, are very common, significant accidents are frequent and major accidents often happen. It's not unusual for five or six people a day to die on Cairo's Ring Road. Such is the density of the traffic on this road that at peak hours it can take several hours for an ambulance to arrive and deliver an accident victim to hospital.

What makes this situation worse is that the roads are in a very bad state of repair. Even on major roads one can find dangers like manholes without covers and blocks of concrete in one's path. There are also many unmarked speed bumps to catch the driver unfamiliar with the road by surprise. Flooded roads from burst water mains are not uncommon. Security checkpoints are also common, and these can cause substantial traffic jams.

Compounds, even those with low occupancy levels, are not exempt from traffic problems. This is because of the extent of car dependence, poor public transport services and the frequency of car journeys in places where there are few facilities and services, and those that do exist may be scattered across a large and pedestrian unfriendly area. It is very clear that if the compounds in New Cairo and surrounding areas were fully occupied, the traffic situation would be total gridlock. Living in such environments ontologically designs a culture wherein people *auto*matically drive everywhere, even short distances. The large number of fleets of private buses operated by schools, universities and language schools taking students to and from compounds also adds to the traffic problems. In contradiction, without these buses the situation would be worse. The inadequate public transport system also reflects a culture where there are actual and imagined issues of security and personal safety, especially among the wealthier classes.

Within compounds this has meant the establishment of a private bus company mostly taking people who work in them (retail staff, services office workers, security staff, maintenance staff, gardeners, etc.) in from and out to a small number of transport hubs that link to the extensive informal transport system that operates in Cairo. This system is almost totally used by the underclasses. It's a cascading system – a worker, or job seeker, may start the day with a bus, train or the metro journey to a station or hub in the city; they continue on by a private mini or micro-bus, or in some cases a taxi or a motor bike taxi (the lowest, cheapest and most informal level of taxi service). One can see bike riders competing for custom at, for example, roundabout that are mini and micro-bus drop-off points. These riders will take two passengers anywhere in New Cairo for a couple of pounds (less than ten pence).

The rate of growth of the Egyptian population is such that the pressure of people on the traffic system is so great that even if there were the means and the will to improve it, the expectation is that the situation is destined to get worse.

From a metrofitting perspective, creating work where people live and repair of infrastructure constitutes a massive design agenda, as does the socialization of de-socialized space. Such change will not come from a utopian master plan but from the proliferation of micro-projects that learn from each other, get a profile, and generate a dynamic as they increase in number.

The women, the young and the old

New Cairo provides few facilities for young mothers, young people in general and the old. Certainly there are the amenities of the sports clubs for those who can afford them, but there is little else. The absence of cultural facilities is extraordinary – libraries, theatres, concert halls, art galleries, cinemas, public swimming pools and so on. This, of course, reflects the nature of how the local state views its population and the role of the family (especially in relation to the care of the old). To a very great extent, the state depends on mosques, churches, charities and families to provide welfare services. All such lacks can be deemed as opportunities to explore.

What is broken?

If one takes this question on face value, instrumentally it is easy to answer, although the list would be extremely long and virtually impossible to close. It would embrace a vast proportion of the fabric of everyday life, evident in the city's traffic system, urban environment, infrastructure, education system, hospitals and the operational structures of civil society. But in actuality, all these manifestations of the broken are systematic of something far more fundamental. At its most general, this can be understood as a socially dysfunctional mode of being-in-the-world – a condition that shows itself in many forms, including social disengagement and withdrawal (into the family, home, compound) indivisibly connected to the lack of non-commercial public space and uncaring relation to the public domain.

This situation, in turn, folds into and reflects a society that has become politically divided between the disenchanted, dispirited and reactionary after the failure of 'the revolutionary moment of the Arab Spring in Egypt'. The collapse of idealism, the loss of hope and the disintegration of the dream of a liberated society has meant large numbers of people, especially the young, have become nihilistic. Layered onto this situation in one direction is the anger, resentment and hostility of the now repressed Moslem Brotherhood, and in the other is the self-interested middle class who support the ruling regime because, while undemocratic, it brings, they believe, the hope of order and control.

While Egypt has in part reverted to a regressive politics of the past it has, and is, doing so with the structural division in society becoming even more entrenched. This is seen in one direction in the huge expansion of compound construction and living, while in another in an even starker abandonment of an underclass. Regional conflict adds another force of unsettlement to the mix with the jihadist extremist militants of 'Daesh', with their objective of creating an Islamic state fuelling conflict in the Sinai which is possibly going to be harder to contain, drawing support from the most radical supporters of the Brotherhood who are still at liberty. The already and increasing dangers coming from Libya mark another threat.

There are points of rupture wherein the broken is not concealed by the aesthetics of late modernity. The appearances of an ordered city, a seemingly viable consumerist society, a high standard of living, and a hegemonic culture holding the difference of 'multiculturalism' in place – no matter the look of the seeming function the reality is not pretty. Moreover, nations and cities that have experienced colonial rule cannot hide evidence of the broken, and the hand of the breakers – its marks are everywhere and get perversely celebrated as history.[19] Egypt, Cairo and New Cairo make this very clear. They present ruin upon ruin: this can be seen in the city – its buildings, in museums, on the streets, at messy peri-urban edges, and even on the faces of many people. These remarks are not supplementary to those on the broken fabric of everyday material life, rather they underscore them. Remembering that the broken never arrives anywhere in a uniform way. So what has been said is merely an orientation towards an infinitely larger and more complex picture, one that acknowledges in nations like Egypt the destructive path of multiple

---

[19] These agents include those political leaders, planners, architects and engineers who globalized the modern city – see, for example, Legg, *Spaces of Colonialism*.

histories of colonization that not only define much of the nation's past but also in less obvious, ontological ways determine much of its present and future. The presence and/or trace of the loss of dignity, the destruction of cultural pride, the everyday inequity of colonial rule, life under dysfunctional governance, the creation of subordinated political culture, the desire for recognition and respect by other nations, the impoverishment of the means to accumulate cultural capital – a myriad stories travel with the manifestation of colonialism's afterlife. But above all what is most evident in such a history is a damaged and broken imagination.

How does all this thinking of the broken connect with the ambition of metrofitting? The most immediate answer is not by simply or idealistically drawing up a list of broken things – even if this list was critically informed, without the means to repair, it would mean very little. Moreover, the task of making a distinction between the irreparable and the repairable is not an easy one. So said, in actuality four actions can be brought into alignment: the acquisition of transformative agency; a well-informed understanding of the possible; the gaining of actual transformative means (practical, intellectual, cultural and financial); and critically viable and situated methods of intervening in the broken *status quo*. None of these actions can come from elsewhere (which is not to say knowledge and experience from the elsewhere is not valid), rather they have to come out of a situated relation with the broken that is not just based on the restoration of the former *status quo*.

Risk analysis was presented in the prior case study as one pathway into metrofitting. Risk analysis in New Cairo, however, is of another order. There are various obstructive economic interests, and there is no potentially receptive system of governance/political agency to engage and influence. Likewise, one cannot instrumentally move to act on any of these four modes of action based on the assumption that appropriate knowledge and capability will be to hand or that a 'change community' already exists. But there are starting points – ones that again can only be established through a process of unlearning, relearning and new learning with others.

New Cairo and metrofitting

Bringing what has been outlined so far closer to New Cairo, it is a place 'which is no place' – for currently it totally lacks any spatial, architectural, environmental, economic or social cohesion that would constitute it as a viable place. What it is in fact is a series of clusters of fragments, marked by dysfunction, abandonment, inclusion or exclusion and unmet social needs. Yet within this situation, and notwithstanding the political disappointment of the failures of the 'Arab Spring', the seeds of a change community exist, out of which contexts for unlearning, relearning and new learning could arrive.[20]

Even if New Cairo had the ability to attract people, to provide employment, to spatially consolidate and articulate its structural elements, very little of fundamental significance is going to change immediately. The broken inhabits the very essence of the polis, the polity and their subjects. By implication, metrofitting starts with people and their becoming. What this indicates is that the formation of change communities is not just a means to create metrofitting but rather is the first evidence of it. To illustrate the point: solving the 'traffic problem' is fundamentally not about roads and the traffic management problem (although both these issues may need attention) but one that most essentially goes to people: why they travel, how the means of travel is configured in their life, who travels and who does not, when people travel and what for, and what can be moved (bringing 'things' to the people rather than the people to the things). Working through and trying to answer such questions opens into not just what has to change instrumentally but a political strategy for collaborative and entrepreneurial action.

As indicated, the broken in the context of New Cairo, like anywhere else, is not a static situation but is fully articulated within the unsustainable. Engagement with this complexity is unavoidable. Food, again taking a very obvious example, and its source, quality and cost has consequences for New Cairo and many other urban conurbations.

Egypt's ability to produce food is delimited by a broken and undeveloped agriculture and distribution sector. Certainly. productivity should be higher and waste much lower (currently a great deal of produce that is damaged in transit arrives in the market place – bad roads, poor handling and lack of refrigeration all contribute to this). Meanwhile as indicated the national population continues to rapidly increase. At the same time, the impact of climate change will mean the availability of agricultural land to produce it will diminish (again as indicated, currently by a projected 20 per cent). Additionally, because of climate change, the nutritional value of food is expected to diminish. There is also another huge and associated problem: the availability of fresh water will decrease as irrigators extract more water from the Nile, while at the same time higher temperatures will increase evaporation levels and reduce soil moisture. Thus the demand for water will increase (a double-bind problem).[21] But along with this situation there is the prospect of a major reduction of water flow in the

---

[20] This claim is not a hollow one but based on direct experience of conversations, small events and meetings in Cairo.

[21] Building desalination plants is another option, but on a scale to supply tens of millions of people represents an economic and energy cost beyond the means of the nation.

Nile due to a large dam being constructed in Ethiopia. So what now exists is the potential for conflict.[22] The pressing question is, therefore, what is the most important strategic question? Even at this still superficial level one can see the relational complexity of many factors starting to converge, including: climate change, water security, soil fertility, food production, roads, transport, population growth and migration patterns, changing 'consumer' tastes, and diet. While addressing all the factors underscoring the problems relationally would be very complex, it is an unavoidable starting point. Without a change community, and a clear understanding of what has to change at a fundamental level, nothing essentially will change.

What can assist in the advancement and growth of a change community? History would suggest it to be the creation of spaces and activities of inclusive cultural exchange wherein ideas are expressed and explored, be they presented via music, literature, theatre, dance, festivals, exhibitions, design workshops or a myriad of other forms of creative events. It sounds very tame, but such is the breeding ground for dialogue, discussion and conviviality – this is exactly what New Cairo must have. Links across social differences and divisions created by compounds are vital to make – this being one key starting point. More generally, created events (conceptualized as *designing events*) out of which a catalyst for a change community could emerge are even more important, with these events being situated and modest exercises that could create and present how things could be other than they are. There are design and architecture schools in New Cairo, there is a creative community, so such events exist in the realm of possibility.

There are two final crucial points on these comments. Pragmatic positions that say that everything is already determined by the existing structure of political power and economic interests have to be rejected – this is the first step in the revitalization of learning and imagination. Second, attempts to visualize what a metrofitted New Cairo might be like – which may be the stuff of speculative conversation – need to be held at bay. Rather, a process of change has to grow out of what metrofitting New Cairo can mean, what modest projects of change can be identified and realized, and how events can be created to expose the possibility of change. It is out of such action that more fundamental change can be visualized as form and credible process. The key question always has to be: how can what is actually broken (as idea, relations, system and structure) be comprehended, and how can things otherwise be imagined?

---

[22] 'Egypt's urgent water problem', *Egypt Daily News*, 25 August 2015 [www.egyptdailynews.com/news].

Selected bibliography

Abourahme, Nasser (2014), 'Ruinous City, Ruinous Time', *City*, Vol. 18, Nos. 4/5, pp. 577–582.

Ackerman, Frank (2005), 'Material Flows for a Sustainable City', *International Review for Environmental Strategies*, Vol. 5, No. 2, pp. 499–510.

Agamben, Giorgio (2005), *State of Exception* (trans. Kevin Attell), Chicago, IL: University of Chicago Press.

Albro, Robert (2014), 'The "Informal City" and Latin America's Urban Future', 17 April [https://aulablog.net/2014/04/17/the-informal-city-and-latin-americas-urban-future/].

Arisaka, Yoko (1995), 'On Heidegger's Theory of Space: A Critique of Dreyfus', *Inquiry*, Vol. 38, No. 4, pp. 455–467.

Auster, Paul (1985), *The New York Trilogy*, London: Faber & Faber.

Badiou, Alain (2005), *Metapolitics* (trans. Jason Barker), London: Verso.

Badiou, Alain (2007), 'The Event in Deleuze', *Parrhesia*, No. 2, pp. 37–44.

Bataille, Georges (1988), *The Accursed Share* (trans. Robert Hurley), New York: Zone Books.

Beck, Ulrich (1999), *World Risk Society*, Cambridge: Polity Press.

Bigon, Liora (2012), 'A History of Urban Planning and Infectious Diseases: Colonial Senegal in the Early Twentieth Century', *Urban Studies Research*, Vol. 2012, Article ID 589758 [https://www.hindawi.com/journals/usr/2012/589758/].

Borsdorf, Axel and Rodrigo Hidalgo (2009), 'The Fragmented City: Changing Patterns in Latin American Cities', *The Urban Reinventors Online Journal*, Issue 3/09, pp. 1–18 [http://urbanreinventors.net/3/borsdorfhidalgo/borsdorfhidalgo-urbanreinventors.pdf].

Bourdieu, Pierre (1977), *An Outline of a Theory of Practice* (trans. Richard Nice), Cambridge: Cambridge University Press.

Bourdieu, Pierre (1990), *The Logic of Practice* (trans. Richard Nice), Cambridge: Polity Press.

Caire, Patrice (2007), 'A Critical Discussion on the Use of the Notion of Conviviality for Digital Cities', *Proceedings of Web Communities 2007*, Salamanca, Spain, February, pp. 193–200 [https://docs.google.com/file/d/0By6DOQr0Mz4JZHI1YXhvNnNxTU0/edit].

Cairns, Stephen and Jane M. Jacobs (2014), *Buildings Must Die: A Perverse View of Architecture*, Cambridge, MA: MIT Press.

Caldeira, Teresa P.R. (2000), *City of Walls: Crime, Segregation and Citizenship in São Paulo*, Berkeley, CA: University of California Press.

Carey, Bjorn (2014), 'Stanford Biologist Warns of Early Stages of Earth's 6th Mass Extinction', *Stanford News*, 24 July [http://news.stanford.edu/news/2014/july/sixth-mass-extinction-072414.html].

Castoriadis, Cornelius (1997), *The World in Fragments*, Stanford, CA: Stanford University Press.

Charvát, Petr, Zainab Bahrani and Marc Van de Mieroop (2008), *Mesopotamia Before History*, London: Routledge.

Chellaney, Brahma (2012), *From Arms Racing to Dam Racing*, Washington, DC: Transatlantic Academy.

Clarke, Desmond M. (2003), *Descartes's Theory of Mind*, Oxford: Clarendon Press.

Crawford, Harriet E.W. (2004), *Sumer and the Sumerians,* Cambridge: Cambridge University Press.

Crysler, C. Greig, Stephen Cairns and Hilde Heynen (eds.) (2012), *The SAGE Handbook of Architectural Theory*, London: Sage.

de Certeau, Michel (1988), *The Practice of Everyday Life* (trans. Steven Rendall), Berkeley, CA: University of California Press.

Deleuze, Gilles (1992), 'What is the Event', from the *The Fold, Leibniz and the Baroque* (trans. Tom Colney), Minneapolis, MN: University of Minnesota Press.

Deleuze, Gilles and Felix Guattari (1987), *A Thousand Plateaus: Capital and Schizophrenia* (trans. Brian Masumi). Minneapolis, MN: University of Minnesota Press.

Directorate of Future Land Warfare (2014), *Future Land Warfare Report 2014.* Canberra, ACT: Directorate of Future Land Warfare [http://www.army.gov.au/~/media/Army/Our%20future/Publications/Key/FLWR_Web_B5_Final.pdf].

Dormer, Peter (1990), *The Meaning of Modern Design*, London: Thames & Hudson.

Dussel, Enrique (1985) *Philosophy of Liberation* (trans. Aquilina Martinez and Christine Morkovsky), Eugene, OR: Wipf & Stock.

Dyer, Gwynne (2008), *Climate Wars*, Melbourne, VIC: Scribe.

Esterman, Isabel (2014), 'Water Shortage Shrivels Dreams of Good Life in New Cairo', 4 September [http://www.madamasr.com/en/2014/09/04/feature/society/water-shortage-shrivels-dreams-of-the-good-life-in-new-cairo/].

Fall, Juliet (2013), 'The Revenge of Geography by Robert Kaplan', *Society and Space* [http://societyandspace.org/2013/06/27/revenge-of-geography-by-robert-kaplan-reviewed-by-juliet-fall/].

Fanon, Franz (1963), *The Wretched of the Earth.* New York: Grove Press.

Findell, Alain (2008), 'Sustainable Design: A Critique of the Current Tripolar Model', *The Design Journal*, Vol. 11, Issue 3, pp. 301–322.

Florida, Richard (2002), *The Rise of the Creative Class*, New York: Basic Books.

Florida, Richard (2012), *Megaregions*, New York: Island Press.

Foster, John Bellamy (2013), 'Marx and the Rift in the Universal Metabolism of Nature', *Monthly Review*, Vol. 65, Issue 07 [http://monthlyreview.org/2013/12/01/marx-rift-universal-metabolism-nature/].

Foucault, Michel (1994 [1966]), *The Order of Things*, New York: Vintage Books.

Fourchard, Laurent (2010), 'Lagos, Koolhaas and Partisan Politics in Nigeria', *International Journal of Urban and Regional Research*, Vol. 35, No. 1, pp. 40–56.

Freire, Paulo (2000 [1968]), *Pedagogy of the Oppressed* (trans. Myra Bergman Ramos), 30th Anniversary Edition, London: Bloomsbury Academic.

Fry, Tony (1994), *Remakings: Ecology, Design. Philosophy*, Sydney, NSW: UNSW Press.

Fry, Tony (1999), *A New Design Philosophy: An Introduction to Defuturing*, Sydney, NSW: UNSW Press.

Fry, Tony (2003), 'Elimination By Design', *Design Philosophy Papers*, Vol. 1, Issue 4, pp. 145–147.

Fry, Tony (2005), 'On Design Intelligence', *Design Philosophy Papers*, Vol. 3, Issue 2, pp. 131–143.

Fry, Tony (2009), *Design Futuring: Sustainability, Ethics and New Practice*, Oxford: Berg.

Fry, Tony (2011), 'Getting over Architecture: Thinking, Surmounting and Redirecting', in Isabelle Doucet and Nel Janssens (eds.), *Transdisciplinary Knowledge Production in Architecture and Urbanism*, Dordrecht: Springer, pp. 15–32.

Fry, Tony (2011), *Design as Politics*, Oxford: Berg.

Fry, Tony (2012), *Becoming Human by Design*, London: Berg.

Fry, Tony (2014), *City Futures in the Age of a Changing Climate*, London: Routledge.

Goldenberg, Suzanne (2014), 'Western Antarctic Ice Sheet Collapse has Already Begun, Scientists Warn', *The Guardian*, 12 May [https://www.theguardian.com/environment/2014/may/12/western-antarctic-ice-sheet-collapse-has-already-begun-scientists-warn].

Gordon, Colin (ed.) (1980), *Michel Foucault, Power/Knowledge: Selected Interviews and Other Writings*, New York: Vintage.

Graham, Stephen and Simon Marvin (2012), *Splintering Urbanism*, London: Routledge.

Hall, David L. and Roger T. Ames (1995), *Anticipating China: Thinking Through the Narratives of Chinese and Western Culture*, New York: SUNY Press.

Hamdi, Nabeel (2004), *Small Change*, London: Routledge.

Hampton, Paul (2009), 'Marxism, Metabolism and Ecology', *Solidarity*, No. 156, July, pp. 20–27 [http://www.workersliberty.org/story/2009/07/30/john-bellamy-foster-marxism-metabolism-and-ecology].

Hayes, William C., M.B. Rowton and Frank H. Stubbings (1964), *Chronology: Egypt, Western Asia, Aegean Bronze Age*, Cambridge: Cambridge University Press.

Heidegger, Martin (1969 [1957]), *Identity and Difference* (trans. Joan Stambaugh), Chicago, IL: University of Chicago Press.

Heidegger, Martin (1971), *Poetry, Language, Thought* (trans. Albert Hofstadter), New York: Harper & Row.

Heidegger, Martin (1988 [1927]), *Being and Time* (trans. John Macquarrie and Edward Robinson), Oxford: Blackwell.

Heidegger, Martin (1990 [1929]), *Kant and the Problem of Metaphysics* (trans. Richard Taft), Bloomington, IN: Indiana University Press.

Heidegger, Martin (1992 [1979]), *History of the Concept of Time* (trans. Theodore Kisiel), Bloomington, IN: Indiana University Press.

Heidegger, Martin (1996 [1926]), *Being and Time* (trans. Joan Stambaugh), New York: SUNY University Press.

Heidegger, Martin (1999), *Contributions to Philosophy (From Enowning)* (trans. Parvis Emad and Kenneth Maly), Bloomington, IN: Indiana University Press.

Heidegger, Martin (2013), *The Event* (trans. Richard Rojcewitz), Bloomington, IN: Indiana University Press.

Hendrix, Cullen S. and Idean Salehyan (2012), 'Climate Change, Rainfall and Social Conflict in Africa', *Journal of Peace Research*, Vol. 49, No. 1, pp. 35–50.

Herbrechter, Stefan (2013), *Posthumanism: A Critical Analysis*, London: Bloomsbury.

Hernades, Felipe, Peter Kellett and Lea K. Allen (2010), *Rethinking the Informal City*, New York: Berghahn Books.

Hetherington, Renée and Robert G. B. Reid (2012), *The Climate Connection: Climate Change and Modern Human Evolution*, Cambridge: Cambridge University Press.

Higgins, Hannah (2009), *The Grid Book*, Cambridge, MA: MIT Press.

Hobbes, Thomas (1996 [1651]), *Leviathan*, Cambridge: Cambridge University Press.

Holston, James (2008), *Insurgent Citizenship: Disjunctions of Democracy and Modernity in Brazil*, Princeton, NJ: Princeton University Press.

Hsiao-yun, Chu and Robert G. Trujillo (2009), *New Views on R. Buckminster Fuller*, Stanford, CA: Stanford University Press.

Hubert, Henri and Marcel Mauss (1964), *Sacrifice: Its Nature and Functions*, Chicago, IL: University of Chicago Press.

Illich, Ivan (1971), *Deschooling Society*, London: Marion Boyers.

Illich, Ivan (1973), *Tools for Conviviality*, New York: Harper & Row.

Jenks, Mike and Nicola Dempsey (2005), *Future Forms and Designs for Sustainable Cities*, Oxford: Architecture Press.

Jullien, François (2007), *Vital Nourishment: Departing from Happiness* (trans. Arthur Goldhammer), New York: Zone Books.

Jünger, Ernst (2013 [1951]), *The Forest Passage* (trans. Thomas Friese), New York: Telos Publishing.

Kamper, Dietmar (1990), 'After Modernism: Outlines of an Aesthetics of Posthistory', *Theory, Culture and Society*, Vol. 7, No. 1, pp. 107–118.

Kaplan, Robert D. (2012), *The Revenge of Geography: What the Map Tells Us about Coming Conflict and the Battle Against Fate*, New York: Random House.

Kearney, Richard (1988), *The Wake of Imagination*, Minneapolis, MN: University of Minnesota Press.

Kennedy, C., S. Pinceti and P. Bunje (2010), 'The Study of Urban Metabolism and its Application to Urban Planning and Design', *Environmental Pollution*, Vol. 159, Nos. 8/9, pp. 1965–1973.

King, Anthony (1990), *Global Cities*, London: Routledge.

Kingsley, Patrick (2015), 'A New New Cairo: Egypt Plans £30bn Purpose-built Capital in Desert', *The Guardian*, 16 March [https://www.theguardian.com/cities/2015/mar/16/new-cairo-egypt-plans-capital-city-desert].

Kolbert, Elizabeth (2014), *The Sixth Extinction: An Unnatural History*, New York: Henry Holt.

Kotkin, Joel and Wendell Cox (2013), 'The World's Fastest-growing Megacities', *Forbes*, 4 August [http://www.forbes.com/sites/joelkotkin/2013/04/08/the-worlds-fastest-growing-megacities/#5605a3a224cd].

Landry, Charles (2000), *The Creative City*, London: Comedia/Earthscan.

Lang, Karen and Arthur Nelson (2009), 'Defining Megapolitan Regions', in Catherine L. Ross (ed.), *Megaregions: Planning for Global Competitiveness*, Washington, DC: Island Press.

Lefebvre, Henri (1991 [1974]), *The Production of Space* (trans. Donald Nicholson-Smith), London: Blackwell.

Lefebvre, Henri (1996), *Writing on Cities* (trans. and ed. Eleonore Kofman and Elizabeth Lebas), London: Blackwell.

Legg, Stephen (2007), *Spaces of Colonialism: Delhi's Urban Governmentalities*, Oxford: Blackwell.

Legg, Stephen (ed.) (2011), *Spatiality, Sovereignty and Carl Schmitt*, London: Routledge.

Levinas, Emmanuel (1969), *Totality and Infinity* (trans. Alphonso Lingis), Pittsburgh, PA: Duquesne University Press.

Lindroos, Kia (1998), *Now-Time/Image-Space*, University of Jyväskylä: SoPhi.

Livesey, Graham (2010), 'Deleuze, Whitehead, the Event, and the Contemporary City' [https://whiteheadresearch.org/occasions/conferences/event-and-decision/papers/Graham%20Livesey_Final%20Draft.pdf].

Locke, John (2014 [1690]), *The Second Treatise of Civil Government*, §5, Adelaide, SA: ebooks@Adelaide.

Luhmann, Niklas (1989), *Ecological Communication* (trans. John Bednarz, Jr.), Chicago, IL: The University of Chicago Press.

Magnus, Bernd (1978), *Nietzsche's Existential Imperative*, Bloomington, IN: Indiana University Press.

Martin, Thomas R. (2013), *Ancient Greece*, New Haven, CT: Yale University Press.

Marx, Karl (1957 [1867]), *Capital*, Vol. 1 (trans. Samuel Moore and Edward Aveling), London: Lawrence & Wishart.

Maton, Karl (2008), 'Habitus', in M. Grenfell (ed.), *Pierre Bourdieu: Key Concepts*, London: Acumen, pp. 49–65.

McGuirk, Justin ((2014), *Radical Cities*, London: Verso.

Meadows, Donella, Dennis Meadows, Jorgen Randers and William W. Behrens, III (1972), *The Limits to Growth*, New York: Universe Books (a report commissioned by the Club of Rome project on the Predicament of Mankind).

Meadows, Donella, Jorgen Randers and Dennis Meadows (2004), *Limits to Growth: 30 Year Update*, White River Junction, VT: Chelsea Green Publishing.

Meier, Heinrich (1995), *Carl Schmitt and Leo Strauss: The Hidden Dialogue* (trans. J. Harvey Lomax), Chicago, IL: University of Chicago Press.

Meikle, Jim (2011), 'Note on: Informal Construction', International Comparison Program, 5th Technical Advisory Group Meeting, 18–19 April, Washington, DC [http://siteresources.worldbank.org/ICPINT/Resources/270056-1255977007108/6483550-1257349667891/01.02_ICP-TAG04_ConstructionNote.pdf].

Mignolo, Walter D. (2011), *The Darker Side of Western Modernity: Global Futures, Decolonial Options*, Durham, NC: Duke University Press.

Milman, Oliver (2015), 'Climate Change Will Hit Australia Harder than the Rest of the World, Study Says', *The Guardian*, 27 January [http://www.theguardian.com/environment/2015/jan/26/climate-change-will-hit-australia-harder-than-rest-of-world-study-shows].

Mitchell, Andrew J. (2010), *Heidegger Among the Sculptors*, Stanford, CA: Stanford University Press.

Mitchell, Timothy (1988), *Colonising Egypt*, Berkeley, CA: University of California Press.

Mumford, Lewis (1961), *The City in History*, London: Penguin Books.

Mundigo, Axel and Dora Crouch (1977), 'The City Planning Ordinances of the Laws of the Indies Revisited. Part 1: Their Philosophy and Implications', *The Town Planning Review*, Vol. 48, pp. 247–268.

Nafeez Ahmed (2014), 'Nasa-funded Study: Industrial Civilsation Headed for "Irreversible Collapse"?', *The Guardian*, 14 March [https://www.theguardian.com/environment/earth-insight/2014/mar/14/nasa-civilisation-irreversible-collapse-study-scientists].

Nietzsche, Friedrich (1968 [1901]), *Will to Power* (trans. Walter Kaufmann and R. J. Hollingwood), New York: Vantage Books.

Njoh, Ambe J. (2008), 'Colonial Philosophies, Urban Space, and Racial Segregation in British and French Colonial Africa', *Journal of Black Studies*, Vol. 38, No. 4, pp. 579–599.

OECD Report (2007), *Ranking of the World's Cities Most Exposed to Coastal Flooding Today and in the Future*, Newark, CA: RMS.

Okyere, Seth A., Seth O. Mensah and Matthew Abunyewah (2014), 'Back to the Future? Caldeira's Fortified Enclaves and the Consequences for Contemporary Developing Cities', *International Journal of Humanities and Social Studies*, Vol. 2, No. 6, pp. 66–71.

Paranagua, Paulo A. (2012), 'Latin America Struggles to Cope with Record Urban Growth', *Guardian Weekly*, 11 September [https://www.theguardian.com/world/2012/sep/11/latin-america-urbanisation-city-growth].

Peckham, Robert (2011), 'Diseasing the City: Colonial Noir and the Ruins of Modernity', *Fast Capitalism*, No. 8/1 [http://www.uta.edu/huma/agger/fastcapitalism/8_1/peckham8_1.html].

Pinceti, Stephanie (2014), 'Urban Metabolism and the Nature of Sustainable Cities', Interview with Jon Christensen, *Huffington Post Green*, 15 September.

Prakash, Gyan (ed.) (2010), *Noir Urbanisms: Dystopic Images of the Modern City*, Princeton, NJ: Princeton University Press.

Pye, David (1974), *The Nature and Aesthetics of Design,* London: Barrie & Jenkins.

Raffoul, François (2012), Book Review: 'The Event of Space: Andrew J. Mitchell, *Heidegger Among the Sculptors: Body, Space, and the Art of Dwelling*', *Gatherings: The Heidegger Circle Annual*, Vol. 2, pp. 89–106.

Robinson, Ken (2011), *Out of Our Minds: Learning to be Creative*, Chichester: Capstone.

Ross, Catherine L. (ed.) (2009), *Megaregions: Planning for Global Competitiveness*, Washington, DC: Island Press.

Rothman, Mitchell S. (2001), *Uruk, Mesopotamia and its Neighbors*, Santa Fe, NM: School of American Research Press.

Sartre, Jean-Paul (1956), *Being and Nothingness* (trans. Hazel E. Barnes), New York: Washington Square Press.

Sartre, Jean-Paul (1972), *The Psychology of Imagination*, London: Methuen.

Schmitt, Carl (2014), *Dictatorship* (trans. Michael Hoelzl and Graham Wood), Oxford: Polity Press.

Scott, David (2014), *Omens of Adversity: Tragedy, Time, Memory, Justice*, Durham, NC: Duke University Press.

Sennett, Richard (2008), *The Craftsman*, New Haven, CT: Yale University Press.

Shenker, Jack (2009), 'Nile Delta: "We are Going Underwater. The Sea will Conquer Our Lands"', *The Guardian*, 21 August [https://www.theguardian.com/environment/2009/aug/21/climate-change-nile-flooding-farming].

Sims, David (2012), *Understanding Cairo: The Logic of a City Out of Control*, Cairo: The American University Press.

Slaughter, Anne-Marie (2012), 'Power Shifts: "The Revenge of Geography" by Robert D. Kaplan', *The New York Times*, 5 October [http://www.nytimes.com/2012/10/07/books/review/the-revenge-of-geography-by-robert-d-kaplan.html].

Sloterdijk, Peter (2009), *Terror from the Air*, New York: Semiotext(e).

Stengers, Isabelle (2000), *The Invention of Modern Science* (trans. Daniel. W. Smith), Minneapolis, MN: University of Minnesota Press.

Sterne, Jonathan (2003), 'Bourdieu, Technique and Technology', *Cultural Studies*, Vol. 17, Nos. 3/4, pp. 367–389.

Stiegler, Bernard (1998), *Technics and Time, 1: The Fault of Epimetheus* (trans. Richard Beardsworth and George Collins), Stanford, CA: Stanford University Press.

Stiegler, Bernard (2009), *Technics and Time, 2: Disorientation* (trans. Stephen Barker), Stanford, CA: Stanford University Press.

Stirling, Bruce (2005), *Shaping Things*, Cambridge, MA: MIT Press.

Stone, Brad Elliot (2003), 'What is Machination', Chapter Two of PhD dissertation, *Dominions and Domains*, University of Memphis, Memphis, TN.

Strategic Studies Group (2014), *Megacities and United States Army: Preparing for a Complex and Uncertain Future* [https://www.army.mil/e2/c/downloads/351235.pdf].

Stringer, Chris (2012), *The Origin of Our Species*, London: Allen Lane.

Taylor, Adam (2013), 'Freedom Ship for the Super Rich', *Business Insider*, Australia, 4 December.

Tlostanova, Madina V. and Walter D. Mignolo (2012), *Learning to Unlearn: Decolonial Reflections from Eurasia and the Americas*, Columbus, OH: Ohio State University Press.

Turner, Graham and Cathy Alexander (2014), '*Limits to Growth* was Right. New Research Shows We're Nearing Collapse', *The Guardian*, 2 September [http://www.theguardian.com/commentisfree/2014/sep/02/limits-to-growth-was-right-new-research-shows-were-nearing-collapse].

Ugbaojah, Paul K.N. (2008), 'Culture-Conflict and Delinquency: A Case Study of Colonial Lagos', *ERAS*, Edition 10, November [http://artsonline.monash.edu.au/eras/files/2014/02/ugboajah-article.pdf].

UN Habitat (2007), *Cities Without Slums*, Nairobi: UN Habitat.

US Census Bureau (2012), American Community Survey B03001.

Vidal, John (2011), 'Drier, Hotter: Can Egypt Escape its Climate Future?', *The Guardian*, 18 November [https://www.theguardian.com/environment/blog/2011/nov/18/egypt-climate-change].

Viljoen, Andre (ed.) (2005), *Continuous Productive Urban Landscapes*, London: Architectural Press.

Virilio, Paul (2005), *City of Panic*, Oxford: Berg.

Webster, Paul and Jason Burke (2012), 'How the Rise of the Megacity is Changing the Way We Live', *The Guardian*, 21 January [https://www.theguardian.com/society/2012/jan/21/rise-megacity-live].

Willis, Anne-Marie (2006), 'Ontological Designing – Laying the Ground', *Design Philosophy Papers: Collection Three*, Ravensbourne: Team D/E/S Publications.

Whitehead, Alfred North (1978 [1929]), *Process and Reality*, New York: Free Press.
Wolman, Abel (1965), 'The Metabolism of Cities', *Scientific American*, Vol. 213, Issue 3, pp. 179–190.
Yovel, Yirmiyahu (ed.) (1994), *Spinoza on Knowledge and the Human Mind*, Leiden: E.J. Brill.
Zafón, Carlos Ruis (2005), *The Shadow of the Wind*, London: Penguin.

Index

www.ingramcontent.com/pod-product-compliance
Lightning Source LLC
Chambersburg PA
CBHW071847270326
41929CB00013B/2135

* 9 7 8 1 4 7 4 2 2 4 1 5 4 *